BIG BROTHER
and the
HOLDING COMPANY

BIG BROTHER
and the
HOLDING COMPANY
THE WORLD BEHIND WATERGATE

Steve Weissman, ed.
Introduction by Noam Chomsky

Ramparts Press
Palo Alto, California

Library of Congress Cataloging in Publication Data
Weissman, Stephen R   comp.
    Big Brother and the Holding Company: the world behind
Watergate.

    CONTENTS: Chomsky, N. Watergate: a skeptical
view. -- Weissman, S.   Crying Wolf in Watergate. -- Weissman, S. Tom Huston's Plan. [etc.]   -- Bibliography
(p.   )
    1.Watergate Affair, 1972-   --Addresses, essays, lec-
tures.
    2. United States -- Politics and government -- 1969-
        -- Addresses, essays, lectures. I.   Title.
E860'W44   973'924   73-90631
ISBN 0-87867-050-5
ISBN 0-87867-051-3 (pbk.)

Published by Ramparts Press, Inc. Palo Alto, California

Library of Congress Catalog Card Number 73-90631
ISBN 0-87867-050-5   cloth
ISBN 0-87867-051-3   paperback

Printed in the United States of America

CONTENTS

FOREWORD

Has Nixon's resignation ended the White House horrors? Or was it the ultimate cover-up—the last-ditch attempt to stop the investigations which threatened to reach into the world behind Watergate? Out of cowardice or complicity and with unprecedented unanimity, Congress has agreed that impeachment (and further revelations) should be forgotten now that Nixon is gone. This book is being published in the hope that it will suggest to the American public the astonishingly wide scope of the further investigation still needed. Was Watergate only a story of CIA bunglers and millionaire fat cats like the invisible Howard Hughes, Wall Street lawyers and gold-plated gangsters from Organized Crime—along with a White House full of characters like smiling John Dean, pious Charles Colson, and the improbable Richard Nixon?

This book tries to answer these questions, and a lot more, offering a hard look at the brute force of the American government and the men of wealth who control it—Big Brother and the Holding Company.

Professor Noam Chomsky sets the tone, asking us to judge Watergate against the backdrop of the government's other crimes, like the mass murder in Southeast Asia. Is Henry Kissinger "clean" if he wasn't bugging his staff? And why the fuss about tapping Chairman Larry O'Brien's telephone at the Democratic Party offices? Washington has been illegally listening in on the left for years. Why isn't that an impeachable offense?

Then the question—"Why Watergate?"

White House drop-out John Dean sees the whole thing as paranoid and irrational—"an inevitable outgrowth of a climate of excessive concern over the political impact of demonstrations, excessive concern over leaks, an insatiable appetite for political intelligence, all coupled with a do-it-yourself White House staff, regardless of the law."

Others, including many of the left, blame it on fanatical former "spooks" like Howard Hunt and his Miami Cubans, who supposedly saw even Richard Nixon as something of a commie symp.

But free-lance journalist and one-time Berkeley activist Steve Weissman "defends" the administration, or at least its rationality. In his first two essays, Weissman pictures Watergate as part of a generally rational—if wholly rotten—effort to build the "emerging Republican majority." From its pre-Watergate crackdown on the Black Panthers and antiwar activists to its psychological warfare against Daniel Ellsberg and the presidential candidates of the Democratic Party, he argues, the Nixon team systematically worked to polarize the electorate, while further centralizing control over the nation's police-intelligence establishment. Weissman sees Tom Huston's spy plan as part of this dual strategy, and suggests that despite the opposition of FBI Director J. Edgar Hoover, the administration never dropped the basic approach of the Huston Plan.

Professor Richard Popkin, who was teaching in San Diego during preparations for the 1972 Republican Convention there, goes on to explore the pre-convention activities of police provocateurs. In grim detail, he shows how the right-wing Secret Army Organization and its FBI-paid leader attempted to assassinate an antiwar activist, setting the stage for a spectacular confrontation between left and right during the Republican Convention. Was that confrontation to include Gordon Liddy's kidnaping of new left activists, bringing to San Diego the tactics the CIA had perfected abroad?

When the scandal over ITT's four-hundred-thousand-dollar offer to the Republicans forced them to shift the convention to Miami, the provocateurs followed, as was shown during the government's prosecution of the highly-infiltrated Vietnam Veterans Against the War. Investigative reporter Fred Cook covered the trial of the Vets, uncovering a pattern of police provocation that went so far that the FBI was caught bugging defense lawyers in the courthouse itself.

Donald Freed, co-author of the film *Executive Action*, starts where Popkin and Cook leave off, suggesting that the police provocation, Watergate break-in, and attempted assassination of George Wallace may have been aiming at America's first domestic coup. In contrast to the other authors in this collection,

Freed moves into the "iffy" world of scenario-building and speculation. But his imaginative reconstruction of "Operation Gemstone" fits all too consistently with the known facts—and with the way American agents foment coups in other countries.

Professor Peter Dale Scott, a professional student of conspiracies, compares the cover-up of Watergate with the cover-up following the assassination of John F. Kennedy a decade before. In Watergate as in Dallas, Scott argues, the central figures—some of them the same—come straight from the overlapping worlds of government narcotics agencies and Organized Crime, right-wing counterrevolution and American intelligence.

Remember the crash of the United Airlines flight that killed Mrs. Howard Hunt and a team of lawyers who were threatening to blow open a scandal involving a multimillion-dollar bribe to Attorney General John Mitchell? Another cover-up kept us from knowing why that plane crashed, argues researcher Barboura Morris Freed. The day after the crash, President Nixon appointed the chief of the Plumbers Unit, Egil "Bud" Krogh, to the post of Undersecretary of Transportation—in charge of the investigation of the ill-fated Flight 553.

Although most critics argue that the Nixon team's "dirty tricks" favored the presidential candidacy of George McGovern, whom Nixon regarded as his weakest possible opponent, a 1972 editorial by the North American Congress on Latin America argues the opposite—that the covert attacks leading to the Watergate break-in grew out of an effort by America's most powerful business leaders to defeat the antiwar McGovern by any means necessary. The editorial points to the unanimity of big business opposition to McGovern, in contrast to the usual practice of backing the presidential candidates of *both* major parties.

Another contemporary interpretation of Watergate came six months after the Paris Peace Agreements on Vietnam, from two leading American Marxists, Paul Sweezy and Harry Magdoff. Instead of asking, "Why Watergate?" they asked, "Who is exposing Watergate, and why?" Their answer suggests a split in the American ruling class over Indochina. As Sweezy and Magdoff see it, those who attacked Nixon over Watergate did so to prevent him from renewing direct American involvement in the

Vietnam War—just as they initially ignored Watergate when they thought that Nixon was winding down the war.

The next three essays look at some of Richard Nixon's ties to the big business elite. Journalists Lowell Bergman and Maxwell Robach profile Nixon's long-time backer C. Arnholt Smith of San Diego, whose shady business dealings have now resulted in scores of criminal indictments. NACLA staffers Stu Bishop and Bert Knorr trace the funds that flowed to Nixon's finance committee through the efforts of Maurice Stans, Herbert Kalmbach, and their friends. And NACLA's Jon Frappier describes the Wall Street law firm of Richard Nixon and John Mitchell—their partners, clients, and interlocking connections with the biggest and best in American business. As Frappier notes, a businessman can do a lot worse than to have his attorney move into the White House.

NACLA's Stu Bishop then paints a short portrait of superspy Charles Colson, whom many think the Watergate mastermind, while investigative reporter Jeff Gerth unearths "The Miami Connection," featuring Bebe Rebozo, Teamster Union pension funds, and Organized Crime.

The book ends on a dispute. Writer Kirkpatrick Sale argues that the murky world of sunbelt capitalists linked to Organized Crime represents a shift in power away from the Eastern Yankee establishment. Steve Weissman denies the existence of any significant Cowboy-Yankee split, and paints the Nixon Administration and Watergate as the bastard child of the entire business elite, North and South, East and West.

Naturally, the authors of all these essays could stir up quite a few fights among themselves on a whole series of questions arising from Watergate. But whatever their differences, they present a view that goes beyond asking, "What did the president know and when did he know it?"—a view that remains vital in spite of Nixon's resignation and the spate of editorials proclaiming that the Watergate crisis has ended and the American system has been vindicated. For whoever the president may be, the American people will have to fight the growing power of Big Brother and the Holding Company.

—The Editors
Ramparts Press

INTRODUCTION

Watergate: A Skeptical View

Noam Chomsky

Since spring 1973, the major preoccupation of the mass media in the United States has been Watergate. Public attention is focused on one crucial question: has the president committed high crimes and misdemeanors of a sort that would justify impeachment or forced resignation? By any rational standards, the question is ludicrous. Richard Nixon is one of the major criminals of the twentieth century, and the same is true of those who have designed and implemented the foreign policy of his administration. The serious question is not whether the president and his advisers are guilty of major crimes. Rather, the question is whether the American system of law, as currently interpreted by Congress and the courts, is so absurd that criminal acts of the highest magnitude are not to be considered violations of law in the technical sense.

But this question has already received its answer. There is no possibility that the president will be impeached, let alone tried for war crimes, on grounds of his criminal actions in Indochina.

The original version of this essay, entitled "Watergate: A Skeptical View," appeared in the *New York Review of Books* © September 1973. Introductory paragraphs have been added from "Watergate and Other Crimes," which appeared in *Ramparts,* June 1974.

It has always been obvious that the judgments of Nuremberg and Tokyo were mere farce, and that apart from defeated nations, any political or military leadership will be exempt from prosecution for crimes committed for reasons of state.

Let's consider, then, the abuses that have so outraged liberal American opinion and evoked a groundswell of agitation for impeachment. Former Attorney General Elliot Richardson explained the central issue succinctly in a Boston press conference, not long after the "Saturday night massacre." The "fatal flaw" of the Nixon Administration, he observed, has been "the proclivity of the White House to perceive critics and opposition as 'enemies,' and the willingness to 'adopt tactics used against an enemy' in handling such criticism." As Hans Morgenthau put it, the Nixon Administration has "attacked American democracy directly by depriving the minority of a chance to compete on approximately equal terms with the majority" and has thus taken a long step toward totalitarianism.

To be sure, Nixon has broken the rules. His petty chicanery has demeaned the office of the presidency, and the majesty of the office serves as a powerful technique for ideological control. His miserable efforts to dismantle progressive programs offended bureaucratic interests and led to perfectly justified irritation and protest. But it is difficult to believe that any of this is what threatens to do him in. On the contrary, his major error is surely the "fatal flaw" identified by Richardson.

Nixon has accused his critics of hypocrisy and pursuit of narrow political advantage. There is considerable force to his charge.

The outrage over Watergate can hardly be explained on grounds of commitment to democratic principle or the belief that criminal actions should not go unpunished. That much, I believe, should be evident from a brief review of the relevant issues.* The wide-ranging counterattack against Nixon is an ef-

* See my article "Watergate and Other Crimes," *Ramparts,* June 1974, from which these introductory paragraphs are taken, for documentation. FBI documents, released on court order since December 1973, reveal ex-

fort to restore the familiar system in which the wealthy and the privileged control American politics. In several ways, Nixon threatened this system. For this transgression, he must pay a price.

Even the most cynical may perhaps be surprised by the antics of Nixon and his accomplices as they are gradually revealed. It matters little, at this point, where the exact truth lies in the maze of perjury, evasion, and of contempt for the normal—hardly inspiring—standards of political conduct. It is plain that Nixon's pleasant crew succeeded in stealing the 1972 election, which probably could have been theirs legally, given the power of the presidency, in spite of Muskie's strength at the polls when the affair was set in motion. The rules of the political game were violated in other respects as well. As a number of commentators have pointed out, Nixon attempted a small-scale coup. The political center was subjected to an attack with techniques that are usually reserved for those who depart from the norms of acceptable political belief. Powerful groups that normally share in setting public policy were excluded, irrespective of party, and the counterattack thus crosses party lines.

The Dean-Colson list of enemies, a minor feature of the whole affair, is a revealing index of the miscalculations of Nixon's mafia and raises obvious questions about the general response. The list elicited varied reactions, ranging from flippancy to indignation. But suppose that there had been no

---

tensive programs of disruption and repression directed against political dissidents through the 1960s. These far exceed in scale anything charged to the Watergate conspirators; furthermore, the programs were implemented and were successful, not merely contemplated, and they constitute a far more serious violation of democratic principle than any of the Watergate or related actions. But the press, typically, has maintained virtual silence on these really crucial matters, no doubt, because it accepts the doctrine that such measures are legitimate when "used against an enemy," that is, against anyone who departs from the political consensus. For a sample of the FBI documents, see appendixes two and three of this volume.

Thomas Watson or James Reston or McGeorge Bundy on the White House hate list. Suppose that the list had been limited to political dissidents, antiwar activists, radicals. Then, it is safe to assume, there would have been no front-page story in the *New York Times* and little attention on the part of responsible political commentators. Rather the incident, if noted at all, would have been recognized as merely another step, inelegant perhaps, in the legitimate defense of order and responsible belief.

The general reaction to the Watergate affair exhibits the same moral flaw. We read lofty sermons on Nixon's move to undermine the two-party system, the foundations of American democracy. But plainly what CREEP was doing to the Democrats is insignificant in comparison with the bipartisan attack on the Communist Party in the postwar period or, to take a less familiar case, the campaign against the Socialist Workers Party, which in the post-Watergate climate has filed suit to restrain government agencies from their perpetual harassment, intimidation, surveillance, and worse. Serious civil rights or antiwar groups have regularly discovered government provocateurs among their most militant members. Judicial and other harassment of dissidents and their organizations has been common practice, whoever happens to be in office. So deeply engrained are the habits of the state agencies of repression that even in the glare of Watergate the government could not refrain from infiltrating an informer into the defense team in the Gainesville VVAW trial; while the special prosecutor swore under oath that the informer, since revealed, was not a government agent.*

Watergate is, indeed, a deviation from past practice, not so much in scale or in principle as in the choice of targets. The targets now include the rich and respectable, spokesmen for official ideology, men who are expected to share power, to design social policy, and to mold popular opinion. Such people are not fair game for persecution at the hands of the state.

---

* John Kifner, " 'Best Friend' of Gainesville 8 Defendant Testifies to Being FBI Informer," *New York Times,* August 18, 1973. See also Fred Cook's article included in this volume.

A hypocrite might argue that the state attack on political dissidence has often been within the bounds of the law—at least as the courts have interpreted the Constitution—whereas Watergate and the other White House horrors were plainly illegal. But surely it is clear that those who have the power to impose their interpretation of legitimacy will so construct and construe the legal system as to permit them to root out their enemies. In periods when political indoctrination is ineffective and dissent and unrest are widespread, juries may refuse to convict. In fact, in case after case they have done so, inspiring tributes to our political system on the part of commentators who overlook a crucial point. Judicial persecution serves quite well to immobilize people who are a nuisance to the state, and to destroy organizations with limited resources or to condemn them to ineffectiveness. The hours and dollars devoted to legal defense are not spent in education, organization, and positive action. The government rarely loses a political trial, whatever the verdict of the courts, as specialists in thought control are no doubt aware.

In the president's "longer perspective," stated in his April 16, 1973 speech, we are to recall the "rising spiral of violence and fear, of riots and arson and bombing, all in the name of peace and justice." He reminds us that "free speech was brutally suppressed as hecklers shouted down or even physically assaulted those with whom they disagreed." True enough. In 1965 and 1966, peaceful public meetings protesting the war were broken up and demonstrators physically assaulted (for example, in Boston, later the center of antiwar activity). Liberal senators and the mass media, meanwhile, denounced the demonstrators for daring to question the legitimacy of the American war in Indochina. Peace movement and radical political centers were bombed and burned with no audible protest on the part of those who were later to bewail the decline of civility and the "totalitarianism of the left"—those "serious people" (in Nixon's phrase) who "raised serious questions about whether we could survive as a free democracy." Surely nothing was heard from

Richard Nixon, who was then warning that freedom of speech would be destroyed for all time if the United States were not to prevail in Vietnam—though when awards are given out for hypocrisy in this regard, Nixon will not even be a contender.

There is nothing new in any of this. Recall the reaction of defenders of free speech when McCarthy attacked the *New York Times* and, by contrast, the *National Guardian.* * Recall the pleas that McCarthy was impeding the legitimate struggle against domestic subversion and Russian aggression, or the reaction to the judicial murder of the Rosenbergs. In fact, the mistake of the Watergate conspirators is that they failed to heed the lesson of the McCarthy hearings twenty years ago. It is one thing to attack the left, or the remnants of the Communist Party, or a collapsing liberal opposition that had capitulated in advance by accepting—in fact, creating—the instruments of postwar repression, or those in the bureaucracy who might impede the evolving state policy of counterrevolutionary intervention. It is something else again to turn the same weapons against the U.S. Army. Having missed this subtle distinction, McCarthy was quickly destroyed. Nixon's cohorts, as recent events have amply demonstrated, committed a similar error of judgment.

The immediate consequence of this deviation is that Nixon's wings have been clipped, and power is being more broadly shared among traditional ruling groups. Congress has imposed constraints on executive actions, and in the changed political climate, the courts have refused to permit executive encroachment on the legislative function through impoundment.

Most important of all, Nixon and Kissinger were unable to kill as many Cambodians as they would have liked, and were thus denied such limited successes in Cambodia as they achieved in South Vietnam, where all authentic popular forces were severely weakened by the murderous assault on the civilian society. Although the failure of the terror bombing of Christ-

---

* Those whose memories are short might turn to James Aronson's review of the record in *The Press and the Cold War* (New York: Bobbs-Merrill, 1970).

mas 1972 may have compelled Nixon and Kissinger to accept the DRV-PRG offer of a negotiated settlement (formally at least),* they nevertheless continued to support the openly announced efforts of the Thieu regime to undermine the Paris Agreements of January. At the same time, they simply shifted the bombing to Cambodia in the hope of decimating the indigenous guerrilla movement. Even in April 1973, Senate doves feared that the "political mood is not right" for a challenge to Nixon's war policy, though they recognized that compliance might be the "final act of surrender" to presidential power. But as Nixon's domestic position eroded, it became possible to enact the legislation urged by opponents of the American war and by politically more significant groups who have come to realize, since the Tet offensive of 1968, that the war was a dubious bargain for American capitalism.

To John Connally, it is "an impressive fact, and a depressing fact, that the persistent underlying balance-of-payments deficit which causes such concern, is more than covered, year in and year out, by our net military expenditures abroad, over and above amounts received from foreign military purchases in the United States."† Rational imperialists who find this fact impressive were, no doubt, less than impressed by the fact that Nixon and Kissinger were able to "wind down the war" over a period equal to that of American participation in World War II, and

---

* To be sure, this is not the official version. With the complicity of television and the press, the government has succeeded once again in imposing on events an interpretation that is wholly at variance with the facts. For some details on government and press deception with regard to the Paris Agreements and the events that led to them, see my "Indochina and the Fourth Estate," *Social Policy*, September 1973.

† May 28, 1971, *Department of the Treasury News*, cited by David P. Calleo and Benjamin M. Rowland in *America and the World Political Economy* (Indiana University Press, 1973), p. 99. The editors of the *Monthly Review* have been particularly effective in explaining the contribution of imperial policy to the economic crisis. One might also recall Seymour Melman's efforts to arouse awareness of the debilitating effects of the policies of the militarized state capitalist institutions, long before the topic became fashionable.

were still intent on pouring resources into an attempt to crush revolutionary nationalism in Indochina. Though the attempt will surely continue, the scale—temporarily at least—will be reduced. This is surely the most significant outcome of Watergate.

Nixon's personal authority has suffered from Watergate, and power will return to men who better understand the nature of American politics. But it is likely that the major long-term consequence of the present confrontation between Congress and the president will be to establish executive power still more firmly. Nixon's legal strategy is probably a winning one, if not for him (for he has violated the rules), then for the position that the presidency is beyond the reach of the law. Kleindienst, Ehrlichman, and Nixon's lawyers have laid the issue out squarely. In spite of their occasional disclaimers, the import of their position is that the president is subject to no legal constraints. The executive alone determines when and whom to prosecute, and is thus immune. When issues of national security are invoked, all bars are down.

It takes little imagination for presidential aides to conjure up a possible foreign intelligence or national security issue to justify whatever acts they choose to initiate. And they do this with impunity. The low point of the Ervin committee hearings was the failure to press Ehrlichman on the alleged "national security issue" in the release of the Pentagon Papers, or his implication that Ellsberg was suspected of providing these documents to the Russian embassy. Mary McGrory has suggested plausibly that the factor that led the White House to such excesses in the Ellsberg affair was the fear that it might inspire further exposures, in particular of the secret military attack on Cambodia.

More generally, the president's position is that if there is some objection to what he does, he can be impeached. But reverence for the presidency is far too potent an opiate for the masses to be diminished by a credible threat of impeachment. Such an effective device for stifling dissent, class consciousness, or even critical thought will not be lightly abandoned. Furthermore, Congress has neither the will nor the capacity to manage the domestic economy or the global system. These related enterprises take on new scope with the increasing internationalization of production and economic affairs and with the Nixon-Kissinger diplomacy, which accepts the USSR as a junior partner in managing what Kissinger likes to call "the overall framework of order,"* much as Stalin seems to have intended in the early postwar years. It is fitting, in more ways than one, that Nixon's most loyal constituency should prove to be the POWs and the Politburo.

If the choice is between impeachment and the principle that the president has absolute power (subject only to the need to invoke national security), then the latter principle will probably prevail. Thus the precedent will probably be established, more firmly and clearly than heretofore, that the president is above the law, a natural corollary to the doctrine† that no law prevents a superpower from enforcing ideological conformity within its domains.

The Watergate affair and the sordid story that has unfolded since are not without significance. They indicate, once again, how frail are the barriers to some form of fascism in a state capitalist system in crisis. There is little prospect for a meaningful reaction to the Watergate disclosures, given the narrow conservatism of American political ideology and the absence of any mass political parties or organized social forces that offer an alternative to the centralization of economic and political power in the major corporations, the law firms that cater to their interests, and the technical intelligentsia who do their bid-

---

* *American Foreign Policy* (Norton, 1969), p. 97. This is properly the concern of the United States, in his view, rather than "the management of every regional enterprise," to be left to subordinates.

† Generally called the "Brezhnev Doctrine," though it was explicit in virtually the same terms in the earlier doctrines of Eisenhower, Khrushchev, Kennedy, and Johnson, as Thomas M. Franck and Edward Weisband have shown in their important study, *Word Politics: Verbal Strategy Among the Superpowers* (London: Oxford University Press, 1971).

ding, both in the private sector and in state institutions. With no real alternative in view, opposition is immobilized and there is a natural fear, even among the liberal opposition, that the power of the presidency will be eroded and the ship of state will drift aimlessly. The likely result will therefore be a continuation of the process of centralization of power in the executive, which will continue to be staffed by representatives of those who rule the economy and which will be responsive to their conception of domestic and global order.

It is true, as critics allege, that Nixon's tactics threatened to subvert the two-party system. The illusion that the people rule rests on the regular opportunity to choose between two political organizations dominated by similar interests and restricted to the narrow range of doctrine that receives expression in the corporate media and, with rare exceptions, the educational institutions of American society. Nixon's tactics thus tend to undermine the conventional basis for stability and obedience, while falling far short of supplying some form of totalitarian doctrine as an ideological alternative.

But the conditions that permitted the rise of McCarthy and Nixon endure. Fortunately for us and for the world, McCarthy was a mere thug and Nixon's mafia overstepped the bounds of acceptable trickery and deceit with such obtuseness and blundering vulgarity that they were called to account by powerful forces that had not been demolished or absorbed. But sooner or later, under the threat of political or economic crisis, some comparable figure may succeed in creating a mass political base, bringing together socio-economic forces with the power and the finesse to carry out plans such as those that were conceived in the Oval Office. Only perhaps he will choose his domestic enemies more judiciously and prepare the ground more thoroughly.

Nixon's front men now plead that in 1969-1970 the country was on the verge of insurrection and that it was therefore necessary to stretch the constitutional limits. The turmoil of those years was largely a reaction to the American invasion of Indochina. The conditions, domestic and international, that have led successive administrations to guide "Third World development" in the particular channels that suit the needs of industrial capitalism have not changed. There is every reason to suppose that similar circumstances will impel their successors to implement similar policies. Furthermore, the basic premises of the war policy in Indochina have not been seriously challenged, though its failures led to retrenchment. These premises are shared by most of the enemies on the Dean-Colson list and by others within the consensus of respectable opinion.

The reaction to recent disclosures illustrates the dangers well enough. While public attention was captivated by Watergate, Ambassador Godley testified before Congress that between fifteen and twenty thousand Thai mercenaries had been employed by the United States in Laos, in direct and explicit violation of congressional legislation.* This confirmation of Pathet Lao charges, which had been largely ignored or ridiculed in the West, evoked little editorial comment or public indignation, though it is a more serious matter than anything revealed in the Ervin committee hearings.

The revelation of secret bombings in Cambodia and northern Laos from the earliest days of the Nixon Administration is by far the most important disclosure of the first half of 1973. It would be difficult to imagine more persuasive grounds for impeachment were this a feasible political prospect. But in this case, too, the reaction is largely misplaced. It seems that congressional leaders and commentators in the press are disturbed more by the cover-up and the deceit than by the events themselves. Congress was deprived of its right to ratify—no one who has studied the Symington committee hearings of the fall of 1969 can have much doubt that Congress would have ratified the bombings and incursions had the opportunity been given.

As for the press, it showed as much interest in the bombings

---

* For some congressional reactions to earlier exposures, see my *For Reasons of State* (New York: Pantheon, 1973), p. 13f.

at the time as it now devotes to the evidence that Thai mercenaries in Laos are being shipped to Cambodia and that casualties of fighting in Cambodia have already arrived in Bangkok hospitals.* The press is much too concerned with past deception to investigate these critical ongoing events, which may well have long-term implications for Southeast Asia. Similarly, when Jacques Decornoy reported in *Le Monde* on the intense bombing of towns and villages in northern Laos in the spring of 1968, the American press not only failed to investigate, but even failed to cite his eyewitness reports. A Cambodian government White Book of January 1970, giving details of American and ARVN attacks, evoked no greater interest or concern. Nor did the reports of large-scale defoliation of Cambodian rubber plantations in early 1969 or the occasional incidents of "bombing errors" that were conceded by the American government since 1966 when American observers happened to be present.† The complaints over government deception ring hollow, whether in the halls of Congress or on the editorial pages.

Still more cynical is the current enthusiasm over the health of the American political system, as shown by the curbing of Nixon and his subordinates, or by the civilized compromise that permitted Nixon and Kissinger to kill Cambodians and destroy their land only until August 15, 1973, truly a model of how a democracy should function, with no disorder or ugly disruption.

Liberal political commentators sigh with relief that Kissinger has barely been tainted—a bit of questionable wire-tapping, but no close involvement in the Watergate shenanigans. Yet by any objective standards, the man is one of the great mass murderers

---

* See Marcel Barang, "Le Laos, ou le mirage de la neutralité," *Le Monde diplomatique*, June 1973.

† As early as January 1962, Roger Hilsman observed the bombing of a Cambodian village by American planes, who then attacked the Vietnamese village that was the intended target. Cf. *To Move a Nation* (Delta, 1967). For a partial record, see my *At War With Asia* (New York: Pantheon, 1970), chapter three.

of the modern period. He presided over the expansion of the war to Cambodia, with consequences that are now well known, and the vicious escalation of the bombing of rural Laos, not to speak of the atrocities committed in Vietnam, as he sought to achieve a victory of some sort for imperial power in Indochina. But he wasn't implicated in the burglary at the Watergate or in the undermining of Muskie, so his hands are clean.

If we try to keep a sense of balance, the exposures of the past several months are analogous to the discovery that the directors of Murder Inc. were also cheating on their income tax. Reprehensible, to be sure, but hardly the main point.

Crying Wolf in Watergate

Steve Weissman

What does "the movement" tell America about Watergate? What do radicals tell people after they've told them that they told them so? Better a break-in at the Democrats' than at the Weathermen's? Not at all. Many radicals say that the *Washington Post* doesn't know the half of it. That it was nearly worse. That next time it will be worse. Do the Special Prosecutor and the Congress pull back from the crimes to attack the cover-up? Not the radicals. They tell the whole story, and then some. With facts and without. Full of secret governments, inner plots, and coups d'état.

Well, they were right before and they may be right again. When God is dead, all things are possible. But until the hard evidence comes in, it seems silly for radicals to create exotic scenarios or conjure up new facts. The old facts are bad enough. The trick is to fit them together.

The puzzle begins in the months before the elections of 1968, when key business leaders from all parts of the country swung to Richard Nixon. According to press estimates, a vast majority of the blue-ribbon Business Council chose Nixon over Hubert Humphrey. With inflation crippling the dollar on the international markets, the businessmen wanted the government to hold down employment and wages, cut back social spending, and keep the lid on discontent. Who was more likely to get the job done? The conservative Wall Street Republican or the free-spending, New Deal Democrat? Nixon was the one.

Backed by big business, Nixon won the election by a narrow margin. He still had to create a popular base for the new business priorities, a working majority for higher profits, more unemployment, lower wages, smaller social benefits, and a long, slow withdrawal from the land war in Asia. How would he do it? By polarizing the country even more than it was. By polarizing "Middle America" against those who favored "permissiveness," "crime in the streets," and "revolutionary violence." Not just a Southern strategy. Not merely a suburban strategy. A generation before, Franklin Delano Roosevelt had forged a hard-to-beat, bread-and-butter alliance of farmers, labor, urban ethnics, liberal intellectuals, and Southern conservatives. Richard Milhous Nixon would bring together the non-young, non-black, and non-radicals.

That much is known. What is overlooked is that the bugging, break-ins, and provocations of "Watergate" became key to the strategy. Nixon and his aides started by "getting" the Black Panthers, shifted to Tom Huston's "domestic security program" to stop antiwar militants, then to the Plumbers' "psy-war" against Daniel Ellsberg, and finally to the Re-Election Committee's "dirty tricks" to disrupt the Democrats. The terms came from the weird world of intelligence and counterinsurgency operations, and the tactics—from spying to provocation—were designed to let Nixon manipulate the climate of violence. Then it was simple. Crush the militants. Silence the center. Build the frightened majority.

Strange as it seems, Richard Nixon came late to "law and order." From his pursuit of Alger Hiss in the late 1940s to his pursuit of the presidency in 1960, he chased communists, not criminals. Only in 1968 did he discover that crime was a winning issue—when Senator Robert Kennedy used it against Eugene McCarthy in Oregon's Democratic Primary. But Nixon learned, running his later campaign against Attorney General Ramsey Clark, whom he accused of "leading an official retreat in the face of crime." To Nixon's growing audience, "crime in the street" became a code word for blacks, and "permissiveness" the enemy of patriotism. It was a fine formula, and not just at election time.

"Above all, the president himself has to take a firm, 'no nonsense' approach," urged Evelle J. Younger, the politically ambitious district attorney of Los Angeles County who headed Nixon's law-and-order task force. Younger's advice to Nixon: appoint tougher judges, use more wiretaps, encourage "space age techniques and hardware," and support local police with better training and equipment. "Most people feel, deep down, that permissiveness toward crime and criminals has gone too far," he warned.

The new president agreed. He used his first press conference to endorse preventive detention, while his campaign manager and later Attorney General John Mitchell wanted "no knock" entry, wiretaps, and federal troops to stop crime in the capital. Mitchell also warned that the Department of Justice would prosecute "hard-core militants" who crossed state lines to incite riots on college campuses. The country was going to go so far to the right that nobody would recognize it, he declared.

Deputy Attorney General Richard Kleindienst was more precise. He was going to crack down on "draft dodgers," "anarchistic kids," and militants of all persuasions. "If people demonstrated in a manner to interfere with others, they should be put in a detention camp," he said. The goal was not simply to stop crime, but to make politics.

Phase I of the evolving strategy started with an all-out attack on the most vulnerable of the "extremists," the black militants and particularly the Black Panther Party. "The Panthers are a bunch of hoodlums. We've got to get them," declared Assistant Attorney General Jerris Leonard, who made the decision to include Panther chairman Bobby Seale in the indictment against the Chicago Eight, whom Leonard charged with inciting riots at the 1968 Democratic convention. Of all the "violence-prone, Black Extremist groups," the Panthers were "the greatest threat to the internal security of the country," added J. Edgar Hoover.

To "get" the Panthers, Mitchell and Kleindienst borrowed from former Attorney General Robert Kennedy. In his war against Teamster boss Jimmy Hoffa and the "conspiracy of evil," Kennedy had mobilized the resources of several federal agencies through a special "Hoffa Squad." Mitchell and Kleindienst formed a similar "Panther Squad," which spent the spring and summer traveling from city to city, supposedly to help bring criminal indictments against the Panthers. Later, FBI and local police informers would be found guilty of crimes and provocations, but in the meantime the police jailed Panther chairman Bobby Seale, Ericka Huggins, the New York Twenty-One, and other Panthers around the country. Police raiding parties also stormed Panther headquarters in Chicago, Los Angeles, and several other cities, shooting it out with those inside and killing at least two Panther leaders, Chicago's Fred Hampton and Mark Clark.

The program was a success. Soon, people everywhere thought of the Panthers as Public Enemy Number One, blaming them for the government's well publicized raids as well as for their own violent acts. What people everywhere didn't know was how much the attacks had left the feared Panthers leaderless. It's hard to say how much of the credit goes to local authorities, how much to pre-existing FBI programs, and how much to the Justice Department's Panther Squad. But whatever the balance, "law enforcement" had become part of political warfare.

By November 1969, the polarization was into Phase II, the anti-antiwar phase. The trial of the Chicago Eight had begun, and the administration was responding to the antiwar movement, newly revived by the nationwide Moratorium on September 15 and plans for the Washington Mobilization in mid-

November. As was his custom, Kleindienst predicted violence at the Washington demonstration and threatened to call out the troops, while John Dean stalled negotiations for the needed permits. "The administration has been following a course calculated to increase the danger that the protest will turn into a violent confrontation," charged the *New York Times*. "The Justice Department has been turned into a funnel for alarmist reports about militant penetration of the peace front—reports of the type that exacerbate tensions and thus serve as self-fulfilling prophecies." But if the administration was against black and antiwar militants, the president announced on November 3 that he was *for* "the silent majority" of "Middle America." Congressional elections were just a year away, and Nixon wanted to keep the choice simple.

To cut away the middle ground, Nixon dispatched Spiro Agnew, the vice president. On November 13, Agnew attacked the "effete corps of impudent snobs" in the media and among the congressional and antiwar liberals, and in the months that followed, assaulted the "nattering nabobs of negativism," "vicars of vacillation," and "hopeless, hysterical hypochondriacs of history." There would be no mercy for those who gave a hearing to the militants or failed to denounce them.

It was weird. Red-baiting had never worked very well against the new movements of the 1960s, and with the opening toward Moscow and Peking, Nixon would hardly want to stir up any excess anticommunism. So the enemies were "anarchists," "violent extremists," and "left-wing fascists," or simply "criminals," while the old "commie-symps" gave way to "rad-libs," the "radical-liberals." The names had changed, but the story was easy to remember.

Agnew carried his alliterative "rad-baiting" to all parts of the country on behalf of "law and order" candidates. He also denounced the Scranton Commission on Student Unrest, which issued its report a month or so before the balloting. Governor William Scranton and his colleagues had shown a sympathy for the students' ends, if not their means, and urged the president "to renew the national commitment to full social justice and to be aware of increasing charges of repression." Agnew accused the commission of "scapegoating" the president and blamed campus disorder wholly on the militants. Don't try to coopt the young and the black and the radical. Crush them.

In the same vein, Special Counsel Charles Colson helped a *Life* magazine reporter put together evidence to charge liberal Senator Joseph Tydings with influence-peddling. Tydings was later cleared, but he lost the election. Colson also organized an ad branding seven senators as "radicals" who favored disorder and dissension in the United States. The ads were so distasteful that three of those listed as sponsors on the ad publicly deplored it.

The White House also dealt in more personal dirt, using a newly created "special investigative unit" headed by John J. Caulfield, a veteran of the Bureau of Special Services and Investigations (BOSSI) of the New York Police Department and Nixon's security chief in the 1968 campaign. Caulfield performed a variety of spying jobs for presidential aide John Ehrlichman and helped Henry Kissinger wiretap his National Security Council staff in search of press leaks, while his assistant Anthony J. Ulasewicz, also of BOSSI, "scouted the potential opposition for vulnerability," as Ehrlichman put it. Paid from a secret fund by Nixon's personal attorney Herbert Kalmbach, Ulasewicz looked into the private lives of political figures, especially the relationship of Senator Edward Kennedy to Mary Jo Kopechne, the woman who died in Kennedy's car at Chappaquiddick.

President Nixon avoided the election fray until late in the campaign, when he toured the country denoucing the militants and at times provoking them. But he had made his views known, especially after March 12, 1970, when bombs exploded in the New York offices of General Telephone, Mobil Oil, and IBM. That evening the president had dinner with Professor Irving Kristol, a veteran of the CIA's campaign to mobilize an earlier generation of intellectuals into the covertly funded Congress of Cultural Freedom. According to the *New York Times,* Kristol and the president attempted "to draw parallels between young, middle-class, white Americans who are resorting to violence and the Narodniki—children of the mid-eighteenth century Russian aristocracy who murdered Czar Alexander II—and between black nationalists here and Algerian revolutionaries." The *Times* did not report what Kristol and the president concluded, but the following day Nixon told his staff to draw up proposals to meet the new threat.

In the following weeks, the president ordered tighter surviellance of radicals, turned the White House police force into an expanded Executive Protection Service, with responsibility for foreign embassies, and told the Law Enforcement Assistance Administration (LEAA) to fund "special training programs" for state and local police, probably in gathering domestic intelligence. The president also asked Congress for stiffer penalties against bombing.

"The anarchist and criminal elements who perpetrated such acts deserve no more patience or indulgence," he explained. They were "young criminals posturing as romantic revolutionaries. . . . They must be dealt with as the potential murderers they are."*

This was shortly before the president sent American troops into Cambodia. It seems likely that he was preparing for the expected reaction, lumping together marchers, strikers, trashers, and terrorists.

---

* The president was in good, if unaccustomed, company—the editorial writers of the *New York Times.* In the lead editorial of the March 13 edition, they too called the bombers "criminals" and "potential murderers": "The actual and threatened bombings of the past few days must not be glossed over as the actions of idealistic if misguided revolutionaries; they are the criminal acts of potential murderers. . . . The mad criminals who threaten and bomb must be recognized for what they are and prosecuted with the full force not only of the law but of the community they would rule and ruin."

White House aides pressed the attack in a series of anonymous interviews which the *New York Times* reported on April
12:

> The officials have concluded that attempts to bring militants back
> into society's mainstream are as futile, as one stated it, "as turning
> off the radio in the middle of a ball game to try to change the
> score."
>
> The official view is that extreme radicals cannot be won over with
> welfare, electoral reforms, or by White House appeals. "It wouldn't
> make a bit of difference if the war and racism ended overnight," said
> a highly placed Nixon assistant. "We're dealing with the criminal
> mind, with people who have snapped for some reason." Accordingly,
> the Administration sees as its prime responsibility as protecting the
> innocent from "revolutionary terrorism." . . .
>
> One of the more conservative aides contended, "We are facing the
> most severe threat this country has seen since the Depression."

"Revolutionary terrorism" was present, to be sure. But the
White House was magnifying the threat, building support for
the Cambodian invasion and the congressional elections by
polarizing the country against the "revolutionary terrorists."

In July, the president further escalated the war on black and
antiwar militants, approving the no-holds-barred Huston Plan
(discussed in full in another chapter of this volume). The plan
authorized increased wiretapping, "mail coverage," informers,
and illegal break-ins ("surreptitious entry"). It also created a
super-secret Interagency Group on Internal Security, with representatives of the White House, FBI, CIA, National Security
Agency, Defense Intelligence Agency, and the three military
counterintelligence agencies. Within days, the FBI's J. Edgar
Hoover forced the president to recall his authorization for the
particular plan. But the interagency approach continued covertly in the Justice Department's Internal Security Division,
while the illegal operations became stock in trade for several
different agencies, as well as for the White House's special
"Plumbers Unit."

On June 13, 1971, the *New York Times* printed the first part of a top-secret history of the Vietnam war and the administration was into Phase III of the grand polarization. Colson, Agnew, and Nixon had already rapped those who would not condemn the lawless militants. Now the administration would attack the rad-libs directly, making a symbol of Daniel Ellsberg and the Pentagon Papers.

Robert Mardian and the Internal Security Division started the attack, going to court for a restraining order to stop the *Times*, *Washington Post*, and two other papers from printing the study. This was prior censorship, and the Supreme Court threw it out as unconstitutional. But Mardian's legal attack helped brand the outdated history as an immediate threat to national security. He followed up by seeking indictments against Ellsberg and his "co-conspirators."

The White House took over from there. By this time, Colson, Ehrlichman, and Dean were considering "how we can use the available Federal Machinery to screw our political enemies," as Dean wrote in an August 16 memo. Most of the "enemies" were rad-libs, and the "federal machinery" they wanted to use included the agencies which awarded grants and contracts, the regulatory and prosecuting bodies, and especially the IRS. Realizing from experience that money was the mother's milk of politics, the White House would harass rich liberals, and especially those who gave to radical groups. All of this was in addition to the dirt-digging skills of Jack Caulfield and Tony Ulasewicz, the FBI, and other investigating agencies.

But Ellsberg was to be a special case, a symbol, and Ehrlichman named his aide Egil "Bud" Krogh to head a special unit, which included David Young from Kissinger's staff, E. Howard Hunt, who had just joined Colson's staff, and G. Gordon Liddy, who had been dismissed from the Treasury Department. Known as the Plumbers, they investigated the "leak" of the Pentagon Papers and information from Henry Kissinger's National Security Council. But their real job wasn't leak-plugging. It was, as Hunt called it, "psy-war," or psychological warfare.

"The plan . . . was to slowly develop a very negative picture around the whole Pentagon study affair (preparation to publication) and then to identify Ellsberg's associates and supporters on the new left with this negative image," Young wrote Ehrlichman on August 26. "The end result would be to show (1) how they were intent on undermining the policy of the government they were supposedly serving and (2) how they sought to put themselves above the law."

Young was ploughing fertile ground. When Defense Secretary Robert McNamara commissioned the study in June 1967, many officials were having second thoughts about the build-up of American troops in what they had originally seen as lower-level counterinsurgency. McNamara probably intended the study to stregthen the position of the doubters, and parts of it probably contributed to the decision in March 1968 to cut back the escalation in Vietnam. At the same time, McNamara ordered the history prepared by the Pentagon's office of International Security Affairs, which worked closely with the CIA and probably had CIA personnel in it. As a result, the study became a defense of Agency analysts who had warned that the build-up wouldn't work and a cover-up of the CIA's counterinsurgents who had helped make the build-up happen. It was easy. The authors blamed the politicians and generals for not heeding the intelligence estimates.

That was the preparation of the Pentagon Papers. Whether their publication was part of the same program is unclear, though it should be remembered that Ellsberg had worked with the CIA in Vietnam and that his "leak" did convey what Fletcher Prouty called the CIA's best cover story—"that it was only an intelligence agency."

Young never planned to raise the CIA's role in the Pentagon Papers. That would have exposed the Agency and created a "national security threat." He and the White House wanted to show only that the doubters who prepared and possibly encouraged publication of the papers were tied to the foreign policy leadership of the Democratic Party. They saw this most clearly in the case of former Assistant Secretary of Defense for International Security Affairs Paul Warnke, a former law partner of former Secretary of State Dean Acheson, present law partner of former Secretary of Defense Clark Clifford, and top foreign policy adviser to Senators Kennedy and Muskie. But they also thought that study director Leslie Gelb and his assistant Morton Halperin were working with the Democrats, and they knew, or should have, that one of the few copies of the study had gone to former Attorney General and State Department official Nicholas Katzenbach. In addition, they probably thought that former ambassador Averell Harriman and Senator William Fulbright had encouraged publication covertly, and saw the *Times* and *Post* as Democratic newspapers. Hardly the new left, but the administration had every right to feel that it was the victim, rather than the initiator, of a psy-war campaign.

Colson, who wanted to turn Ellsberg into "another Alger Hiss," had also wanted to tie him to "the real enemy," which the White House tried to do by arguing—without evidence—that a copy of the Pentagon Papers had gone to the Soviet Embassy. But the line never got off the ground.

The White House attack, or counterattack, took many forms. Hunt thought that the case would be tried in the newspapers, and using a little "resourceful engineering," he and the Plumbers managed to plant an article about his left-wing attorney, Leonard Boudin. Hunt also put together for Colson some "politically damaging material on the Democratic hierarchy," and fabricated documents to strengthen the case that President John Kennedy had ordered the assassination of South Vietnam's Catholic Premier Ngo Dinh Diem. The hope was to plant a story that would undermine Catholic support for Senator Edward Kennedy. But as the president's chief speech writer Pat Buchanan explained, the situation was too big to be undermined by planting leaks among the friendly press. By late August, Young was pinning his hopes on using the negative information in a full-scale congressional investigation.

The White House also sought to make use of "surreptitious

entry," which the president had approved earlier in the Huston
Plan. According to John Caulfield, Colson had asked him early
in July to get "some national security documents" from Leslie
Gelb's office at the Brookings Institution. "Colson suggested
that one way of getting the information was to have the District
of Columbia fire regulations changed and have the FBI respond
to all arsons. Colson suggested that there could be a fire at the
Brookings Institute and then the FBI could take the file out of
Gelb's office," Caulfield explained. The administration would
blame the fire on the militants.

Colson's break-in and fire were never approved. Caulfield told
the story to Dean, who flew to San Clemente, returned, and
told the ex-cop to forget it. But other break-ins did get approval. On August 11, Young and Krogh recommended to Ehrlichman "that a covert operation be undertaken to examine all
the medical files still held by Ellsberg's psychoanalysts covering
the two-year period in which he was undergoing analysis." The
Plumbers wanted personal "dirt" on Ellsberg, in part for a CIA
personality profile, and they probably hoped to find clues on
Ellsberg's relationship to the leading Democrats. Ehrlichman
agreed, initialing the August 11 memo and noting "if done
under your assurance that it is not traceable." He would claim
later that he did not suspect that the "covert operation" would
be a burglary. According to Dean, Nixon also gave approval. But
Dean's source was Krogh, who claimed full responsibility himself. In any case, Hunt and Liddy assembled a team of Cuban-
Americans from Miami, and on September 3 they broke into
the Beverly Hills office of Dr. Louis Fielding.

Another covert operation against Ellsberg was more violent.
Back in May of 1970, during the Cambodian invasion, construction workers had attacked student protestors in the Wall Street
area. According to reports at the time, Colson had a hand in the
attack and following it he urged the president to invite the
hardhats to the White House. Hunt and Liddy staged a similar
attack in Washington the evening of May 4, 1972. Ellsberg and
radical lawyer William Kunstler were speaking at an antiwar rally

on the steps of the Capitol, while inside the recently deceased J. Edgar Hoover lay in state. The symbols were perfect—Hoover and patriotism, hippies and traitors—and Hunt's Cuban cadre started a series of fights, disrupting the rally and shaking up Ellsberg. As Ellsberg saw it, the White House had organized the attack to make him appear violent, though it might have been to make him appear as an effete intellectual.

From the phony cables to the break-ins and vigilantes, the anti-Ellsberg operation looked like something the CIA does overseas, and for good reason. Hunt had worked for the agency for twenty-one years; his Cubans were CIA veterans; and the CIA provided false identification, disguises, business cards, a recording device, a voice-altering device, and an experimental camera in a tobacco pouch. The CIA also developed photographs of Fielding's office and prepared a personality profile on Ellsberg, supposedly the first they had ever done on a domestic political figure. CIA. CIA. CIA. Was the Plumbers unit a CIA operation? No more than was the publication of the Pentagon Papers. From the available evidence, it was a White House operation, controlled by the president's most loyal aides, if not by the president himself.

By the May 4 attack on Ellsberg, the White House and the Justice Department had moved their forces into the Committee to Re-Elect the President; John Mitchell had become the official campaign director on March 1, and Robert Mardian political coordinator on May 1. Haldeman's aide Jeb Magruder was deputy director, serving in CREEP since late 1971, while G. Gordon Liddy became general counsel and chief of intelligence in December, moving over to the finance committee in March or April. Hunt remained in the White House, but continued to work with Liddy and the new security chief, James McCord, another longtime CIA veteran.

Little else had changed. Nixon would continue to run against the black militants, student terrorists, and rad-libs. Spies and burglars would gather intelligence. Saboteurs, strategists, and political spokesmen would put the intelligence to use. Sometimes the spy would be the saboteur. Sometimes a single operation would do the dirty tricks and bring back information that could be used in later dirty tricks. It was the Panther Squad, the Huston Plan, the Internal Security Division, and the Plumbers all rolled into one. It was perhaps different in that Nixon would be waging "psy-war" on the entire Democratic Party rather than the Panthers, or even Ellsberg. But why not? The nation's future was at stake. Not just four more years for Nixon, but a lasting Republican majority and a massive mandate for the social and economic priorities of his big business backers.

The campaign actually began the night Nixon won the presidency in 1968, and re-election had been part of every move the administration made. But in 1970, the more partisan effort picked up, as Haldeman secretly put $400,000 or so into the race for governor of Alabama, trying to stop George Wallace. That failed, and by late October 1971, Magruder and possibly Mitchell were in California, paying $10,000 in an equally abortive effort to re-register members of Wallace's American Independent Party and knock the party from the ballot. The money, or at least part of it, went to members of the Nazi Party. (Rightwing publicist William K. Shearer also blames the Nixon team for the "Draft Wallace" effort at AIP's convention in August 1972, seeing it as a way to disrupt the party at a time when Wallace wouldn't run.)

As might be expected, the campaigners showed an early interest in intelligence, and like the intelligence community, they used the word to mean both information *and* "dirty tricks." Sometime in 1971 Caulfield proposed a modest program he called Sandwedge, while as early as February of that year, the president's appointments secretary Dwight Chapin and Haldeman's aide Gordon Strachan had started to put together a nationwide department of dirty tricks for the Democratic primaries. As it was later described by one of their victims, McGovern's campaign director Frank Mankiewicz, the apparent goal was to create "such a strong sense of resentment among the

(Democratic) candidates and their followers as to make unity of the party impossible once a nominee was selected."

A key agent in the program was Donald Segretti, a young lawyer and Vietnam veteran whom Chapin and Strachan had known in their college days at USC. Using several aliases, Segretti began work that summer, flying across the country to recruit campaign workers. Starting early, the recruits put together dossiers on the Democratic candidates and backers, stole documents, forged campaign literature and press releases, disrupted fundraising parties and political rallies, harassed campaign workers, picked fights, and the like. In the Florida primary, Segretti and his recruits sent out a press release on Henry Jackson's stationery accusing Muskie of stealing Congressional typewriters for the campaign and one on Muskie stationery accusing Jackson of homosexuality and Humphrey of suppressing reports of an automobile accident in which he was caught with a call girl. The "tricksters" also produced a leaflet with the slogan, "If you like Hitler, you'll love George Wallace."

Ken Clawson, the Communications Director of CREEP, went Segretti one better. During the New Hampshire primary he authored a letter supposedly from a Florida voter to William Loeb's Manchester *Union-Leader,* accusing Muskie of calling French-Americans "canucks" and his wife of using un-ladylike language. Muskie responded publicly, his eyes wet and his voice shaky, turning thousands of New Hampshire voters against him and destroying his previously unbeatable edge in the Democratic race.

The only one to get through the primaries relatively unscathed was George McGovern, who seemed the easiest opponent for Nixon. "We're out to destroy all candidates except McGovern," Segretti told a campaign recruit in Indiana. But once McGovern neared the top of the Democratic heap, the dirty tricksters opened fire. They made bogus phone calls setting up phantom meetings with labor leaders at which McGovern never showed, canceled television ads, and generally widened the rift among Democrats. According to Mankiewicz,

Segretti and his recruits distributed "leaflets deliberately distorting the record and maligning the character of Senators Humphrey and McGovern . . . in the name of the other, rival candidate." "Dirty tricks" were anything but pranks.

It was a remarkable operation, and it ran on information. According to Strachan, it was common knowledge in the Nixon camp that they were getting information from Senator Muskie's driver. "Fat Jack" (John Buckley) covered Muskie's Washington headquarters. "Chapman's Friends" (Seymour Freidin and Lucy Goldberg) posed as reporters on the campaign planes, and "Sedan Chair II" (Michael W. McMinoway) posed as a volunteer security guard at the Democratic Convention. It was "Sedan Chair II" who reportedly overheard Mankiewicz discuss the health problems of Senator Thomas Eagleton.

Hunt, Liddy, and McCord had other work as well. While still at the Justice Department, Mitchell had ordered Liddy to work up an intelligence plan for the campaign, which he did with help from Hunt. Liddy presented the plan on January 27. He and Hunt wanted to use electronic bugs and call girls to get information from Democratic National Chairman Larry O'Brien and other prominent party leaders, and to kidnap radical activists to keep them out of the way during the Republican convention. "They would be detained in a place like Mexico and returned to the country at the end of the convention," Magruder later testified. Liddy and Hunt figured that the plan would cost a million dollars, but Mitchell balked, and Liddy had to present scaled-down versions on February 4 and again on March 30 at Key Biscayne. Mitchell later testified that he never approved the plan, but Magruder said that Mitchell did, authorizing a quarter of a million dollars. Magruder also testified that Colson had pushed the plan, telling Magruder "to get off the stick and get the budget approved for Liddy's plan to get information on Democratic Chairman Lawrence O'Brien."

Whoever gave the go-ahead, McCord and some of the Cubans broke into the Watergate offices of the Democratic National Committee over the Memorial Day weekend, planting bugs on the phones of O'Brien and another party official and searching

the files for interesting information. They repeated the performance again on June 17, in part to replace a defective device
on O'Brien's phone. This time they were caught.

O'Brien was an obvious target. The White House considered
him the shrewdest of the Democrats, and according to Dean,
Caulfield and Ulasewicz had been trying to get something on
him. He was a Kennedy man, and would know of any last
minute efforts to draft Edward Kennedy. As party chairman, he
would be in the center of the kind of gossip that the dirty
tricksters could put to use, and his files would contain advance
schedules, political strategies, and lists of top financial contributors.

All this was reason enough for the break-in. But another
consideration might have weighed as heavily. Back in the 1960
elections, it became known late in the campaign that billionaire
industrialist Howard Hughes had loaned Nixon's brother Donald
$205,000. The story hurt Nixon at the polls, and Robert Ken-
nedy credited it as a major factor in *his* brother's victory. By
1972, Donald Nixon had new ties to the Hughes organization,
as well as to financier Robert Vesco, and had played some part
in a mysterious $100,000 contribution from Hughes. Since
O'Brien was in a position to have the inside information, having
served as a high-priced consultant to Hughes, it was vital to
know if he knew and if he was planning any surprise use of the
information. If "Watergate" was a four-year program to polarize
America, the break-in itself might well have been a smaller,
family affair.

Evidently, "the same crowd" chalked up other break-ins, possibly at the home of the Democratic treasurer Robert Strauss
and the law office of vice-presidential contender Sargent
Shriver. They also contemplated a break-in at the office of Las
Vegas publisher Hank Greenspun, who might have had additional evidence of Hughes's activities. But as with the campaign
against Ellsberg, break-ins were only a prelude to open assault,
though this time on a grander scale.

At the time the Republicans were planning the convention in
San Diego, FBI informer Howard Barry Godfrey was leading the

right-wing Secret Army Organization in a campaign of terror bombings and shootings against the San Diego left and was planning to do even more at the convention. According to informer Louis Tackwood, the Los Angeles Police Department had a special squad to provoke left-wing violence at the convention. Once the convention site had been moved to Miami, Hunt and Liddy evidently had a similar confrontation planned, pitting anticommunist Cubans against antiwar Vietnam veterans. Little ever came of the plan, in part because Guy Goodwin and the Internal Security Division got an indictment against the vet leaders for planning to disrupt the convention. This helped cover up for the Watergate arrests, which had come less than a month before, tied the vets up during the convention, and created the aura of violence needed to polarize the voters even more.

It was, of course, this premature ending that encouraged radical speculation about what might have happened if the Watergate burglars hadn't been caught, or if the convention hadn't been moved from San Diego, where the prospects for violence were much greater. From the experience at the Democratic convention in Chicago four years before, as well as the experience in Watts and Berkeley, it is likely that the authorities would have used more than a minimum force to handle any demonstrators. The right-left clash might have gotten out of hand; Governor Reagan might have called in the National Guard; Hunt and Liddy might even have kidnaped some radical leaders, if the San Diego police hadn't arrested the radicals first.

But bad as it might have been, there is no reason to think that the president and his backers would have pushed for ongoing martial law or called off the elections. Why should they? The forms of democracy were working in their favor, so much so that the president would overwhelm McGovern in an unprecedented landslide and go on to cut back even more Great Society and New Deal programs. Thanks to four years of psy-war and Watergate, Nixon and his backers had successfully polarized America.

Tom Huston's Plan

Steve Weissman

To look at Tom Charles Huston, no one would think he had anything to do with secret police. Thin and scholarly-looking in his wide-rimmed glasses, the former White House aide looks like an assistant professor from some small college in the mid-West. But in June 1970, Huston drafted an internal security program which increased the role of the CIA and Defense Intelligence Agency in domestic spying and authorized the FBI to use illegal wiretaps, bugs and break-ins.

The existence of the Huston Plan, and the conflict it caused between the White House and FBI Director J. Edgar Hoover, were among the more startling revelations of former White House Counsel John Dean. But Dean's Watergate testimony left two key questions unanswered. Where did the Huston Plan come from? And where did it go after Hoover forced President Nixon to call back his initial approval?

As Huston explained it, he simply wanted to stop the black militant and Weatherman-type terrorists before they created a real right-wing backlash. More likely, the White House wanted to use the terrorists to provoke a backlash in its favor. But whatever the political purpose, the Huston Plan clearly tried to tighten White House control over the nation's police apparatus. The Administration was already using the CIA, DIA, and National Security Agency to follow the Panthers and new leftists abroad, looking for possible links to Havana, Algiers, Moscow, Hanoi, and Peking. Now it would make new use of these ostensibly overseas agencies and also take charge of the FBI.

Huston was particularly interested in the problems of the DIA, which coordinated the military intelligence agencies and their role in domestic counterinsurgency. He had come to the White House from a top-security army intelligence post at the Pentagon and knew the problems the DIA faced.

Back in the 1950s, the Eisenhower administration had asked the military to teach its Brazilian, Indonesian, and Greek counterparts the "nation-building" and "civic action skills" they would need to play "new roles." Once the "bulwark" against external aggression, the military of the poorer nations was now to guard against "internal subversion," act as an "internal motor" of development, and "prepare to assume the reins of power themselves." Many of America's professional soldiers didn't like the new counterinsurgency, but following President John F. Kennedy's embarrassment at the Bay of Pigs, his brother Robert worked with General Maxwell Taylor and the CIA to force the new doctrine through the still-traditional Pentagon, the State Department, and the Agency for International Development.

Inevitably the new thinking also took hold within the United States, especially in riot control and surveillance.

The core cities "can offer better security to snipers and city guerrillas than the Viet Cong enjoy in their elephant grass and marshes," explained Colonel Robert Riggs. But advance intelligence could "identify hide-outs, areas where weapons are stored, sources of arms, guerrilla means of transportation, access and escape routes, and probable resistance spots." It could also help "to warn of secret subversive plans, to pinpoint leaders, and to disrupt the organization itself."

The military worked hard to counter the domestic insurgents, and also to strengthen its role in internal affairs, much as it had taught its counterparts to do abroad. The Military Police School at Fort Gordon, Georgia, ran courses in civil disturbance control for state and local police, as well as the National Guard. Army advisers worked with the FBI and the Katzenbach Commission on Law Enforcement in preparing the Federal Riot Manual, and with Attorney General Ramsey Clark and the International Association of Chiefs of Police in providing consultants and technical skills to the grassroots riot controllers. The Army, Navy, and Air Force also gathered intelligence secretly, storing it in their own files and computers and supplying it to the Justice Department's Interdivisional Information Unit (IDIU), which had been created by Attorney General Clark. To pinpoint leaders, the Army distributed a two-volume compendium, or "blacklist," of people "likely to cause trouble to the Army." This made it possible for the police, National Guard, and Army to "kidnap" potential insurgent leaders, particularly with the Nixon administration's views on preventive detention.

The problem for the White House and the counterinsurgents was that former Captain Christopher Pyle had uncovered the Army surveillance program in the January 1970 issue of *Washington Monthly*. This caused an uproar in Congress, especially from Senator Sam Ervin, who noted that the Army was not "concerned solely with nonestablishment political activities which they thought might develop into or be aligned with violent actions," but "was actively covering the activities of individuals and groups against whom no charge of political extremism can possibly be made." The Army replied that it was spying on civilians because it might be called upon to put down civil disturbances and because the FBI and Justice Department lacked the manpower to do the job. Then, in March and April 1970, the Army told Kleindienst that it was cutting back the program. Senator Ervin discovered later that the Army only unplugged some of its computers and that it continued much of the spying, both in the United States and on civilian groups in

West Germany. But the furor raised the possibility that the administration would have to find other agencies to do the spying.

The CIA's domestic interests were more closely related to local police. The agency had maintained front groups and surveillance activities within the United States almost from its creation in 1947, even though the National Security Act forbids it "police, subpoena, law enforcement powers, or internal security functions." But it had stepped up its domestic activity while working on counterinsurgency, especially through AID's Office of Public Safety and International Police Academy, for which it helped recruit local police and FBI men to train foreign police. It also contributed to the Katzenbach Commission, reportedly briefed Chicago police at CIA headquarters in Langley and at secret paramilitary camps in Virginia and the Carolinas in 1968, and later admitted training police from about a dozen cities in handling explosives, detection of wiretaps, and organization of intelligence files.

Several CIA veterans were also moving into direct supervision of police forces. The head of the agency's youth and student operations, Robert Kiley, became Associate Director of the Police Foundation in 1970, then Deputy Mayor of Boston, with responsibility for the police department. A former CIA clandestine agent, Don Harris, was a consultant to the New York Police Department under a grant from the Law Enforcement Assistance Administration (LEAA). A third former agent, E. Drexel Godfrey, became director of the Pennsylvania State Crime Commission, while a fourth, Manuel Aragon, became deputy mayor of Los Angeles after the election of Tom Bradley. "The whole police field in Washington is all mixed up with the intelligence community," a Boston official told Andrew Kopkind.*

Much of this domestic activity was probably the work of the

* See Andrew Kopkind, "The Politics of Police Reform," *Ramparts,* October 1973.

CIA's Special Division for Internal Operations, which had been set up in 1964 under Tracy Barnes, a top CIA official and liaison to the State Department during the Bay of Pigs. Many observers also regarded LEAA as something of a CIA outpost and a direct copy of the Office of Public Safety. Despite this obvious domestic interest, Huston had worried that the CIA might refuse to go along with the new program, possibly out of competition with the rival DIA. He was pleasantly surprised to find CIA Director Richard Helms "most cooperative and helpful."

The FBI was more uncertain. Ever since FDR, it had been *the* domestic intelligence agency, and to do the job it had regularly resorted to illegal bugs, wiretaps, burglaries, mail coverage, and even safe-cracking, as a number of G-men have testified. But on June 30, 1965, after the FBI disclosed it had used electronic devices in the criminal investigation of President Lyndon Johnson's former protegé Robert G. "Bobby" Baker, the president banned all the wiretaps and bugs except in national security cases, and only then with the approval of the attorney general. As far as anyone knows, Attorneys General Katzenbach and Clark generally refused Bureau requests on electronic devices and also on break-ins.

On his own, Hoover reportedly dragged his feet on ghetto intelligence, and his new left coverage was so inadequate that FBI informers at the December 1969 SDS meeting in Flint, Michigan, apparently failed to note that the Weathermen had decided to go underground and begin a campaign of bombings. An old fashioned anticommunist, the director lacked the agents and the understanding to penetrate the new radical milieux. As Huston saw it, Hoover had "wiped out the whole domestic security system."

That was one side of the story. The other was more positive, at least from Huston's point of view. Despite rules and regulations, the FBI had continued to use wiretaps and break-ins, sometimes without the attorney general's consent, sometimes with local police or army intelligence agents. The Bureau's counterintelligence programs had infiltrated new left and "black extremist" groups to disrupt them and topple their leaders, and on May 11, 1970 Hoover started a "Counterintelligence and Special Operations" assault on the Black Panthers. As Hoover explained it, the Bureau would prepare false police or FBI documents "pinpointing Panthers as police or FBI informants; ridiculing or discrediting Panther leaders through their ineptness or personal escapades; espousing personal philosophies and promoting factionalism among BPP members; indicating electronic coverage or other counteractions; revealing misuse or misappropriation of Panther funds; pointing out instances of political disorientation."

An unnamed college professor later described one of the Bureau's successes to the Boston *Phoenix*. As he put it, FBI officials "told me quite frankly that the Bureau informers within the Black Panthers had been told to align themselves with either the Cleaver faction or the Newton faction and intensify the split."

FBI informers played a big part in police raids and indictments against the Panthers, while the Counterintelligence Program (COINTELPRO) effectively planted a number of anti-Panther stories with "responsible news media sources." Bureau informers like Larry Grathwohl and "Tommy the Traveler" were even provoking a good part of the "revolutionary terrorism" that fueled the White House anti-student campaign, especially in the Cambodia spring of 1970.

The Bureau also supplied special services to the White House. In 1969 Nixon learned that Franklin Roosevelt and Lyndon Johnson had used the FBI to dig up dirt on their enemies, cover up for their friends, and conduct special operations. Nixon wanted the same, and the Bureau started a special "Intelligence Letter for the President," telling local agents to flag certain "security-related" items for Nixon's attention. This included significant "inside information concerning demonstrations, disorders or other such disruptions." Project Inlet also flagged "items with an unusual twist concerning prominent person- alities," whether related to security or not.

At least part of the questionable activity was the work of William C. Sullivan, longtime chief of the Domestic Intelligence Division and, after July 21, 1970, Assistant to the Director—the number three post in the Bureau. As he explained it, things had to be kept from Hoover during his last three years because the chief had become "mentally incompetent." This attitude made Sullivan a natural ally of the White House. "Those individuals within the FBI who have day-to-day responsibilities for domes- tic intelligence operations privately disagree with Mr. Hoover and believe that it is imperative that changes in operating pro- cedures be initiated at once," explained Huston.

These were the various perspectives within the intelligence community in early June 1970, when the president asked Huston to head an ad hoc committee to suggest improvements in the domestic security system. Huston presented the com- mittee's proposal on June 25, and by any reckoning it was a hodge-podge. To former Colonel L. Fletcher Prouty, who served several years as an Air Force liaison with the CIA, it read as if it had come from a DIA position paper, while the ACLU's Frank Donner suggests that William Sullivan might have written most of it. In any case, Nixon approved the Huston Plan, as Halde- man told Huston on July 14, 1970, and Huston gave the agencies the go-ahead on July 23. The United States had a new and highly illegal security program.

The Huston Plan called for a stronger attack on the militants and terrorists, authorizing illegal break-ins, mail checks, bugs, wiretaps, monitoring of international communications, and "coverage" of American students (and others) traveling and liv- ing abroad. But it left unspecified "present restrictions" on "the use of military undercover agents." As Huston explained it, "the intelligence community is agreed that the risks of lifting these restraints are greater than the value of any possible intelligence which would be acquired by doing so." The plan also created a permanent Interagency Group on Domestic Intelligence and Internal Security, composed of the chiefs of the FBI, CIA, DIA, NSA, and military intelligence agencies. The Group was to oversee all domestic intelligence, prepare intelligence estimates and evaluations, and "perform such other duties as the President shall, from time to time, assign." It was to work in secret, its existence and purpose known only to those with a "need to know." The goal: better coordination and greater "responsiveness to the White House."

Huston was delighted, and then disappointed. He had told Haldeman that "the only stumbling block was Mr. Hoover." The old man had "refused to go along with a single conclusion drawn or support a single recommendation made," and had "entered his objections as footnotes to the report." But Hoover continued to object, and evidently got to Mitchell, who had not been included in the interagency group. Mitchell backed Hoover's request that the plan be reconsidered, the president gave in, and on July 28 the White House was forced to telephone the agencies and ask them to return the memoranda giving the president's approval.

"For Mr. Hoover, jurisdiction was paramount," explained an FBI loyalist. He had run the Bureau for over 50 years and he didn't want an interagency anything looking over his shoulder. He also wanted to protect his flanks from the civil libertarians. In describing the program to Haldeman, Huston had noted that "covert mail coverage" and "surreptitious entry" were "clearly illegal," "risky," and potentially embarrassing. "We don't want the President linked to this thing with his signature on paper," he warned. "All hell would break loose if this thing leaks out." Hoover evidently agreed. According to one account, neither the president nor the attorney general would give explicit authorization for the illegal activities, and Hoover refused to take responsibility on his own. Nor could he be coerced. He had evidence that Henry Kissinger had wiretapped his National Security Council staff, and the old fox knew how to use it.

With the Huston Plan out of the way, the confusion in the FBI continued, at least from the White House point of view. Huston had seen the campus as "the battleground of the revolutionary protest movement," and had called for more student informers, especially under twenty-one. Hoover had reportedly balked, but on September 16 he approved hiring "student informers," and on November 4 he ordered "an increase in both quality and quantity of intelligence information on black student unions and similar groups which are targets for influence and control by the violence-prone Black Panther party and other extremists." Hoover also started in October to hire a thousand new agents, even though Congress hadn't yet voted the money, and the Bureau continued to pay local police to run informers, giving the Bureau "deniability." According to Frank Donner, the use of local police was most advanced on the West Coast, where it was used against SDS, Venceremos, and the Revolutionary Union.

FBI provocations also continued, particularly in Camden, New Jersey, where sixty-dollar-a-day informer Robert Hardy led a group of antiwar Catholics in a raid on the draft board the night of August 22, 1970, bringing the arrest of twenty-eight militants. "It definitely wouldn't have happened without me," Hardy explained in a later affidavit. "I provided 90 percent of the tools necessary for the action. They couldn't afford to pay for the tools so I paid and the FBI reimbursed me. It included hammers, ropes, drills and bits. They couldn't use some of the tools without hurting themselves, so I taught them."

Hardy claimed that the FBI had followed the planning for a period of two months, promising him that they would make the arrests before the raid took place. But the Bureau broke its promise, possibly at a time when Director Hoover was on his summer vacation. "I was told," Hardy testified, "that against the wishes of some of the local FBI people, the higher-ups, 'someone at the little White House in California,' they said, wanted it to actually happen." Someone at the little White House wanted the draft board raided.

On the other hand, Hoover continued to go his own way. In August he broke all liaison with the other agencies; in October he began sending agents as "legal attachés" to gather overseas intelligence. He also broke with the Justice Department over the antiwar "plot" to kidnap Henry Kissinger and blow up underground electrical conduits and steam pipes near the Capitol, about which he learned in late August, mostly from informer Boyd Douglas. The Justice Department found the evidence insufficient even to bring a grand jury. But Hoover used his November 27 appearance before the Senate Appropriations Committee to unmask the conspiracy, giving himself the credit and forcing the indictment of the Harrisburg Seven.

During this whole period, the Bureau was under continual attack by civil libertarians and other critics. Then in early March 1971, radical activists "liberated" some embarrassing files from the FBI office in Media, Pennsylvania, and on April 25 House Democratic leader Hale Boggs accused the FBI of "secret police tactics" and of infiltrating campuses, unions, and church, business and black organizations. Three days later, Hoover called off the counterintelligence programs, though the Bureau later admitted that it continued to conduct similar programs under different names. Hoover also moved against White House ally William Sullivan, placing W. Mark Felt into a new post above Sullivan on July 24, 1971, and forcing Sullivan to resign on October 4. Seeing the end, Sullivan took the logs of the Kissinger wiretaps from the Bureau files, and in July gave them to Robert Mardian, who flew them to San Clemente. For this act of loyalty, Nixon later appointed Sullivan Director of National Narcotics Intelligence.

It was a messy business, replete with rumors that Sullivan had been locked out of his office. But, ironically, the purge showed that the FBI had not stopped its illegal operations, as Huston had charged, a year or so before. As an FBI man told right-wing journalist Ralph de Toledano, "Strangely enough, where they locked horns, the Director was taking the 'civil rights' position and Sullivan was gung-ho for action. Everybody was jumping on the Bureau for taking the law into its hands. The Director was sensitive about this and he put a partial 'hold' on the use of wiretaps and microphone surveillances. He also put his foot down on what we call 'surreptitious entry' and the 'bag job'—that's where agents enter a house or office and go through papers, effects, and so on—even in national security cases."

The Huston Plan was dead, the White House grip on the FBI dying, and army intelligence still under fire—if Nixon and his aides were to push ahead with their war on the "revolutionary terrorists," they would have to do it piece by piece. The options were plentiful, both in the federal government and by working through state and local agencies, where extralegal methods would cause few problems—at least for the White House.

The possibilities of the hand-me-down approach were clearest in California, where Ronald Reagan was running again for governor and Los Angeles District Attorney Evelle Younger for a first term as attorney general. According to later accounts, the California Council on Criminal Justice had a Task Force on Riots and Disorders, headed by Dr. William Herrmann, a retired Los Angeles policeman, an expert on counterinsurgency for the Systems Development Corporation, and a government adviser on Vietnam. Both during and after Huston's attempt to give Nixon a new security program, Herrmann was giving Reagan a secret plan "to forestall revolution." To the experts, it was a model for dealing with national emergency.

The Herrmann Plan, which was called "Saving America," included electronic surveillance, deeper penetration of dissident groups by undercover agents, mathematical probability models to predict the time and place of future violence, and the use of a nationwide computerized intelligence system. The plan would cost $24 million, with $18 million from LEAA. It would coordinate civil, military, and police agencies in the collection of intelligence. And it would use everything from income tax records and traffic violations to information on sexual behavior and drug use.

A follower of the British counterinsurgent and Nixon-adviser Sir Robert Thompson, Dr. Herrmann wanted to use intelligence much as Thompson had used it to crush the rebels in Malaya. Governor Reagan had admitted that "a great majority of students" stood behind the youthful radical groups. Herrmann would "split off those bent on destroying the system from the mass of dissenters." As an aide explained, the state would no longer allow "these people" to misuse democratic rules to play the revolutionary game. The Herrmann Plan would be a militant defense of the laws, aimed at troublemakers whom Herrmann saw as part of a communist-inspired campaign to make impossible America's "worldwide peace-keeping task."

As it happened, Dr. Herrmann talked about this plan to the *Los Angeles Times*, explaining that the National Guard would do much of the spying. That led to a public outcry, and Reagan was forced to cancel the National Guard's role in "Saving America." But the state and the Los Angeles Police Department continued with much of the plan with LEAA funding, while in December 1970 Attorney General Mitchell and the FBI secretly took control of the computerized intelligence system.

The White House also looked to other federal agencies. On August 25, for example, Huston urged an Executive Order expanding the powers of the nearly defunct Subversive Activities Control Board. "We cannot afford to let the Board sit idle or content itself with investigating old-line Communist fronts which are largely irrelevant to our current problems," he wrote Haldeman. A month later, on September 21, he urged a larger role for the Internal Revenue Service, which had formed a Special Services Group in mid-1969 to investigate the tax records of "known militants and activists" and their organizations. As Huston explained, "What we cannot do in a courtroom via criminal prosecution to curtail the activities of some of these groups, IRS could do by administrative action. Moreover, valuable intelligence-type information could be turned up by IRS as a result of their field audits."

Several other agencies either got or kept intelligence, including the Secret Service and the Treasury Department's Bureau of Alcohol, Tobacco and Firearms. The White House also found intelligence possibilities in the newly created Bureau of Narcotics and Dangerous Drugs (BNDD) and the Drug Abuse Law Enforcement (DALE) agency. Of those who would come to play major roles in Watergate, several worked at one time or another in drugs. Another outside possibility was the CIA. In 1971, James Schlesinger did a big reorganization study of the CIA while still at the White House Office of Management and Budget, and then helped implement it as CIA director. It seems possible that the Schlesinger Plan touched on the problems of replacing the Huston Plan. "Unlike most of the bureaucracy, the intelligence community welcomes direction and leadership from the White House," Huston had noted.

But the clearest consequence of the Huston Plan, or its demise, came in the Internal Security Division of the Department of Justice, organized in 1954 to conduct Smith Act prosecutions against those who taught or advocated the overthrow of the United States by force and violence. Something of a white elephant, or red herring, ever since the Supreme Court declared the Smith Act unconstitutional, the ISD got a new lease on life and an energetic new boss, Robert Mardian. A personal friend of Kleindienst and ardent foe of the militants, Mardian came in November from the White House, where he had served under Vice President Agnew as executive director of a special group to help Southern schools deal with court-ordered desegregation. For his new post, Mardian had hoped to bring in Huston as his deputy, but Huston didn't trust the older man's ardor. As he saw it, "Mardian didn't know a kid with a beard from a kid with a bomb."

One of ISD's first tasks under Mardian was to take on the coordination of domestic intelligence, a central concern of the Huston Plan. Back on September 18, White House Counsel John Dean had sent a memo to Attorney General Mitchell, suggesting that the anti-riot Interdivisional Information Unit (IDIU) might make a good "cover" for "an interagency intelligence unit for both operational and evaluative purposes." Dean, on whose staff Huston had worked, urged Mitchell to meet with Hoover and ask his help. Haldeman would be happy to join the meeting, he added.

"I believe we agreed that it would be inappropriate to have any blanket removal of restrictions [on illegal surveillance]; rather, the most appropriate procedure would be to decide on the type of intelligence we need, based on the recommendation of the unit, and then proceed to remove the restraints as necessary to obtain such intelligence," Dean wrote.

Two months later Mardian had moved to Mitchell's department, and in December the covert Intelligence Evaluation Committee (IEC) was at work, staffed by member-agencies—the CIA, NSA, and DIA, along with the Secret Service and Justice Department. The White House and Treasury were also members of the IEC, as was the FBI, though Hoover refused to provide any of the initial staff.

Much as Dean had suggested, the IEC moved step by step. On February 10, 1971, Mardian sent out an IEC memo on intelligence for civil disorders, claiming "access to all pertinent intelligence in the possession of the United States Government." Later he expanded the committee's scope to cover a broad range of radical and antiwar activity. For whatever reason, probably bureaucratic, the cover IDIU was not put into Mardian's Division until February or March, but public accounts of *its* activity suggest the scope of the secret IEC.

"Officials in the department [of Justice] say that the Interdivisional Information Unit, known as IDIU, concentrates on black militant opponents of the war in Vietnam and New Left advocates of overthrow of the nation's political and economic system," the *New York Times* reported on April 2, 1971.

"But it also maintains dossiers on elected political officials and moderates who are thought to condone or stimulate civil disobedience. One official says that 'anybody like that, no matter what his politics are or what his position might be, would go into the file,'" the *Times* continued. Back on July 29, 1970, the day after the president moved to reconsider the Huston Plan, army intelligence had given the entire printout of its civilian surveillance computers to ISD, which was defending in court the Army's right to spy on the homefront. ISD was still receiving material for its files from the Army, as well as from other agencies.

The IEC-IDIU was "particularly active" in planning for coming May Day demonstrations in Washington, the *Times* noted. The plan was more polarization. Riot-geared police and regular army troops ringed the capital, arrested over thirteen thousand people, and packed them into local prisons and JFK Stadium. The courts declared the mass arrests illegal and freed the protestors. But the show of force was just what Mitchell and Kleindienst had wanted ever since Inauguration Day.

What else the IEC-IDIU did is unclear, particularly in the area of illegal surveillance. Dean, who suggested that it "remove the restraints as necessary," later told the Watergate Committee that he knew of no illegal activity by the unit. In his statement of May 22, 1973, President Nixon said the same: "I did not authorize nor do I have any knowledge of any illegal activity by this Committee. If it went beyond its charter and did engage in any illegal activity, it was totally without my knowledge or authority."

On the other hand, the president never rescinded his approval of illegal surveillance, not even on July 28 when the White House asked the agencies to return the memo giving approval to it. If the president had taken back his go-ahead, the much beleaguered White House would have come up with the proof. This is key, since police records show several suspicious break-ins against lawyers and defendants in political cases handled by Mardian and the ISD.

Besides the IEC-IDIU, Mardian's ISD took over prosecution of some forty-five hundred draft cases and all political bombings and fires. It also maintained contact with FBI informers Larry Grathwohl in Detroit and William Lemmer in Gainesville. But the most telling thrust against the antiwar militants was its special grand juries, which ISD conducted all over the country under authority of the Organized Crime Control Act of 1970. The grand juries brought a few key indictments, notably those against the Reverend Phillip Berrigan and the Harrisburg Seven, Leslie Bacon, and the alleged bombers of the Mathematics Research Center at the University of Wisconsin. But their real job was to gather political intelligence.

The sessions were secret, except where ISD wanted to leak a story embarrassing to the radicals. Special Prosecutor Guy Goodwin and his colleagues in ISD's Special Litigation Section asked radical witnesses the broadest questions: where they spent their time, who they saw, what they did, what their friends did. The law forced witnesses to answer, jailing for contempt those who refused. The FBI, with which the prosecutors worked closely, lacked the power to subpoena witnesses. Not the grand juries. Director Hoover fell short on informers, wiretaps, and break-ins. The grand juries granted immunity from prosecution and forced radicals to inform on themselves and their friends, or risk jail. No right to counsel. No right to know who was being investigated on what charge.

"Obviously you can't give witnesses before a grand jury the rights of the accused," Mardian explained. "It would stop the wheels of justice from turning."

From LEAA's support of the Herrmann Plan to Robert Mardian's transformation of the Internal Security Division, the administration pushed far beyond Tom Huston's plan, but what began as an effort to tighten control over domestic policing led even farther—to the creation of the Plumbers Unit within the White House itself. This came in July 1971, right at the time William Sullivan's star was beginning to wane at the FBI, and its job was to carry out many of the wiretaps and break-ins which the president had authorized a year before. Tom Huston was gone, but his secret police went marching on.

The San Diego Coup

Richard Popkin

San Diego is a strange town, where the niceties of Western civilization cannot hide the power of the buck and the hint of brute force. It is the city built with the largesse of twenty-five years of imperial sway: a stronghold, a haven of anti-communism, a base for racketeers. Richard Nixon considered it his lucky city. He wanted the Republican Convention to be held there, and though the city fathers and the people of San Diego were not terribly enthusiastic, the plans went forward until May 1972, when the president abruptly changed his mind.

Included in these plans, it turns out, was a tumultuous, massive, bloody riot—on such a scale as to justify the most extraordinary preventive measures, including burglary, bugging, sabotage, and perhaps even kidnaping. Watergate, we learn from the likes of John W. Dean, was simply a part of a strategy to maintain domestic tranquillity in the face of a serious left-wing threat.

The original version of this essay, entitled "The Strange Tale of the Secret Army Organization (USA)," © 1973, appeared in *Ramparts,* October 1973. Reprinted by permission of the author.

Presumably, this Red Menace existed in San Diego as well as Miami. But San Diego has never been a radical stronghold, and while local activists did undertake extensive perparations for antiwar demonstrations during the GOP convention, the Committee to Re-elect the President seems to have had a far higher opinion of their organizing successes than they themselves dared to entertain.

Unless, of course, CREEP and its local San Diego allies were hell-bent on making certain that bedlam did in fact occur. That is precisely what a defecting *agent provocateur* named Louis Tackwood suggested almost a year before. Tackwood told an incredible story back in October and November 1971, one which suggested the Republicans were doing their utmost to turn San Diego into a bloodbath during the convention, with the aim of annihilating the left, smearing the Democrats, and coasting comfortably into four more years of conservative rule. His allegations were regarded as the ravings of a madman until testimony in the Senate caucus room appeared to corroborate some of his wildest stories. He told of preparations to seal off and then bomb a hundred thousand demonstrators attending a rock concert on Fiesta Island in Mission Bay, San Diego. All sorts of mayhem were supposed to occur. Bombs were to be smuggled into Convention Center in hollow furniture, which was already being built in Los Angeles. At least one major Republican official would perish in the melee. The Democratic Party would be tied in to the events, discredited, possibly outlawed. The Republican candidate would then win an easy victory with the overwhelming support of an outraged citizenry. Today, Tackwood sticks by his original story, though he now adds that the plan also called for blowing up the podium as President Nixon was making his acceptance speech!

Civil War in San Diego

Incredible as the Tackwood scenario seemed back in 1971, it sounded less outlandish to San Diego radicals than to those on the outside. For two years, they had quite literally been engaged in protracted warfare with right-wingers determined to drive them out of the area. As early as 1970, activists associated with the San Diego *Street Journal*, an underground newspaper, were living in an armed fortress which they guarded around the clock against the attacks of night riders who would shoot into their houses, firebomb their cars and threaten their lives. (Curiously, this terror campaign intensified as the paper exposed more and more illegal activities of San Diego kingpin C. Arnholt Smith.) On one occasion, for example, sentries spotted two men crouched behind a car with a high-powered rifle trained on the house. It was late at night, but they were prepared for such emergencies. At a signal, they switched on floodlamps which bathed the house in light and they announced over a loudspeaker system that they would open fire if the men did not withdraw. The gunmen waited a moment, then dismantled their rifle, and drove off into the night.

By late 1971, the vigilantes had stepped up their attacks and had chosen their principal targets. One of these was a certain Peter Bohmer, a radical who at the time was teaching economics at San Diego State College. He began receiving threatening phone calls, and on November 13, 1971, a car parked in front of his house was firebombed. Then on December 27, 1971, a group calling itself the Secret Army Organization put out a Special Bulletin on Peter Bohmer. After listing his antiwar activities, and his background, the letter said: "For any of our readers who may care to look up this Red Scum, and say hello, here is some information that may help." Then his address, phone number, and car license were given, plus a physical description. "Now, in case any of you don't believe in hitting people who wear glasses, to be fair, I guess we will have to tell you he wears contact lenses."

On January 6, 1972, cross-hair stickers (the symbol of the SAO) were placed on the doors of three San Diego State College professors, including Bohmer. Then, an anonymous caller telephoned Bohmer's residence to say, "This time we left a sticker, next time we may leave a grenade. This is the SAO." Bohmer's friends were called and told to say goodbye to him. That evening, two shots were fired into Bohmer's home and a woman named Paula Tharp was wounded.

The right-wing terror campaign continued for six more months, marked by death threats, menacing phone calls, and warning messages. Its climax came on June 19, 1972, when an SAO member bombed a local porno movie house, the Guild Theatre. This last event finally aroused the San Diego police to drive the group underground.

Police action brought a halt, at least temporarily, to right-wing terrorism in San Diego. But this is not the end of the tale. For in the months that followed a very bizarre story began to unravel, one which involved the SAO, the FBI, and some mysterious contacts between the terrorists and agents of CREEP. The pieces began to appear as early as mid-1972, but it is only in recent months that they have been pulled together by reporters for another San Diego alternative newspaper, the *Door*.

Secret Army—USA

The SAO, it seems, grew out of the demise of the Minutemen. According to a recently discovered document entitled "History of the Secret Army Organization," it all began one morning in February 1970, when ". . . a group of six Minutemen leaders from four states met secretly in Northern Arizona to discuss the crisis that the arrest and imprisonment of two top Minutemen leaders and the assassination of a third had brought on the organization. Although some of these men had met before in their roles as Minutemen group leaders, others were meeting for the first time." These men agreed that "the Minutemen as a national coordination organization of militant right-wing groups had effectively been destroyed by the pro-communist elements inside the Justice Department," and they further agreed that the need for a coordinating organization was greater than ever "in view of the increased revolutionary activity by communists in the United States." The new organization was the Secret Army Organization, and it would save America from its leftward drift under Nixon's regime.

The initial SAO documents speak of the immediate need to set up paramilitary groups to carry on guerrilla warfare, and even open and conventional warfare. A letter from "General Headquarters" dated November 8, 1971, outlines the nature of SAO operations—combat teams, organization, transportation, travel procedures, weapons and equipment, training lessons, intelligence work, security, etc. They say that the country has entered "Stage II": a time when most people think they can still get along with the government, but "a few real patriots are willing to take part in underground activity." Stage II "will be a time of assassination and counterassassination, terror and counterterror." It is a period marked by "the communist infiltration and control of the present United States government."

SAO thus set out to wage total resistance to communism, a small band determined to risk all in the struggle for America. Nationwide, the group probably numbered less than two hundred members, thirty of whom were active in San Diego County. There the group was founded by two men—Jerry Lynn Davis (Southland Coordinator) and Howard Barry Godfrey (San Diego Commander and Intelligence Officer).

In late 1971 and the first half of 1972 the SAO put out bulletins on how to make booby traps, how to use ammonium nitrate in high explosives, and how to gain forced entry into buildings. (Much of this information was taken from Department of the Army technical manuals on "Unconventional Warfare Devices and Techniques.") The San Diego SAO also put out bulletins about local liberals, radicals and antiwar activists, all of whom were lumped together as communists. (These missives went out to a mailing list of two hundred twenty-seven names in the area, including a naval commander, a county supervisor, a vice admiral, a Marine Corps brigadier general, a rear admiral, and some San Diego police officers.)

The group was organized into small, semi-autonomous cells.

Members were listed by code numbers, and were given mail drops for their contacts.

The FBI Connection

SAO thrived in San Diego until the June 1972 bombing of the Guild Theatre led to the group's fall from grace. A former Birchite named William Francis Yakopec was arrested and charged with the bombing, and in September 1972 he was brought to trial in the Superior Court of the State of California in San Diego before Judge Robert W. Conyers. Much to the astonishment of the SAO supporters, the star witness against Yakopec turned out to be San Diego Commander Godfrey. Then a local fireman, Godfrey admitted he had worked for the FBI since early 1967 as an undercover agent. He did it, he said, because "I felt it was my duty to my country." Before accepting the role, he had talked it over with J. Clifford Wallace, then the Stake President of the Mormon Church for San Diego, and more recently a federal judge by appointment of Richard Nixon. Wallace put Godfrey in touch with the FBI, and he was assigned to agent Steve Christianson, to whom he reported verbally every day. Godfrey was to work on the militant right wing, and was paid two hundred fifty dollars per month by the FBI. At first he was assigned to the Minutemen and then with the demise of that group in San Diego, he helped start and run the SAO in November 1971. Godfrey testified that his FBI contacts knew all of his activities, including his stockpiling of illegal explosives in his house. This, he said, was done with their permission. (He later gave some of the explosives to Yakopec to "save them for after the Communist takeover of this country.")

Godfrey functioned as a one-man plumbers' operation within the SAO. He knew how to pick locks, burglarize, bomb and handle guns. The FBI paid his dues and covered his expenses. All this enabled him to carry on effectively as a terrorist. At Yakopec's trial, he said that he actively recruited for the group.

What kind of people did he look for? "People with previous right-wing connections." Did he enlist potentially dangerous elements? "Yes, sir."

Apparently, Godfrey himself was among the more dangerous elements in the SAO, and agent Christianson among the more dangerous *eminences grises* of the operation. During the Yakopec trial, Godfrey admitted that he had driven the car from which another SAO member, George Hoover, had fired into Bohmer's house, wounding Paula Tharp. Subsequently, he had taken the weapon to Christianson, who had hidden it for six months. (This was evidently insufficient grounds for the FBI to take disciplinary action against agent Christianson. He continued as Godfrey's contact until the bombing of the Guild Theatre, at which point he was removed by L. Patrick Gray himself. He currently resides in Kanosh, Utah.)

In addition, Godfrey confessed to publishing a certain leaflet on February 18, 1972, the day on which President Nixon left for China. The bulletin was headlined "Wanted for Treason," and it featured a picture of Nixon and an inflammatory text which accused the president of high treason because of his China policy. The SAO symbol appeared at the bottom of the text, and the group distributed it in fifteen cities—including San Diego, Phoenix, Yuma, San Francisco, and Bellingham, Washington.

At the Yakopec trial, Godfrey testified that he had paid the printer for the posters, picked them up, and was reimbursed by the FBI, and that the FBI understood the nature of his expenditures and saw all of his SAO publications. As for poor Yakopec, who had joined the SAO through Godfrey, his next door neighbor, he admitted to owning several of the posters: he said he stored them under his mattress. Why there? "I thought they were kind of corny." Later, he testified that he kept a bomb with the Nixon posters. Did he generally keep bombs under his bed? "No, I like to sleep too well." (When I visited

the San Diego Court House to see the exhibit in question, the
custodian located a stack of thirty-three posters, with the bomb
casing still attached!)*

* It was not noted at the time, but in fact these posters bear a remarkable
resemblance to leaflets which were distributed in Dalls, Texas, just one or
two days prior to the assassination of President Kennedy. That poster
likewise bore the headline "Wanted for Treason" and it also featured
pictures (front and profile) of JFK and an inflammatory text about the
president's allegedly treasonous activities. On the hunch that the leaflet
might have some connection with the assassination, the Warren Commission sent Secret Service agents to track down its author and printer.
They worked from late November 1963 to May 1964 until they found
that Robert. G. Klause had printed the flyer and that Robert Allan Surrey,
an associate of General Walker, had ordered it. When Surrey testified
before the Commission on June 16, 1964, he pled the Fifth Amendment
on all questions concerning the leaflet. The late Hale Boggs, a member of
the Warren Commission, pointed out that Surrey "is the only witness out
of hundreds who has pled the Fifth Amendment." Klause denied any
interest in or involvement with the contents of the leaflet, and there the
matter was allowed to rest. By that point, the Warren Commission was
determined to prove that Oswald had acted alone, and therefore lost interest in trying to connect the assassination with the leaflet.

WANTED
for TREASON

NIXON

DESCRIPTION

FULL NAME: Richard Milhous Nixon. DATE OF BIRTH: January 9, 1913 at Yorba Linda, California. FORMER OCCUPATIONS: Used car salesman, law clerk, second rate congressman, and mediocre Vice President. PRESENT OCCUPATION: Professional liar and double-crosser (part time employment as United States President). WEIGHT: 170 pounds. EYES: brown. HAIR: black. HEIGHT: 5'11". RACE: White. NATIONALITY: Claims American citizenship but actions prove this unlikely. LAST KNOWN ADDRESS: 1600 Pennsylvania Avenue, Washington, D.C. (Rumored to have a California hideout.)

CRIMINAL RECORD

RICHARD NIXON (alias Cry-Baby Nixon, alias Tricky Dicky) is an expert in disguises and has successfully passed himself off as an anti-communist in the past. He may again try using this disguise if pressed for votes in 1972. Saying one thing, then doing the opposite is Nixon's MOA. While he campaigned in 1968 on a platform of curtailing socialism he has in fact done more to establish a socialistic dictatorship than either of the last two Democrat administrations. His economic policies have continued to enrich Big Industrialists while rising prices and higher taxes have all but reduced the average worker to a state of financial slavery. This criminal has even made vicious attacks on small children (forced busing to acheive "racial balance") and has caused the destruction of local school systems. WARNING: Nixon suffers from an EMPEROR COMPLEX and becomes extremely dangerous when criticized.

CAUTION

Trickery and deceit are Nixon's trade-marks. At the present time Nixon and his chief henchman HENRY (CZAR) KISSINGER are engaged in forming an alliance with another gang of criminals, the Red Chinese. The RED CHINA GANG have slaughtered an estimated fifty million of their own people since coming to power. This Godless horde of barbarians killed thousands of Americans in the Korean War (shooting captured soldiers and starving and torturing prisoners of war). The RED CHINA GANG have been supplying the NORTH VIETNAMESE BANDITS with weapons and bullets to kill American soldiers in another no-win war in Vietnam. The very fact that Nixon is dealing with these ARCH ENEMIES OF FREEDOM is enough to convict him of treason. DO NOT LET THIS CRIMINAL STEAL YOUR FREEDOM. DEMAND HIS ARREST BY PROPER AUTHORITIES AND HIS TRIAL FOR THE CRIME OF HIGH TREASON.

⊕ **Secret Army Organization**

Godfrey's surfacing as an FBI agent rattled the remnants of the SAO. They were angry at having been set up by the FBI, and when reporters for the *Door* began approaching their old adversaries for information earlier in 1973, they found that many were willing to cooperate; some were even friendly. And as the SAO began to open up, a pattern began to emerge which seemed to link the San Diego events to Watergate.

Breakthrough

The breakthrough came in the spring when an editor of the *Door* made contact with a former SAO militant named Jerry Busch. From November 1969 to the summer of 1971, said Busch, Howard Barry Godfrey made frequent visits to the Gunsmoke Ranch in El Cajon. "It was also during June, July, and August of 1971 that Barry Godfrey and Donald Segretti (posing as 'Don Simms') visited Gunsmoke and though supposedly not 'knowing each other,' they spoke together on at least one occasion," in a quiet conversation aside. The Segretti connection is important in itself; it is particularly interesting insofar as—according to Busch's account—Segretti was in touch with SAO *while* contacting his old college chums Dwight Chapin and Gordon Strachan in June 1971, but *before* commencing work as a dirty trickster in September 1971.

Busch did not say what Segretti discussed at the Gunsmoke Ranch, but he did report that following "these casual conversations" Godfrey came up with bizarre ideas to take care of what he called "those red punks"—in the event that the GOP held its convention in San Diego. Among Godfrey's plans in October 1971 were:

(1) the use of massive dosages of LSD, cyanide or strychnine introduced into the punch at antiwar group meetings;

(2) bombing of the VVAW headquarters, the Guild Theatre, and several porno shops;

(3) bombings of the homes or offices of antiwar leaders;

(4) kidnaping or assassination of antiwar leaders and activists;

(5) fire bombing of vehicles and other property belonging to antiwar activists.

By November and December 1971, Busch continued, Godfrey had become more ambitious: he wanted to acquire drone planes which would carry payloads of high explosives and phosphorus to be dropped on the demonstrators. In addition, Godfrey spoke of using similar air craft, loaded with TNT or C-4 plastique, to blow up Air Force One and assassinate Nixon. The idea was to fly a bomb into the presidential jet as it landed either at Lindbergh Field or at El Toro Marine Base. Busch claimed that he had expressed horror at the suggestion and told Godfrey he had lost his mind suggesting anything as insane as an attempt on the life of the president. Shortly thereafter, Busch and Godfrey parted ways after the former grew suspicious that he was being set up to take the rap on the shooting of Paula Tharp. By March 1972, he had left San Diego and has not yet returned.

Even before Busch left the SAO, the "Wanted for Treason" leaflet was printed and distributed. Another former SAO member corroborates that in this same period—January-February, 1972—Godfrey tried to find someone to build a plane that would carry a load of high explosives. (In addition, he was apparently trying to obtain another plane for the purpose of gassing or bombing demonstrators on Fiesta Island.) After Busch's departure, the SAO issued its April 1972 bulletin which began with a quote attributed to Abraham Lincoln, "A tyrant would not come to the United States from across the sea. If he comes, he'll ride down Pennsylvania Avenue from his inauguration and take up legal residence of the White House." Then followed detailed instructions on the manufacture of explosives which might be used to destroy a large bridge (Tackwood's scenario included the demolition of two bridges on and off of Fiesta Island) and on various methods of forced entry into buildings.

A Sinister Plot?

Was there a right-wing plot to kill the president? Tackwood says so. Busch says that FBI informer Barry Godfrey talked about it. The "Wanted for Treason" poster certainly indicated no loss of love between the extreme right and the president, and Godfrey *was* checking out the availability of drone planes.

The *L.A. Times* reported on July 13, 1973 that a former Minuteman had requested political asylum in Fiji, saying he had secret information on Watergate and feared assassination.

All of this proves nothing, of course, but it suggests that the Dirty Tricks operation may have been much more complex than we have been led to believe. Perhaps there was a plot to kill Nixon. In August 1973, Godfrey reportedly admitted to the San Diego *Door* that there was a real plot to kill Nixon. He blames the plan on his erstwhile cohort, Gary Lynn Davis. Then again Godfrey's plot may have been a further hoax aimed at discrediting the left and the Democratic Party. What did Segretti discuss with Godfrey, and why and how did he meet Godfrey in the first place? How did it happen that the FBI financed a threat on the life of a president (a crime which carries a penalty of up to five years in jail and a thousand-dollar fine)? In the past, the Secret Service has taken such threats very seriously. A check of the *New York Times* index shows that at least eleven people were arrested between January 1972 and May 1973 for doing much less than Godfrey. Most seem to have been psychopaths or drunks, with no positive plan—just verbal threats.

But then there are other instances: Arthur Bremer's Ottawa visit on April 13-14, 1972, for example, when he supposedly stalked Nixon. On May 30, three bombs demolished the tomb of the father of the Shah of Iran an hour before Nixon was scheduled to lay a wreath there. On August 11, a certain A. B. Topping was arrested in New York after paying an undercover agent a thousand dollars to kill Nixon. Topping, it developed, was well-to-do, of the American Nazi political persuasion, and interested in having the president killed the week after the payoff. No trial has been held. And then in late May 1973, one of Nixon's helicopters went down in the Bahamas. It subsequently came out that the president has three helicopters ready at all times and chooses which to use one minute before the flight.

Watergate has uncovered an administration racked by factionalism. Under Hoover, the FBI was at odds with the White House—to such a degree that Hoover was willing to use secret documents to blackmail the president. In addition, Nixon was having his difficulties with the leaders of the CIA, and James McCord wrote to John Caulfield at Christmas 1972 that if Nixon pushed out Helms and involved the CIA in Watergate, "every tree in the forest will fall." Could there have been other tensions as well? Were there elements which opposed Nixon for his policy of rapprochement with China and Russia, and which would have preferred, say, Spiro Agnew as President?

After returning from San Diego in July 1972, acting FBI director, L. Patrick Gray, talked to Nixon and said: "Mr. President, there is something I want to speak to you about. Dick Walters and I feel that people on your staff are trying to mortally wound you by using the CIA and the FBI . . ." His words may have carried greater import than any of us has heretofore suspected.

Setting up the Vets

Fred Cook

"The government is not on trial in this case," federal Judge Winston E. (Beau) Arnow insisted in repeated rulings against the Gainesville Eight—seven members of the Vietnam Veterans Against the War and a supporter, all accused by the government of plotting the violent disruption of the Republican National Convention in Miami in 1972.

Never was a judge more wrong. For the government, even more than the defendants, was on trial in the Gainesville Eight case; and when the jury returned its verdict on August 31, 1973, the government, in effect, was found guilty.

None of the politically motivated trials brought by the Nixon Administration's Internal Security Division of the Justice Department collapsed of its own weight as abjectly as did this one—not even the Berrigan case or the prosecution of Daniel Ellsberg in the Pentagon Papers imbroglio or the resounding defeat of the prosecution in the Camden Twenty-Eight draft

The original version of this essay, entitled "Justice in Gainesville: The Real Conspiracy Exposed," © 1973, appeared in *The Nation,* October 1, 1973. Reprinted by permission of the author.

board raid. The striking different in Gainesville was that virtually the only evidence presented to the jury (no defendant took the stand) was the government's evidence; and so damning was this to the government that, when the jurors got the case, ten were so determined on acquittal that they did not even need to discuss the issues.

If the Gainesville verdict makes the kind of impact on official minds that it should, it could be a case of historic importance. For what a jury composed of middle-class Florida citizens said, at least by implication, was this: it is time to stop framing dissidents for political purposes through the use of unreliable and sometimes psychotic informers turned *agents provocateurs*; it is time to stop using authoritarian methods, for they are destroying the credibility of the government itself to the point that even the most solemn word of the Justice Department's representatives becomes almost worthless.

To understand all that is implied in the Gainesville verdict, it is necessary to take a step-by-step overview of this complicated case, the manner in which it developed and what ultimately became of the sensational charges.

In the defense view, the prosecution was intertwined with the Watergate scandal. As one defense attorney told Judge Arnow during legal arguments, the defense believed "that this prosecution is the ultimate Watergate cover-up." Here is the sequence of events cited as lending credence to this belief:

On June 17, 1972, former CIA agent James McCord, at the time the security chief for the Committee to Re-Elect the President, was arrested with a group of helpers in the act of burglarizing the Democratic National Committee's Watergate headquarters.

On June 23, 1972 his attorneys (see Gerald Alch's testimony before the Ervin committee) discussed as a possible defense the patriotic need to counteract projected domestic violence.

On June 27, a special federal grand jury was convened in the Northern District of Florida by the unusual device of having the clerk telephone jurors to appear for the special session. Guy L.

Goodwin, chief of the special litigation section of the Internal Security Division, was in charge. Goodwin is the nattily dressed *éminence grise* of a whole series of Internal Security cases that have been almost invariably (like the Berrigan case) based on the word of informers.*

On July 3, the jury issued subpoenas for twenty-three VVAW leaders who had gathered in Miami Beach for proclaimed peaceful demonstrations at the Democratic National Convention. The VVAW leaders were summoned before the grand jury in Tallahassee on July 10.

On July 9, a Sunday, Carol Wild Scott, a Gainesville attorney who had represented Scott Camil, southeast regional coordinator of the VVAW, discovered that her law office had been burglarized. Desk drawers had been pulled out, papers scattered about, some vitamin pills strewn on the floor—but twenty-five dollars in petty cash had been left untouched on her secretary's desk; a new electric typewriter, an adding machine, and other articles of value had not been taken. Just one item was gone— Ms. Scott discovered in an office check the following day that the entire file, including biographical material and notes on VVAW activities of Scott Camil, was missing. Ms. Scott also noticed that someone had apparently tampered with the telephone box in her office and the terminal box in the hall outside. There was a little pile of plaster on the floor under the box in her office and the terminal box bore evidence of having been jimmied. Police who were called made a routine investigation, found no traces of fingerprints, and went away.

On Monday, July 10, the twenty-three VVAW leaders were called before Guy Goodwin's grand jury. Thirteen were released after perfunctory questioning; the others were grilled more rigorously. By Wednesday four had been thrown into jail for contempt (Supreme Court Justice William O. Douglas later ordered their release); and that night, the grand jurors were summoned by telephone for an extraordinary session. They in-

* See "The Grand Jury Network," by Frank Donner and Eugene Cerruti, *The Nation*, January 3, 1972.

dicted six of the veterans, including Scott Camil; subsequently, a superseding indictment was voted, naming the eight who eventually went to trial in Gainesville.

The indictment charged the veterans with conspiring "to organize numerous 'fire teams' to attack with automatic weapons fire and incendiary devices police stations, police cars and stores in Miami Beach." The plot contemplated, according to the indictment, the firing of "lead weights, 'fried' marbles, ball bearings, 'cherry' bombs, and smoke bombs by means of wrist rocket slingshots and cross bows." These were scary, headline-making accusations.

A fourteen-month legal battle followed. At the outset the defense theorized that its ranks might have been infiltrated by informers—and so it put Guy Goodwin on the spot. It demanded that the U.S. Attorney state whether any of the twenty-three VVAW members originally summoned before the grand jury had been an informer for the government. Goodwin replied categorically under oath that none had. Later, when the case came to trial in the summer, this statement was revealed as untrue. The government put one of the twenty-three, Emerson L. Poe, on the witness stand; and Poe, who had been a close friend of Scott Camil and who had been represented originally by attorneys for the defense, testified he had been an FBI informer since January 1971. According to reliable sources, Guy Goodwin may still be required to explain that one.

In the months of pretrial maneuverings, Judge Arnow aligned himself with the Establishment, not only by his repeated refrain, "The government is not on trial in this case" but by rulings that almost invariably upheld the Justice Department at the expense of the defense. His bias showed most clearly in pretrial hearings on June 20 and 21, 1973. Defense attorneys filed motions seeking to determine: "whether and to what extent employees or agents of the White House, CREEP, the FBI, the CIA, military intelligence or other agencies of the government participated in espionage, infiltration, sabotage, provocateurism, and electronic surveillance of the defendants or the Vietnam Veterans Against the War, the organization with which the defendants are affiliated." They also sought to probe the mystery of the theft of Scott Camil's file from Ms. Scott's law office.

Judge Arnow granted the defense an evidentiary hearing, but then so hedged it with rulings as to inhibit any genuine discovery. He refused to consider the issue of infiltration and provocateurs, limiting the hearing to just two issues: electronic surveillance, which is extremely difficult to prove, and the burglary of Ms. Scott's office, a crime never solved.

Defense attorneys, anticipating that they would be allowed to question witnesses on the electronic surveillance issue, subpoenaed a number of high officials, including former Attorney General John Mitchell and Robert Mardian, who had headed Internal Security in the Justice Department before he joined CREEP. The importance of such potential witnesses insured media coverage.

The Columbia Broadcasting System was especially active. It sent an artist to draw sketches of the scene in the courtroom, an accepted procedure. Judge Arnow, seeing her sketching, confiscated her work and ordered her out of the courtroom. She sketched from memory what she had seen, and CBS exhibited some of her sketches along with a number of interviews on its nighttime news telecast.

Judge Arnow responded by issuing an order charging Robert Salant, head of CBS News, with contempt of court. CBS fought the action, arguing its right to cover the news under the First Amendment to the Constitution guaranteeing a free press. Judge Arnow ignored the First Amendment, convicted CBS and fined the network five hundred dollars—a decision that was promptly overturned by the U.S. Court of Appeals.

The tempest with CBS was indicative of the more important tempest in the courtroom, when the defense tried to question its subpoenaed witnesses. Guy Goodwin met this threat by presenting affidavits in which each of the witnesses declared he had no knowledge of electronic surveillance. Goodwin himself, his credibility not yet called in question by the Poe matter, filed a blanket affidavit, saying that he had checked every source and had found no evidence of the wiretapping or bugging of any of the defendants.

This mere assertion of collective innocence was sufficient for Judge Arnow. Defense attorney Morton Stavis argued passionately and persistently that he was entitled to put witnesses on the stand and examine them. He cited precedents (especially the Justice Department's cover-up efforts in the Ellsberg case) to show that time and again the government's original professions had proved to be false and that admissions had been forced only by constant pressure. Judge Arnow quashed one subpoena after another on the mere representations of innocence in the Goodwin-filed affidavits.

Two developments were, however, noteworthy. FBI Agent Robert L. Pence, apparently in response to the defense's original motion which Judge Arnow had crimped to the single issue of electronic surveillance, had filed a sweeping affidavit. He averred: "I have caused inquiry to be conducted and as a result thereof have determined that no information in this case was derived from acts of espionage, infiltration, sabotage, provocateurism or electronic surveillance" conducted by employees of the White House, CREEP, CIA, military intelligence or "other agencies" of the federal government—all this in anticipation of a case which, when it came to trial, was marked by a parade of FBI and other informers telling their lurid stories!

Then there was Pablo Fernandez, a Cuban refugee and an informer who, it developed, had been paid by the Miami Police Department but whose information had been made almost instantly available to the FBI. Fernandez was an acute embarrassment to the prosecution. He had committed the indiscretion of giving an interview to Rob Elder of the *Miami Herald,* and in this he had said two startling things: he had played the role of *agent provocateur* by trying to get the VVAW to buy guns from him to disrupt the Republican convention, but the veterans had turned him down; and he had spied on the antiwar vets with electronic devices. Fernandez allegedly had given some testimony to this effect when he had been called before a federal grand jury investigating the activities of Donald Segretti, the ubiquitous dirty-tricks operator for President Nixon's CREEP. Defense attorneys requested the right to examine the grand jury minutes, but were denied it. Then they tried unsuccessfully to subpoena Fernandez, who soon disappeared.

Major Adam Klimkowski, commander of the Miami Police Department's special investigative section, confirmed to the *Miami Herald* that Fernandez had indeed attempted to sell guns to the veterans. "We were hoping for the overt act necessary to produce a charge of conspiracy," he said. And he added: "In fact, I guess he [Fernandez] might make a good defense witness"—only, of course, Fernandez could not be found.

More tenuous indications of some kind of linkage between the Florida prosecution and Watergate kept seeping out from under the prosecution's rug. Fernandez, it developed, had been an associate of Bernard L. Barker, the former CIA operative and kingpin of the Cuban contingent that had gone from Miami to Washington for the Watergate burglary. In a deposition filed in Broward County, another undercover man with Cuban and CIA ties, Vincent J. Hanard, declared he had received a telephone call from a man using the name "Eduardo" (the admitted alias of convicted Watergate conspirator E. Howard Hunt, Jr.) offering him fifteen hundred dollars a week to infiltrate the VVAW and cause trouble. Hanard, who had his hands full informing for the CIA, the FBI and the Miami police, and who described himself as "an instigator rather than an investigator," turned down the offer because the size of the stipend made him suspicious about what might be required of him. And anyhow, as he said in his deposition, he was already working trying "to expose the VVAW [as] being pink and Communist and all this stuff."

Such disclosures had no effect on the judicial process. Judge Arnow refused to recognize any indications that this was a

politically motivated case; the evidentiary hearings were so
limited as to be virtually worthless—and so the trial of the
Gainesville Eight began later in July.

In an atmosphere of transparent provocateurism and entrap-
ment, the case of the Gainesville Eight came to trial on July 31.
And, almost instantly, there occurred an incident that seemed
to many to confirm all the earlier suspicions about electronic
surveillance.

Defense attorneys and their clients had been assigned a room
in the courthouse in which they could confer during the trial.
As they were walking along the corridor toward this room on
the opening day, Peter Mahoney, one of the accused veterans,
happened to glance at the glass vent of the door of an adjoining
cubicle. He saw the shadows of two men inside, reflected on the
glass. The defense party halted. While some remained grouped
outside the door, the lawyers raced off to find Judge Arnow.
The judge sent U.S. marshals to the scene; the door was opened
—and out tumbled two FBI agents, dripping with electronic
gear.

The agents had been working in the closetlike space that
shared a common wall with the room assigned to the defense.
They had with them a large Samsonite attaché case packed with
such electronic gadgets as a battery pack, an amplifier, an out-
put transmitter, a receiver, "a couple of little earphones," and
other gear and tools. The defense was convinced—especially in
view of all that had transpired earlier—that the FBI agents had
been huddled in the closet, known as the telephone terminal
room, for the purposes of eavesdropping on lawyer-client con-
ferences during the trial.

Not so, the prosecution protested vigorously. In a quick informal hearing before Judge Arnow, the two agents—Carl
Ekblad and Robert Romann—asserted that they had been only
"checking the FBI [telephone] lines" that ran through the terminal room. Romann protested that he "had no knowledge"
about the use of electronic devices and had been "only holding
the paper" on which they were to take notes.

Defense attorneys tried to cross-examine the FBI agents, but Judge Arnow, adhering to the pattern of accepting as truth whatever the government professed to him, blocked most of their questions.

The jury that was impaneled to hear the case gave defense attorneys more reason to hope than had the judge. The average age was thirty-one. Seven were women, three were blacks, and one was a veteran of Vietnam. One of the women was the wife of a college professor; another, an elementary schoolteacher; a third had been seen eating lunch at a counter-culture health food store.

With the first witness, the credibility of the prosecution was again called into question. The witness was Charles R. Marshall, Jr., a one-time private detective who managed the old frame house in Gainesville where defendant Scott Camil lived. Marshall testified that Camil had showed him "wrist rocket slingshots," along with steel balls and "fried" marbles that would shatter on impact. He declared that Camil had told him the VVAW intended to disrupt the Republican convention violently.

Defense attorneys asked whether the prosecution had any Jencks Act material they should see—in other words, any records of pretrial questioning of the witness that should be given to the defense to determine whether the story he originally told matched the one he testified to in court. Jack Carrouth, who was handling the prosecution's case—Guy Goodwin, as always, stayed in the background, an evasive figure seen slipping in and out of the FBI offices but never in court—denied that the government had any such material.

Grilled by Larry Turner, however, Marshall testified that he had been interviewed by Claude Meadow, the FBI agent in charge of the Gainesville office. "He transcribed what I said and he asked me to read it and sign it and I did," Marshall testified. Carrouth still insisted: "We do not have any signed statement."

Judge Arnow was becoming annoyed and ordered Meadow to

search his files. The FBI agent returned with a three-page document that he testified was a transcript of his dictated notes of
an interview with Marshall on August 17, 1972. A heated de-
bate followed about whether Marshall had signed such a statement and whether it qualified as Jencks material. At one point,
William Patterson, who was acting as his own attorney, jumped
up and told the judge that one of the prosecutors "is shaking his
head at the witness"—the shaking coinciding with Marshall's
transparent attempt to modify his earlier testimony about signing the statement. Judge Arnow, increasingly angry, admon-
ished the prosecutor: "Now, if you're shaking your head at the
witness, you stop." Obviously unhappy about the prosecution's
tactics in this instance, the judge finally cut short the argument
and ordered Marshall's original statement turned over to the
defense.

It was an opening skirmish that, like so much else in this
checkered case, seemed significant not so much for the testimony as for what it seemed to say about the ethics of the
prosecution.

The government's principal witness against the veterans was
William W. Lemmer, a stocky man with long hair and a walrus
mustache. Lemmer had been a paratrooper in Vietnam, and he
had told a congressional committee on one occasion that the
army had threatened him with a psychiatric discharge. The
VVAW had long been aware of his role as an FBI informer and
probable *agent provocateur.*

Pausing at time to breathe heavily, Lemmer testified that
Scott Camil had told him he was forming "political assassination squads" to disrupt the Republican convention. He quoted
Camil as saying training sessions had been conducted at a re-
mote farm with facilities for "rifle, pistol and mortar" practice
and that the VVAW were obtaining guns by selling drugs. Since
there had been no mention in the indictment of drugs, mortars
or political assassinations, defense attorneys objected to this
testimony, but Judge Arnow permitted it.

The crux of Lemmer's testimony involved his account of a rally of the VVAW at Camil's home on May 27, 1972. He declared that the veterans had exhibited fishline bolos designed to trip up police horses; fire bombs made from drugstore chemicals; and hand grenades made from cherry-bomb firecrackers. Defendant Kniffen, he said, had fired a shaft from a crossbow through six to eight inches of wood; others had demonstrated their wrist rocket slingshots; and Camil, for no reason at all, had whipped out a derringer and fired a bullet through a mound of papers.

The least believable bit of Lemmer's testimony came in this sequence: he acknowledged that at this very meeting the VVAW had unmasked him as an FBI informer. They had become suspicious after finding that, when arrests were made, Lemmer somehow always managed to be released fairly quickly, as if he had a guardian angel somewhere, and Lemmer, when taxed with this, had admitted his role as a spy. Yet, if Lemmer was to be believed, it was *after* this exposure that Scott Camil invited him to a clandestine meeting of the VVAW and propositioned him to "fill a contract" for a gangland-type slaying.

Another fierce legal battle raged about Lemmer's testimony. Defense attorneys had a fourteen-hour tape-recorded confession that Lemmer had made to two of his former VVAW comrades after he had been exposed at the Gainesville meeting. From the tape, it appeared that Lemmer had developed an almost paranoid fear of military intelligence, whose agents he felt were harassing him for his antiwar activities after he left the army. And so he had fallen into the clutches of the FBI because "I had security problems that I was worried about and for self-protection. I used my position [as an informer] to cover a lot of people, myself included."

The FBI was only too happy to "protect" him in return for his services. Lemmer became head of the VVAW apparatus in Arkansas, and according to the veterans, he was always in the forefront, advocating the most violent measures. This agitation for extreme action was coupled with a sudden affluence. His former wife, Mary, later recalled that her virtually penniless husband showed signs of unusual prosperity about October 1971 (Lemmer, in his confession to the VVAW in May 1972, said he had been an FBI informer for nine months). His wife said that he bought new clothes, flew all over the country to VVAW meetings, and traded in his old car for a new $3,847 Toyota sports model.

The available evidence indicates that this sudden affluence entailed obligations; that Lemmer became the ever more helpless puppet of his FBI controllers. Thus he had no choice but to follow orders when the FBI directed him to go South to attend the late May meeting in Scott Camil's home.

Lemmer had been involved in a demonstration in Washington before he left and had met Barbara Stocking, a forty-three-year-old teaching fellow at Boston University, who planned to attend the political conventions. He offered her a ride South, and she accepted. In an affidavit she later filed with the court, she said that, during the entire two-day trip, Lemmer talked almost constantly about violence. He warned her against attending the Republican convention because "all the VVAW leaders were going to be picked up and taken out of circulation."

"Whenever we stopped along the way," Ms. Stocking's affidavit continued, "as soon as we were at a table or counter, he began talking in a loud voice about shooting, bombing and the like. I asked him to stop but he still did not. When we got to Gainesville and went to the home of Scott Camil, which was where he was going to stay, he again talked of shooting and bombing."

Lemmer's increasingly erratic conduct had precipitated a break with his wife. In June 1972, shortly after the Miami meeting, Mary Lemmer retained a divorce lawyer and had her husband held for a sanity hearing. In affidavits filed in Fayetteville, Arkansas, at that time, Mary Lemmer charged that he kept a loaded weapon with him and that he had threatened both her and her lawyer. Police confiscated a loaded .22-caliber pistol and a loaded .22-caliber rifle that Lemmer kept. Lemmer himself was released after being examined by a young general practitioner, who recommended that he see a psychiatrist.

Mary Lemmer subsequently turned over to the VVAW defense three rambling letters she had received from her husband after their separation. In these, he bragged of his importance to the government, boasted about his grand jury testimony against the veterans, and threatened vengeance on some of the VVAW leaders whom he blamed for his marital breakup. In one letter he wrote that, if he came to get the veterans, it would not be noisily but in "tennis shoes" with a "length of piano wire."

The defense struggled desperately to get this picture before the jury, and the prosecution protested that any reference to Lemmer's psychiatric background would be prejudicial because it would lead the jurors to infer that he "was crazy." Judge Arnow followed his usual pattern of siding with the prosecution. When he did permit questions about Lemmer's state of mind, it was usually out of the presence of the jury; and when the defense tried to show that Lemmer had been an *agent provocateur*, the judge ruled that they were ranging too far afield.

At only one point did the judge become annoyed at the prosecution. This again involved a dispute over Jencks Act material. The judge had ordered the prosecution to turn over such material, if it had any, to the defense, but the prosecution stalled. Not until Lemmer had left the stand on direct examination did the government suddenly give the defense two written statements and ten hours of cassette tape recordings. Judge Arnow, angry at this tardy implementation of his earlier order, suspended trial for a day to give the defense an opportunity to study the material, then summoned Carrouth and U.S. Attorney William Stafford into his chambers. The session lasted forty-five minutes and apparently was not pleasant. The attorneys emerged grim and tight-lipped; and when asked what the judge had told them, they muttered, "No comment." (Even this apparent judicial bawling out had little effect in making the prosecution toe the ethical line. At the end of the trial, after the defense had rested its case, FBI Agent Claude Meadow, who had been in the courtroom throughout, suddenly gave defense attorneys forty-eight more pages of Lemmer material that the prosecution had still withheld.)

Lemmer was followed to the stand by a parade of other informers and police undercover agents. By their very number, they demonstrated the truth of Angelica Rohan's earlier comment in one interview when she said: "Darling, the spies were spying on the spies that were spying on the spies."

Perhaps the most dramatic confrontation of the trial took place when the government called Emerson L. Poe—the informer who had not been an informer, according to Guy Goodwin's sworn word. Poe, who had been the principal friend and confidant of Scott Camil, turned out to be almost as helpful to the defense as to the prosecution. He testified about a newsletter the VVAW had issued, detailing plans for demonstrations at the Republican convention. The newsletter, however, had emphasized that the demonstrations must be *peaceful* and had cautioned that any acts of violence would play into the hands of the Nixon Administration.

The document did refer to a "supply of extremely well-made slingshots that have proven themselves," and it urged members to order these devices promptly. It continued: "Marbles, ball-bearings and lead weights are extremely effective defensive projectiles." Throughout, the letter recommended action only if the demonstrators were attacked by police; and Poe, on cross-examination, admitted that the newsletter contained the *only* knowledge he had about convention plans.

There is not much else that needs to be said about the trial of the Gainesville Eight. The defense called only one witness, an expert who testified that the type of bombs described by prosecution informers would never work. Then the defense rested, deciding to let the government's case collapse of its own weight.

And it did just that. When the jurors got the case on August 31, only two felt there was anything to discuss; and as they said afterwards, this was mainly because they felt jurors were supposed to discuss *something*. After staying out three and a half hours, the jurors, all wearing broad smiles on their faces, filed into the courtroom and gave their verdict, acquitting all defendants. While the veterans and their lawyers, half-laughing, half-crying in relief, hugged each other and slapped each other's shoulders, the defeated prosecution team slunk out of a side door of the courtroom to avoid the press.

Gemstone — the Bottom Line

Donald Freed

The arrests at the Watergate on June 17, 1972 aborted the agenda of Operation Gemstone—was it luck alone?—and the nation was spared the real crisis. Yet, in all the subsequent furor, investigators have never really followed the trail back from the five men caught inside the Watergate office of the Democratic National Committee. None of the five had descended on the nation's capital from Mars. All were human, and all left human tracks that point directly to those who had sent them—their spymasters, the arch conspirators above *them*, the rivers of cold cash that financed the clandestine scenario, and *its* sources in industry, intelligence and organized crime.

What follows is an attempt to follow that trail and reconstruct Gemstone. Hopefully, it can help to uncover the "Watergate" beyond bugging and burglary, and show how an experienced team of Cold War professionals could engineer the shooting of Alabama Governor George Wallace, prepare murder and mayhem for the Republican National Convention, and implicate the opposition by planting evidence in—not stealing it

This essay is a chapter from a new book, *Operation Gemstone,* by the Citizens Research and Investigation Committee, edited by Donald Freed.

from—the offices of the Democratic National Committee at the Watergate. There, except for the bungled cover-up, Operation Gemstone was stopped. But the bottom line was already in sight—the end of constitutional rule through a paramilitary coup d'état.

Paramount to any clandestine operation is the chain of command and the "compartmentalization," as it is called. In Gemstone, the president's Special Counsel Charles W. "Tex" Colson played the role of a "station chief" in foreign intelligence work. His job was to oversee the spymasters, who in turn "controlled," "handled," and "ran" the secret agents. John Mitchell and the two presidential assistants, Bob Haldeman and John Ehrlichman, were equivalent to diplomatic heads of an American mission, ambassadors and the like. Together with their secret police, headed by Assistant Attorney General Robert Mardian, they were to handle the cover-up and the subversion of the Justice Department, the FBI, the CIA, etc. But, we shall argue, of the four highest Nixon agents—Mitchell, Haldeman, Ehrlichman, and Colson—one acted with a divided loyalty, was essentially a double agent, and in the end set up the other three.

As of 1970, there were basically three covert operations. One was under the aegis of Haldeman's "November Group" and could be called political propaganda/espionage. This group's field controls were former New York City policemen John Caulfield and Anthony J. Ulasewicz on the East Coast and "prankster" Donald Segretti on the West. A second team of amateur political agents worked out of the Committee to Re-Elect the President (CREEP). These young, middle-level bureaucrats began to panic as Nixon slipped behind Edmund Muskie and George Wallace in some of the 1970 polls.

The third operation was Charles Colson's "Attack Group" or "black advance." This was the Hunt-Liddy network, the Gemstone axis of the conspiracy. *By February 1972 this group had taken over the Segretti "dirty tricks" network, the CREEP "political propaganda" operation, the White House Special Intelligence Unit (the "Plumbers"), and the intelligence fronts*

using narcotics control as a cover (DALE, Operation Intercept).
The paramilitary, unofficial Gemstone net not only controlled
all of the other political efforts of the presidential campaign,
but *had penetrated and was beginning to use and compromise
the FBI, CIA, Treasury, Office of Economic Opportunity, Internal Revenue Service, Department of Justice, Bureau of Narcotics and Dangerous Drugs* and perhaps a dozen other federal
agencies, plus local intelligence or "Red Squads" across the
country. This was the magnitude of Operation Gemstone.

Colson was the key figure. Publicly, as Special Counsel, he
was liaison between the White House and various political
groupings—the Reverend Carl McIntire, the Liberty Lobby, and
similar right-wing extremists; the Eastern European ethnics,
many of them neo-fascists; the American Security Council and
the National Rifle Association; Teamster officials and organized
crime; ITT, the multinationals, and the CIA. Covertly, he was
liaison *to* the White House *from* the secret government, with
primary responsibility for Operation Gemstone. Charles Colson
was the double agent, and his plan was simplicity itself:

1. Prepare to re-elect the president. Eliminate Wallace. Isolate
the left.

2. Seize the government. Disrupt the GOP convention. Blame
the left *and* the center. Declare a state of national emergency.
Rule with Nixon, or without him. More a *coup de main* than a
coup d'état.

3. Cover up. Eliminate anyone who could "talk."

4. Build new mass base. Use four-year American Bicentennial
Celebration to drown all remaining dissent.

The president, the political wheelhorses like Mitchell and
Mardian, the public relations men like Haldeman and Ronald
Ziegler, the Arrow Collar killers-on-the-make like Gordon
Strachan and Jeb Magruder, the heartbreak kids like John Dean,
the Southern California "old boys" like Dwight Chapin and
John Ehrlichman—at one point or another they all went along,
thinking they could exploit and profit from the Gemstone plan.
But, by the night of the Watergate arrests in July 1972, they

were all pawns of Colson and his Cold War professionals.

Colson would use the politicos. But his plan was essentially paramilitary, as were his leading operatives. His "cut-off" and chief spymaster was E. Howard Hunt. Ever since his days in the wartime Office of Strategic Services, through two decades in the CIA, Hunt had been known as an assassin. He even admitted to a secret Watergate grand jury that he had headed an aborted mission to kill the anti-American president of Panama. Hunt's aide Frank Sturgis was a CIA sharpshooter. Both men figured in a number of known assassination plots, including the one that killed John F. Kennedy.

G. Gordon Liddy, James McCord, Bernard Barker, and their "Cubans" all brought particular skills to the Colson team. But they were all specialists in violence, and as the violence grew— the burning, rioting, kidnaping, sexual blackmail, explosives, and use of *agents provocateurs*—they, the paramilitary professionals, would inexorably gain a stranglehold over their "civilian" superiors. In vain would John Mitchell and Richard Nixon protest that they "never intended Gemstone to go so far." The deeds would be done and the invisible, psy-war pros— Colson, Hunt, Liddy, McCord, et al.—would be calling the shots. Put another way, Haldeman, Ehrlichman and the political "November Group" were being taken over by Colson's "Attack Group" and its paramilitary arm, Operation Gemstone.

Richard Nixon set the tone. He was appearing in Burlington, Vermont, early in the 1970 congressional elections, and as Air Force One taxied in, officials allowed a group of protestors onto the landing strip. One of the protestors threw a single stone about the size of a fifty-cent piece, which landed approximately eighty feet from the president. Striding ahead, Charles Colson picked up the stone and turned to Nixon.

"These rocks will mean ten thousand votes," he crowed. Such was the Executive mentality, the worldview of Richard Nixon and those in power, as America veered toward its intended fate.

Later Colson would arrange anti-Nixon incidents at the AFL-CIO convention in Miami and hard-hat attacks against antiwar demonstrators in New York.* It seems likely that he was also involved in an early rehearsal of Gemstone at a Nixon appearance in San Jose, California, in late October. According to Congressman Paul McCloskey and the local police chief, the ultra-conservative Young Americans for Freedom (YAF) sent its members to pose as anti-Nixon demonstrators. Both Hunt and Colson were founders of YAF.

Wherever the president appeared, he referred to the violent demonstrators somewhere else, and the ugliness began to spread. In Philadelphia, for instance, the police publicly beat peaceful protestors, while Mayor Frank Rizzo covertly organized his own secret police, which spied on and wiretapped, among others, the governor of the state of Pennsylvania!

Resentful men of the Nixon ilk bulked larged against the urban skylines, preparing for a landslide . . .

If George Wallace had been able to stand for election in 1972 as an independent candidate for president, the election might well have been thrown into the heavily Democratic House of Representatives, where Richard Nixon was not a popular name. Nixon knew this, and while on a plane from Mobile to Birmingham in 1971, he had urged Wallace to run as a Democrat instead of at the head of the American Independent Party. Wallace agreed, and the Department of Justice dropped a pending indictment against the governor's brother.

But Wallace only promised to run as a Democrat in the primaries. He anticipated a showdown with the left wing of the party at the Miami convention, and expected to lead a dramatic walkout. He would then stage an electoral blitzkrieg across the

---

* Colson's aide in the hard-hat demonstration was Edward Butler of the Information Council of the Americas (INCA), a right-wing industrial intelligence front. During the summer of 1963, Butler had worked with Lee Harvey Oswald, helping to set up a left-wing, pro-Castro cover for the alleged assassin.

nation as the standard bearer of the American Independents. Based on the primaries, the balance of the power would have been his. CREEP spent upwards of $600,000 to stop the populist, but to no avail.

More and more the paramilitary was crowding the politicos. Mitchell and his amateurs had only one last chance to stop Wallace their way. In 1970, Haldeman had spent $400,000 in an unsuccessful effort to defeat the Alabama governor in his state race for re-election. Now, in November 1971, in a meeting at the Los Angeles Hilton, Mitchell and Jeb Magruder agreed to finance a re-registration drive against Wallace's American Independent Party. They reached this agreement with operatives close to the American Nazi Party!

"Mitchell started the conversation," recounted Glenn Parker, an activist of the far right. "He said he had heard there was a way to remove the American Independent Party from the ballot. He said they had run a poll between Muskie, Nixon and Wallace that showed that without Wallace four fifths of the Wallace vote would go to Nixon. He emphasized they thought they were in trouble, and that Nixon especially wanted to win California."

That was November. By March 1972 Mitchell and CREEP had to admit defeat. They had been able to stop neither Wallace nor the antiwar demonstrators. The FBI had halted its CO-INTELPRO plan to "disrupt" dissident groups, while Senator Sam Ervin's Subcommittee on Constitutional Rights had exposed and the Supreme Court had rejected the Army's surveillance of American citizens, a practice which had gone on during the Johnson administration and through 1970. There was no alternative except to sign on to Operation Gemstone, which was being run by Colson and Hunt. Colson now had them all—Haldeman, Ehrlichman and Mitchell.

Two months later, on May 15, 1971, Arthur Bremer was arrested for the attempted assassination of George Wallace. The question is the classic cui bono, who benefits? The answer, Operation Gemstone.

From the media the American people learned that Wallace's would-be assassin Arthur Bremer was a disturbed twenty-one-year-old, an unemployed ex-busboy and janitor's helper. He had been laid off his janitorial job in Wisconsin in January 1972 and had no record of any income from that time until his arrest in Maryland in May. His tax return for 1971 shows earnings of $1,611. His automobile, purchased in September 1971, cost some eight hundred dollars, half of his total income for the year. Where, then, did Bremer get the money for his "mad scheme" to kill George Wallace, by far the most heavily guarded of all the presidential candidates, with a double set of body guards and a bullet-proof speakers' podium?

It is relatively easy to compute the minimum amount that Bremer would have needed from January to May. Setting to one side the cash outlay for stopping at expensive hotels (the Waldorf-Astoria in New York, the Lord Elgin in Ottawa); automobile repairs for a machine driven constantly for weeks at speeds up to seventy-five miles per hour in order to keep pace with presidential candidates who flew to their destinations; any miscellaneous expenses such as his records, specially constructed ammunition found in his car, and the expensive clothes Bremer wore into court when he pled not guilty; setting aside all these and any other contingency costs, *Bremer could not have spent less than five thousand dollars* on his eighteen-week, ten-state odyssey.

The figure is conservative. It includes the price of the guns he purchased, court fines for speeding and carrying a gun, and the $135-a-month rent for his occasionally used Milwaukee apartment.

On May 15, 1972, Arthur Bremer stepped from a crowd in a shopping center in Laurel, Maryland, and gunned down George Wallace. To this day no one has explained how Bremer could have known weeks in advance where in Laurel Wallace would speak. Nor has the FBI been able to identify the bullets used as coming from Bremer's gun, since they were special and had no rifling marks. Somehow the "lone fanatic" had gotten advance

intelligence for what appeared to be a thoroughly professional
job.

Early wire-service reports said flatly that more than one suspect was involved, and that Maryland and Pennsylvania State
Police had issued an all points bulletin for a 1971 light blue
Cadillac, driven by a white male with light blond hair, about six
feet two inches, wearing striped trousers, a light blue shirt, and
a yellow tie. The suspect was seen near Savage, Maryland, across
the Patuxent River from Laurel, changing Georgia for Maryland
license plates on the car.

After the shooting the Special Assignment Squad of the Milwaukee Police Department began looking for a possible conspiracy, but the higher-ups quashed the investigation. A Milwaukee Police Department intelligence officer says that the
Alcohol, Tobacco and Firearms Division of the Treasury
Department sealed the squad's files and took them away. The
squad was told to concentrate instead on possible subversion
stemming from Milwaukee at the forthcoming national political
conventions.

Within hours of the shooting—and before Bremer's address
had been released to the press—Charles W. Colson was moving.
First, he called Hunt and told him to break into Bremer's Milwaukee apartment to "look" for left-wing literature. Then,
when Hunt complained that this would not work, a Gemstone
agent in Milwaukee (using the press credentials of a small news
service) planted a copy of the *Black Panther* newspaper in
Arthur Bremer's apartment—that from a Milwaukee policeman.
Over a year later, in June 1973, Hunt told the grand jury in
Washington about Colson's orders to break into Bremer's apartment. The night before a fellow inmate in prison assaulted the
super-agent and beat him badly.

Meanwhile, at the White House, Colson and others attempted
to soothe Nixon. The president was near hysteria. He was
certain that his re-election campaign would be linked to the
Wallace shooting, in part because Washington and the Maryland
area were crawling with Gemstone agents. Only two nights be-

fore the assassination attempt on Wallace, Sturgis had led a "national security" break-in of the Chilean Embassy, while the "Cubans" assaulted Daniel Ellsberg during an antiwar demonstration on the steps of the Capitol. Two weeks later, on Memorial Day, James McCord would lead the first break-in at the Watergate.

But "Tex" Colson was not worried. Wallace was expected to die at any moment. CBS radio and other media had announced that "authorities" were looking for a group of black men seen fleeing from the scene and soon someone would find the *Black Panther* newspaper in the assassin's lair. A thoughtful man, Colson knew what could happen. He remembered the scene after the assassination of Dr. Martin Luther King, the riots and the threat of race war. Dr. King had been a black man. Governor Wallace was white, his followers had a strong base in police departments throughout the country, and the shooting had just plunged them from the heights of his stunning success to the depths of impotence and rage. The stage was set for possible state of siege.

The full story remains to be told. But during 1972-73, our research group, the Citizens Research and Investigation Committee (CRIC), received several bits of unconfirmed information which are worthy of note:

—On July 13, 1973 Roger Gordon, fifty-three, a member of the right-wing Secret Army Organization (SAO) fled from a hiding place in Australia to beg asylum in Suva, Fiji. According to the Associated Press, Gordon "had secret information concerning Watergate" and feared for his life. His information: that the heavy-set man with the "Joisey brogue" seen giving orders to Bremer on an Ohio ferry was Anthony Ulasewicz, a White House operative.

—Secret Army Organization (SAO) and FBI sources in the San Diego area reported that White House agent Donald Segretti gave money to Bremer.

—During 1970 Tom Huston, a Nixon aide, prepared a series of memoranda which attempted to tighten White House control

of the FBI, CIA, etc., and intensify the use of electronic surveillance, "penetration agents," and illegal break-ins. According
to a staff member of the Ervin Committee, White House files
contain a still undivulged memo in which Huston justifies selective assassination.

—On May 18, 1972, three days after the Wallace shooting,
Charles Colson staged a "Victory in Vietnam" march and rally
in Washington, under the auspices of the right-wing preacher
Carl McIntire. Mr. and Mrs. Calvin Fox of the Secret Army
Organization drove from San Diego to attend, passing en route
near the site of the Wallace shooting. Sources in San Diego
reported that while the Foxes were away, FBI Special Agent
Steve Christianson entered Mr. Fox's office files and planted
documents which could implicate him in the assassination attempt. A group of Washington-based former intelligence agents
have since confirmed this.

With Wallace out and the election assured, most of Nixon's
politicos signed off the Gemstone plan. The hardliners under
Colson did not. Moving into the temporary vacuum, they
stepped up their drive for power. Their immediate object—to
implicate the opposition in the violence planned for the GOP
convention.

How? By planting forged documents, a second specialty of
Howard Hunt.

Where? In the offices of the Democratic National Committee
at the Watergate Complex.

It wasn't difficult. Once inside the complex, the contract
team moved into the office of Dorothy V. Bush, which was
located next to that of Lawrence O'Brien, the Democratic
National Chairman. It was their third raiding party and they
moved with a familiarity of the surroundings. They carried with
them the necessary tools: false documents prepared by the CIA,
lockpicks and door jimmies, a shortwave receiver, gas guns, two
cameras and forty rolls of film, a walkie-talkie, and an assortment of electronic surveillance equipment.

The team had several objectives. One was to install a bugging device to monitor O'Brien's telephone conversations. Another was to search for evidence of contributions from foreign governments. A third grew out of an earlier break-in over the Memorial Day weekend. The team had discovered that the Democrats had nothing in their files which could later be used to link them to the "violent, left-wing militants," or to justify emergency measures against the party in the name of "national security." So, while McCord checked listening devices, and one of the Cubans handed the security plans for the Democratic Convention to a compatriot to photograph, Frank Sturgis prepared to put several forged documents deep in a filing drawer where no one would be likely to find them before the time was ripe. According to a source close to some of the men arrested that night, Sturgis was planning to plant something which purported to tie the upcoming convention violence to the Vietnam Veterans Against the War (VVAW), the Black Panther Party, the antiwar movement, and the presidential campaign of Senator George McGovern. Sturgis was Hunt's man, and he was acting without the knowledge of McCord, Barker, and the others.

Over the Labor Day weekend of the previous year, 1971, Howard Hunt and Gordon Liddy broke into the Beverly Hills office of Daniel Ellsberg's psychiatrist. While in Southern California, they also made two contacts with Louis E. Tackwood, a black *agent provocateur* who had worked for both the FBI and the Los Angeles Police Department's secretive Criminal Conspiracy Section (CCS).

In an interview with CRIC after the Watergate arrests, Tackwood told the story. "I'm giving up only two names. There's Martin and there's White. All right. Now, Martin was the code name for my contact, and I'm gonna tell you, he's CIA all the way," Tackwood explained.

"Now the control, the man over Martin is White. I only heard a little about him, but they say he's the money man, nobody's over him but the top dogs. Martin and White, that's all I'm gonna give you now. This is my life insurance."

Much later, before the Ervin Committee, Hunt revealed that Colson used a code name. It was "White." As early as 1963, the name "Martin" had appeared around the Dallas assassination.

According to the Gemstone scenario, Tackwood was to head a team of black and Chicano provocateurs, which would foment street violence during the GOP convention. Inside the convention hall, other agents would ignite explosives built into the furniture, maiming and killing GOP delegates. Together with similarly staged "attacks" from the right, the "left-wing" violence would persuade James McCord to recommend that the president declare a "State of National Emergency" as authorized by the pre-existing Executive Order 1140. McCord would make the recommendation in his capacity as one of the chiefs of the Pentagon's Special Analysis Division, the agency which would censor all news and round up "subversives" during the "emergency." In the ensuing "crisis," someone would find the Hunt-Sturgis documents in the Democratic offices. The government would move against the Vietnam vets, Black Panthers, antiwar activists, and members of the McGovern campaign. After that the government would call off the elections, or permit them to be held. It would not really matter.

Officers Keel and Thomas of CCS and Special Agent Burch of the FBI would "run" Tackwood and his team, which would be known as "Squad 19." It is possible that Keel, Thomas, and Burch were acting without the consent of their agencies, or that the agencies were playing along in order to break open the conspiracy to glean evidence for use in a power struggle with the White House. It is also possible that top officials of CCS and the FBI wanted Gemstone to work.

At any rate, Tackwood opted out. The "mad dogs" would put him into the concentration camps, too, he concluded. It was better to talk, to blow open the plans for San Diego—which is what he did in late September 1971, nearly a year before the Watergate arrests.

On January 27, 1972, CREEP chief John Mitchell turned down Gordon Liddy's plan to kidnap radical demonstrators at the San Diego convention. That is the testimony before the Ervin Committee at least. But Mitchell's veto no longer counted. Gemstone agents intended to carry out the kidnaping anyway.

In March, two months after Mitchell first said no, saboteur Donald Segretti traveled to San Diego. Using the code name "Donald Simmons," he met at the U.S. Grant Hotel with Ronald Johnson, thirty, a right-wing student from San Diego State College. Segretti wanted Johnson to work on the convention activities.

"One thing that Segretti said ... stood out in my mind," Johnson recalled in June 1973. "He told me that if I located any trouble-makers, they could be 'gotten rid of.' I asked him what he meant and he said, 'They could be sent out of town for a limited time.' " In the end, Johnson refused to work with Segretti. He disliked radicals, but he didn't think it was right to kidnap them.

Segretti had already worked San Diego the previous summer. On that occasion he discussed convention plans with members of the SAO, which had just been formed to fill the vacuum left by the demise of the Minutemen. According to an FBI informant, Segretti also furnished funds.

Segretti was now a paramilitary operative. He had hired on under Haldeman and the politicos, but Hunt and Liddy had "turned" him, possibly when they were in Southern California for the Ellsberg break-in and the contacts with Tackwood. "Squad 19," along with CCS and FBI "controls" would work the "left" half of the operation, Segretti the "right."*

Besides Segretti, Gemstone had a second operative working with the San Diego SAO, an FBI informer and provocateur named Howard Barry Godfrey. Godfrey had worked over four years for the San Diego office of the Bureau. He had worked in the Minutemen, engaged in fire-bombing and sabotage, infiltrated various radical groups, and stolen files from the Peace

---

* For a full discussion of the "right" half of the San Diego operation, see Richard Popkin's essay in this volume.

and Freedom Party and subscription lists from local underground newspapers. He had also helped organize the SAO,
which he used to spy on the radical community.

The FBI was only one of the government agencies to help
Godfrey and his fellow militarists. SAO agents in the California
National Guard and at nearby military bases supplied arms, and
also recruited for special operations. According to a Los Angeles
policeman who was serving a stint in the Guard, two SAO
members approached him and asked him to join a special assassination squad. They called themselves "Reagan's Army," and
they were probably preparing for the Republican convention.

Tackwood and his *agents provocateurs* would cause violence
from the "left." Godfrey and the SAO would kidnap real
demonstration leaders and trigger violence and even assassination from the "right." Then the government would impose
Executive Order 1140, a state of national emergency. No
wonder Colson and the paramilitary agents insisted on holding
the GOP convention in San Diego long after Haldeman, Mitchell
and the politicians wanted to move to Miami.

With the exposure of ITT's $400,000 offer to fund the
San Diego Republican convention, CREEP was able to override
the Colson group and move the convention to Miami. After this
change in site, Bernard Barker, Frank Sturgis, and Eugenio
Martinez all became involved in recruiting pro-war and pro-
Nixon demonstrators to counter the much smaller antiwar
demonstrations planned for the Republican convention at its
new site.

But the Gemstone plan remained, and the Colson agents hur-
riedly found substitutes for the San Diego SAO and Tackwood's
"Squad 19." In Miami the "right" would be members of YAF
and Cuban refugees; the "left" Gemstone infiltrators and provocateurs would be inside the Vietnam Vets. An FBI
provocateur, William Lemmer, has since admitted that a group
posing as VVAW cadres, but with a special lightning flash in-
signia for recognition, would fire on convention delegates with

automatic weapons. As it turned out, the Watergate arrests drove Lemmer and a host of agents out of Gemstone and back into official law enforcement, where provocation was generally confined to shouting.

The arrests set all of Gemstone a-run, except for the cover-up. Predictably, only the paramilitary professionals—Colson, Hunt, and Liddy—knew how to "go to ground." The politicos—Mitchell, Haldeman, Ehrlichman and the young careerists—proved helpless, running around in circles, lying, confessing. But the compartmentalization held, and at this writing at least, the investigations and indictments have barely touched the inner workings of Gemstone.

Yet, it was all so very obvious, and so much a copy of what Colson, Hunt and McCord had been engineering in other countries. They swell both right and left with provocateurs, who then attack the center. Forged documents and propaganda demoralize and undermine established institutions. The center no longer holds, and the secret government seizes power.

Mainstream sources include all the major news and magazine media in the United States as well as selected British and French newspapers.

Special information is credited to: the Citizens' Research and Investigation Committee (C.R.I.C.); the North American Committee on Latin America (N.A.C.L.A.); the Peoples Bicentennial Committee (P.B.C.); the Indochina Peace Campaign (I.P.C.); members of the Secret Army Organization (S.A.O.); the Black Panther Intercommunal News Service (B.P.I.N.S.); the San Diego *Door* Collective; Professor Richard Popkin and Professor Peter Dale Scott; the Committee to Investigate Political Assassination (C.I.P.A.), Washington D.C.; ex-members of the American Nazi Party; Committee for Action/Research on the Intelligence Community (C.A.R.I.C.), the Fifth Estate, Washington D.C.; Robert Gottlieb for E. Howard Hunt literary research; Mae Brussell; Timothy R. Heinan, undercover operative H-680 for the Milwaukee Police Department; Stan Stang, contributing editor of *American Opinion* magazine; the *Washington Watch*; and C.R.I.C.'s necessarily nameless informants.

Obviously, the deductions, conclusions and projections of the Gemstone "bottom line" are the sole responsibility of C.R.I.C.

From Dallas to Watergate:
The Longest Cover-Up

Peter Dale Scott

The discovery of the Watergate break-in on June 17, 1972, has led slowly but irreversibly to wider revelations about the government's use of crime, past and present. At first glance, it might seem the burglars' long record of covert activities would have made such revelations inevitable. Most of those arrested in the Democratic National Committee offices had been employed by the CIA in anti-Castro activities, and one of them—Eugenio Martinez—was still on a CIA retainer. Another, Frank Sturgis *alias* Fiorini, had defied President Kennedy's ban on U.S.-based raids against Cuba, and continued them with the support of former Havana casino operators with strong links to organized crime. His activities immediately before and after the Kennedy assassination had made Sturgis suspicious in the eyes of some private assassination buffs, long before Watergate made him a public figure.

E. Howard Hunt, the man chosen by Nixon's re-election team to mastermind the Watergate break-in, had served as political

The original version of this essay, entitled "From Dallas to Watergate: The Longest Cover-Up," © 1973, appeared in *Ramparts,* November 1973. Reprinted by permission of the author.

officer in the CIA's Bay of Pigs operation, which Richard Nixon had almost single-handedly pressed on the Eisenhower Administration, and for which Nixon was the White House Action Officer. In connection with the Bay of Pigs, Hunt had proposed the assassination of Castro to his CIA superiors, and, according to some sources, continued to propose similar assassination projects, the latest of these against the president of Panama in 1971.

Yet the Watergate cover-up almost succeeded—not despite the exotic records of the defendants, but precisely because of them. Complicity in their past crimes, such as the burglary against Dan Ellsberg's psychiatrist—and who knows what others —left the Nixon Administration with little alternative but to obstruct justice in the case of the Watergate Seven. By 1972 the chain leading from crime to cover-up to new crime was becoming a major preoccupation at the White House. But the establishment consensus necessary for a successful cover-up had been so eroded during the past ten years that the cold warriors could no longer keep their conspiracies secure.

In my opinion it is no coincidence that the key figures in Watergate—Liddy, Hunt, Sturgis, Krogh, Caulfield—had been drawn from the conspiratorial world of government narcotics enforcement, a shady realm in which the operations of organized crime, counterrevolution, and government intelligence have traditionally overlapped. Nor is it a coincidence that one of these men—Watergate burglar Frank Sturgis—played a minor role in the cover-up of the Dallas assassination ten years ago. On the contrary, I believe that a full exposure of the Watergate conspiracy will help us to understand what happened in Dallas, and also to understand the covert forces which later mired America in a criminal war in Southeast Asia. Conversely, an analysis of the cover-up in Dallas will do much to illuminate Watergate and its ramifications, including that Miami demimonde of exiles, Teamster investments, and Syndicate real estate deals with which Nixon and his friend Bebe Rebozo have been involved.

I hope to show that what makes this Miami connection so dangerous, and what links the scandal of Watergate to the assassination in Dallas, is the increasingly ominous symbiosis between U.S. intelligence networks and the forces of organized crime.

Cover-Up in Dallas

The experience of the Ervin Committee suggests a new approach to the Kennedy assassination: to focus on the cover-up rather than on the crime itself. Although many vital records of the Watergate break-in were successfully destroyed, the cover-up actions themselves became new evidence of an ongoing conspiracy. Thus the Ervin Committee has learned more about the mechanics of the cover-up than of the original break-in. In Dallas, too, the actual circumstances of the three shootings—of Kennedy, Oswald and Officer Tippit—have been largely obliterated. But if we focus only on the ensuing Dallas cover-up, the evidence of conspiracy, and the identity of some of the principals, are unmistakable—as is the central presence of criminal and intelligence networks also evident in the politics of Watergate and Vietnam.

The Watergate investigations revealed that many men in government will conspire against the law when two justifications are offered—whether or not these justifications are credible or are actually believed. The first is the possibility of a national security threat (as when Ellsberg's revelation of the Pentagon Papers was alleged to have threatened current truce negotiations, or to have involved a leak to the Soviet Embassy). The second is the alleged involvement of a governmental intelligence network or operation (as when on May 22, 1973, Nixon justified his participation in the cover-up by explaining that he had believed, erroneously, that the CIA was implicated).

The second justification flows from the first. E. Howard Hunt was no fool when he used a CIA Minox camera to photograph G. Gordon Liddy in front of the office building of Ellsberg's psychiatrist. Although the photograph was irrelevant to the ensuing burglary, by implying CIA involvement it insured that Hunt and Liddy would be protected by an administration cover-up—and that, if the cover-up ever collapsed, it could be credited to national security instead of political expediency. By the same logic it was by foresight, not oversight, that Bernard Barker had CIA-veteran Hunt's name and White House phone number in his notebook at the time of the break-in (*New York Times*, June 24, 1972, p. 24), and that Frank Sturgis was allegedly "carrying a false passport prepared by the CIA at Hunt's request" (*New York Times*, January 14, 1973, p. 38).

In Dallas, allegations both of a security threat and an intelligence involvement were available to justify federal intervention into the investigation, and thus also to justify a massive *ex post facto* cover-up. Following the assassination, a large number of rumors linked Oswald (and sometimes Ruby) in a left-wing conspiracy extending to Castro's Cuba and possibly the Soviet Union. Some of these rumors seemed to be backed by evidence; one, interestingly enough, was "corroborated" by Frank Sturgis.

The Secret Service in Dallas intercepted a letter to Oswald, postmarked Havana, November 28, 1963, and signed by Pedro Charles. The letter indicated that "Oswald had been paid by Charles to carry out an unidentified mission which involved accurate shooting" (CE 2763, 26 H 148).* Meanwhile the FBI possessed a letter from Havana to Robert Kennedy, "written by one Mario del Rosario Molina [which] alleged that Lee Harvey Oswald assassinated President Kennedy at the direction of Pedro Charles, a Cuban agent. . . . According to the writer, Oswald met with Charles in Miami, Florida, several months ago [i.e. in early 1963] and was paid $7,000 by Charles" (26 H 148).

---

* Citations to the Warren Commission's twenty-six volumes of Hearings (H) and one-volume Report (R) follow the Commission's format: in this instance, to Commission Exhibit 2763, *Hearings*, Vol. 26, p. 148.

By now this story seems absurd: the elaborate FBI chronology of Oswald's movements gave no indication that he ever visited Miami. But at the time the letters arrived, a reporter in the Miami area named James Buchanan was publishing stories (attributed to Frank Sturgis *alias* Fiorini) that Oswald *had* been in Miami and also had been in contact with Cuban intelligence (CD 59.2-3, CD 395.2; cf. CD 1020).* Later reports from James Buchanan's brother Jerry placed Oswald in Miami in March 1963 (CD 1020.7). These concatenating pieces of misinformation from Miami and Havana suggest, in retrospect, a conspiracy to mislead.

The stories today are much less important than Buchanan's sources for them, all of whom came from two Miami-based anti-Castro groups. The first group (CD 49.26), the DRE (Student Revolutionary Directorate), was Cuban, and the CIA used it to infiltrate Cuba in connection with the Bay of Pigs; the DRE was named in Oswald's notebook (16 H 67), since Oswald had been in contact with them in New Orleans (R 728), and perhaps in Dallas (CD 205.646). The second, American, group—which included both James Buchanan and his brother Jerry—was the International Anti-Communist Brigade. It was a small band of mercenaries headed by a named source of Buchanan's articles—Frank Sturgis alias Fiorini, the future burglar of Watergate.

Sturgis, like the DRE, had been employed by the CIA in connection with the Bay of Pigs invasion. But after the Cuban Missile Crisis of 1962, Kennedy had begun to crack down on anti-Castro raids launched from the continental United States. Jerry Buchanan had been arrested by the British in the Bahamas in April 1963 on board a boat formerly used in CIA missions, and now being used (without presidential authorization) for an intended raid against a Soviet tanker (New York *Times,* April 2, 1963, pp. 1, 9; April 3, 1963, p. 3). In September, the Federal

---

* Citations from the Warren Commission's unpublished documents, available in the U.S. National Archives, Washington, will follow this format: in this instance, Commission Documents 59, pp. 2-3, 395, p. 2; cf. Commission Document 1020.

Government had issued "strong warnings" to six Americans for their anti-Castro activities, including Frank Fiorini (Sturgis) and Alexander Rorke, the owner of Jerry Buchanan's boat (New York *Times,* Sept. 16, 1963, p. 39). As for James Buchanan, the Brigade's secretary and propaganda director, Sturgis allegedly broke with him in December 1963 because of his "excessive" attacks on the FBI and the CIA, "even going so far as to describe former President John F. Kennedy as a communist" (CD 1020.6).

Similar anti-Kennedy sentiments were allegedly expressed by Carlos Bringuier, Oswald's contact with the DRE in New Orleans, and a right-winger who later headed up the Cuban-Americans for Nixon-Agnew. Another witness told the Warren Commission that Bringuier, because "the United States didn't help to overthrow Castro . . . hates the United States almost as much as he hates Russia" (11 H 353). Because these sentiments were so widely held among Cuban exiles, many students of the Dallas assassination have theorized that a group of anti-Castro terrorists (Cuban and/or American) may have killed Kennedy in revenge for having been abandoned by the CIA in 1963.

Murder, Incorporated

According to an article in the July 1973 issue of *The Atlantic,* former President Lyndon Johnson also had doubts about the findings of the Warren Commission despite his public support of its "lone assassin" hypothesis. Interviewed not long before his death, Johnson

> expressed his belief that the assassination in Dallas had been part of a conspiracy. . . . Johnson said that *when he had taken office* he found that "we had been operating a damned Murder Inc. in the Caribbean." A year or so before Kennedy's death a CIA-backed assassination team had been picked up in Havana. Johnson speculated that Dallas had been a retaliation for this thwarted attempt (p. 39).

Johnson's recollection is corroborated by E. Howard Hunt in his memoir on the Bay of Pigs. Hunt admits to having personally proposed an attempt to assassinate Castro. And although he claims that nothing came of his proposal, this is not true. The CIA's assassins nearly succeeded, but were caught and executed in Havana on the day of the Bay of Pigs invasion.

Another detail suppressed by Hunt is that the CIA's assassination plan involved giving the legal green light (and other aid) to a Cuban conspiracy against Castro sponsored by Las Vegas mobster Johnny Roselli and his organized crime allies in gambling—who wanted back their old Havana casinos. A detailed account of the assassination attempt by Andrew St. George—himself a one-time U.S. intelligence agent—suppresses the Mafia angle but confirms that this attempt was but one of a series, in which a prominent role was played by Frank Sturgis' co-conspirator, Alexander Rorke (*Parade,* April 12, 1974, p. 4). In fact Rorke, according to St. George, died in an assassination attempt when his plane crashed in the Caribbean in September 1963 (cf. CD 1020.29). Rorke's 1963 attorney, Hans Tanner, had already published an account of his own assassination attempt in July 1961. His book gave several informed details about the International Anti-Communist Brigade of Frank Sturgis, which he considered to be "financed by dispossessed hotel and gambling room owners who operated under Batista."*

Hunt is said to have been the CIA's contact for an assassination conspiracy against Castro in 1966, involving Rolando Cubela Secades, who confessed after being captured in Havana. Cubela, a former military leader of the DRE in Batista days, admitted that he had planned, with help from the CIA and Bay of Pigs leader Manuel Artime, "to shoot Premier Castro with a high-powered telescopic rifle and later share in top posts of a counter-revolutionary regime with Mr. Artime" (*New York Times,* March 6, 1966, p. 25). These facts help explain why Artime—for whose child Hunt is a godfather—organized a defense fund for the Watergate burglars, whom he has since continued to visit regularly in prison (*New York Times,* July 9,

---

* Hans Tanner, *Counter-Revolutionary Agent* (London: Foulis, 1962), p. 127.

1973, p. 25, cf. June 19, 1972, p. 20). The same facts may also help us to understand what was being covered up in Dallas.

Bernard Barker testified that he carried out two burglaries for Hunt in the expectation that this would eventually help to depose Castro. He also claimed that up to ten minutes before the Ellsberg break-in he knew only that he was working on a case involving espionage by a Soviet embassy. Such exploitation of anti-Castro militants had long ago been offered as an hypothesis for the Dallas assassination. According to this theory, evidence involving Oswald in a left-wing conspiracy had in fact been planted by militant anticommunists, to make a case for a retaliatory U.S. invasion of Cuba. This would, for example, explain the oddly self-incriminating letter from "Pedro Charles," which the FBI quickly exposed as fraudulent, having been written on the same typewriter as the second warning letter from Havana (26 H 148).

According to a more sophisticated version of this hypothesis (involving a "two-tier conspiracy"), the clumsy fraud was *meant* to be exposed. Having first served as a pretext to engage the services of anti-Castro Cubans, its ultimate intention was to justify not an invasion but a massive federal debunking of all traces of conspiracy—the false and also the true.

We know at any rate that the direct result of such stories was to justify the creation of the Warren Commission. As Lyndon Johnson wrote in his memoirs, *The Vantage Point:*

> We were aware of stories that Castro . . . only lately accusing us of sending CIA agents into the country to assassinate him, was the perpetrator of the Oswald assassination plot. These rumors were another compelling reason that a through study had to be made of the Dallas tragedy at once. Out of the nation's suspicions, out of the nation's needs for facts, the Warren Commission was born (p. 26).

The Oswald Nexus

As the Commission's investigative arm, the FBI, with little other legal authorization, proceeded to expose Buchanan's stories of conspiracy, and others like them. For demonstrating that Oswald was not a Castro agent, but "acted alone," the FBI and the Warren Commission drew applause not only from liberals but even from left-wing critics such as I. F. Stone. Yet in their efforts to establish the "lone assassin" hypotheses for Oswald and Ruby, both the FBI and the Warren Commission were guilty of covering up much evidence to the contrary.

A seemingly minor but significant example is the cover-up of Oswald's relationship (still unclear) to the FBI. On January 24, 1964, the Warren Commission first heard from Dallas District Attorney Henry Wade and Texas Attorney General Waggoner Carr of a rumor that Oswald had been an FBI informant since September 1962. Wade's evidence included hearsay that the name, phone and license plate number of FBI agent Hosty (who was responsible for surveillance of pro- and anti-Castro Cubans) were in Oswald's address book (just as Hunt's phone was in Barker's), and also that Oswald had a government voucher for $200 at the time of his arrest (5 H 242). The first piece of hearsay turned out to be true (16 H 64), but the Commission did not learn this easily: the FBI had supplied it with an itemized list of names in Oswald's notebook, from which Hosty's had been omitted (5 H 112). You will look in vain for any of this information in the Warren Report. Instead, the Commission concluded from the sworn testimony of two CIA and five FBI officials, "corroborated by the Commission's independent review of the Bureau files," that "there was absolutely no type of informant or undercover relationship between an agency of the U.S. Government and Lee Harvey Oswald" (R 327). In fact, Chief Justice Warren declined on security grounds to inspect the FBI file on Oswald noting that others "would also demand . . . to see it, and if it is security matters we can't let them see it" (5 H 13). According to the Commission lawyer in charge of this matter, no "independent review" was ever made of the file.*

In any case, the question of Oswald's FBI links is only one part of the puzzle. There is considerably more evidence to indi-

* See Edward Epstein, *Inquest* (New York: Viking, 1969), p. 38.

cate Oswald's involvement with U.S. intelligence—evidence that is obscured rather than laid to rest by the Commission Report.

Let us look at a few of the instances in which this "intelligence angle" was covered up. Oswald's mother, trying vainly to convince the Commission her son was "an agent of the government" (1 H 142, cf. 1 H 191), cited his "special work" in the Philippines (apparently in connection with the CIA military intervention in Indonesia) and in the Taiwan crisis (1 H 233, cf. 22 H 723). The Warren Report, without directly refuting this last claim, implied that Oswald had only been in Taiwan for a day or so around September 30, 1958 (R 684); it relied on Oswald's personnel file, and a related Pentagon memo, which placed Oswald's Marine Air Group 11 in Atsugi, Japan (23 H 796, cf. 19 H 658). In reality, MAG-11 had moved from Atsugi to Taiwan, in response to the Quemoy crisis, for an extended period beginning September 8 (Department of Defense Annual Report, 1958-59, pp. 228-29).

This change of status is noted in Oswald's pay records, which only reached the Commission nine days before its report went to press (26 H 709, 715). The pay records also show, in contradiction to the personnel file, that on returning to Atsugi (the base for CIA U-2 and covert commando operations in the Far East), Oswald left MAG-11 (now in Taiwan) and was attached to its replacement MAG-13 (26 H 715). That Oswald's personnel file could put him in one unit, while his pay records put him in another, suggests that Oswald, at least in 1958-59, was engaged in some kind of activity so sensitive that some of his records were altered to conceal it.

There are also discrepancies with regard to Oswald's "hardship discharge" from active duty in September 1959 to support his mother. The Warren Report cites affidavits that Mrs. Oswald "had been injured at work in December 1958 and was unable to support herself" (R 688). In fact, both Mrs. Oswald's regular doctor (CD 5.298) and an Industrial Accident Board denied that she had suffered a loss of wage-earning capacity. Nevertheless, Oswald received his release with an ease and rapidity that surprised some of his colleagues (8 H 257).

In Oswald's group at Santa Ana, California, where a "secret clearance . . . was a minimum requirement" (8 H 298, cf. 232), the basic function was "to train both enlisted [men] and officers for later assignment overseas" (8 H 290). The swift handling of Oswald's release suggests that it was a cover: Oswald was being "sheep-dipped," just as U-2 pilot Gary Powers before him had been "released" from the Air Force for assignment to a covert intelligence role. Oswald's immediate application for a passport on September 4 "to attend the Albert Schweitzer College in Switzerland and the University of Turku in Finland" (22 H 78) suggests that that role concerned his "defection" in October to the Soviet Union.

Here, too, the Warren Commission chose to overlook discrepancies. How was the trip paid for? The Report blandly repeats Oswald's own story that he had saved fifteen hundred dollars from his Marine Corps salary (256), ignoring the fact that his only known bank account contained a total of two hundred three dollars (22 H 180). How did Oswald fly to Finland from London Airport, where his passport was stamped "Embarked 10 Oct. 1959" (18 H 162)? If he had taken the only commercial flight, he would have arrived too late to register before midnight (as claimed) at his Helsinki Hotel (26 H 32). The Report's solution was to conclude that Oswald had departed from London October 9, ignoring both the evidence of the conflicting date stamp and the possibility that his flight was not a commercial one at all.*

The desire of U.S. intelligence agencies to interview even casual visitors to the Soviet Union is well known. In June 1962, Lee Harvey Oswald was a returning Marine defector who had once served at a CIA base and had told the U.S. Embassy in Moscow of his intention to pass information to Soviet officials (18 H 98). For two years he had worked in a sensitive Soviet factory and was now married to the niece of a colonel in Soviet intelligence. Yet the Report tells us that the returning Oswalds were met in New York City, not by the FBI or CIA, but by

* R 690, cf. Sylvia Meagher, *Accessories After the Fact* (New York: Bobbs-Merrill, 1967), p. 331.

"Spas T. Raikin, a representative of the Traveler's Aid Society" (R 713).

The FBI interviews did not point out that Spas T. Raikin was also the Secretary-General of the American Friends of the Anti-Bolshevik Bloc of Nations, a small but vigorous group of right-wing revanchiste East Europeans in direct touch with the FBI and Army Intelligence—and also with the Gehlen spy organization in West Germany, the Kuomintang in Taiwan, the mother of Madame Nhu, right-wing Cubans like Oswald's DRE contact Carlos Bringuier, and other elements of a shadowy "World Anti-Communist League." This WACL had contacts with U.S. anti-communists in New Orleans, in the building with the Camp St. address used by Oswald on his pro-Castro literature, and also by the CIA's Cuban Revolutionary Council of which Bringuier had once been press secretary. As I have indicated in my book, *The War Conspiracy,* Mr. Raikin's personal correspondents in Taiwan (the Asian Peoples' Anti-Communist League) were intelligence agents involved in the Kuomintang's narcotics traffic—a fact dramatically illustrated by the 1971 arrest in Paris of the Chief Laotian Delegate to the APACL, whose suitcase containing sixty kilos of high-grade heroin would have been worth $13.5 million on the streets of New York.

Unfortunately, there has not been space to show the ways in which many if not most of the Commission's staff, like most of the FBI agents involved, did attempt an honest and thorough investigation. I have focused narrowly on some of the indications that there was a cover-up where security and intelligence matters were involved. And, as we have learned from the Watergate and "plumbers" break-ins, the cover-up of an intelligence matter can become a priority, thereby protecting perpetrators of crimes which have no intelligence justification.

The Ruby Connection

Jack Ruby, the second "lone assassin," was a more difficult subject for a cover-up; his personal and business ties with the police and underworld in Dallas were widely known, and there is evidence they extended considerably beyond Texas. Nevertheless, the Commission went to great lengths to argue that Ruby, like Oswald, "acted independently" (R 373), and in particular to downplay his close links to the Dallas police and also to organized crime. According to a brief and unconsciously humorous section of the Report, "the evidence indicates that Ruby was keenly interested in policemen and their work" (R 800). Nothing is said of the testimony of Detective Eberhardt, a veteran of the Special Services Bureau (SSB), "that he regarded Jack Ruby as a source of information in connection with his investigatory activities" (13 H 183)—i.e., as a police informant, specifically in the area of narcotics.

A word must be interpolated here about the SSB of the Dallas Police. Like similar "Special Units" in other police forces across the country (all of which work with one another), the Dallas SSB had had a consolidated responsibility, in collaboration with the FBI and other agencies, for investigating subversive activities (allegedly the world of Lee Harvey Oswald), and also organized crime (the world of Jack Ruby). It also had responsibility for the area of vice, and particularly for supervising nightclubs such as Jack Ruby's. Thus SSB Vice Chief Gilmore, a "close friend" of Ruby (23 H 78, 25 H 290), was said to visit his clubs "every night they are open" (23 H 207). SSB also had a Narcotics Unit. Last but not least, the SSB was given the responsibility of protective intelligence for the visits of important government officials—such as President Kennedy—who visited Dallas (5 H 48).

Ruby's status as a high-level police informant would explain the repeated stories, from sources inside and outside Dallas, "that Ruby is the payoff man for the Dallas Police Department" (CD 4.529) and "had the 'fix' with the county authorities" (23 H 372). One of these reports is particularly credible, inasmuch as it was received by the FBI seven years before the assassination. According to a Mrs. James Breen, who with her husband acted "as informants for the Federal Narcotics Bureau," her husband "had made connection with large narcotics setup operating between Mexico, Texas and the East. . . . In some fashion James got the okay to operate through Jack Ruby of Dallas" (23 H 369).

The Warren Report discounted the even more numerous stories (one of them from a former Dallas County Sheriff) that Ruby was linked to organized crime. Commission Exhibit 1268 (22 H 372) is a typical example of the FBI's and Commission's reluctance to explore more deeply Ruby's underworld connections. In it a Dave Yaras (unidentified) "claims 'Sparky' " [i.e. Ruby] "knew Lenny Patrick 'like he knows him' but was 'positively on his own and not outfit connected.' " Yaras further described "Sparky" as a " 'romeo' who was most successful in picking up girls." In the Report only the trivial part of this testimony remains: "one friend regarded him as a 'Romeo,' who was quite successful in attracting young women" (R 792).

We must turn to the Kefauver and McClellan Crime Hearings to learn (in answer to the obvious question not asked by the FBI) that the link between Yaras and Patrick (and hence, inferentially, Ruby) was intimate. Both men were top Syndicate gambling figures on Chicago's Jewish West Side. They had been arrested and indicted together for the syndicate murder in 1946 of wire service king James Ragen, an indictment dropped after the murder of a key witness. The police captain most active in the investigation was himself subsequently murdered, right after he reported to the Kefauver Committee (through his lawyer Luis Kutner) that he had a "hot new witness who will . . . name Leonard Patrick, Dave Yaras, and Willie Block as the killers" (*Newsweek,* October 9, 1950, p. 37). In 1963, news stories that Luis Kutner had intervened for Ruby with the Kefauver Committee also noted (correctly, it would appear), that Ruby was "linked" to Dave Yaras, Lennie Patrick and Willie Block" (*Washington Post,* November 26, 1963, A6).

Dave Yaras himself should have particularly interested the Warren Commission, since the McClellan Committee's counsel, Robert F. Kennedy, had charged him with the same connections later attributed to Ruby: corrupt Teamster interests, and "some gambling in Cuba" (McClellan Hearings, pp. 7416, 12522). Yet it asked no questions about Yaras and instead misspelled his name (as Yeres) when Ruby's sister began spontaneously to reminisce about him and Patrick (14 H 444).

This studious disinterest in Ruby's alleged Teamster connections appears to have been systematic. The Commission asked no questions about Ruby's two telephone calls in November 1963 with Barney Baker (25 H 244), a convicted Teamster hoodlum who phoned Dave Yaras on the eve of the assassination (25 H 295). Nor about Ruby's call to top Teamster bondsman Irwin Weiner (25 H 246)—an organized crime associate of narcotics overlord Sam Battaglia. When Ruby himself began to talk about his phone call to Dusty Miller, head of the Teamsters Southern Conference (25 H 244), this was transcribed in the Warren Hearings as a call to "Deutsch I. Maylor" (5 H 200).

It is of course quite possible that all these calls were innocent, but the Commission did not bother to find out. None of those called were witnesses, and their names will not be found in the Report. Instead the Report claims that Ruby's friendships with criminals "throughout his life ... were limited largely to professional gamblers," and adds, even more astonishingly, that "there is no credible evidence that Ruby, himself, gambled on other than a social basis" (R 370). The Commission had received numerous disinterested reports to the contrary (e.g. 23 H 48, 23 H 363, CD 360.115). One of these, from a south Texas businessman, recalled Ruby saying in 1960 that "he had recently been to Cuba, as he and some associates were trying to get some gambling concessions at a casino there but it did not work out" (22 H 858).

The Commission knew that Ruby in fact had visited Cuba in 1959, probably twice. Its Report mentions the eight-day August 1959 trip on one page (R 802), the two-day September trip (22 H 859) on another (R 370), and treats the two trips as one: "Ruby traveled to Havana as a guest of a close friend and known gambler, Lewis J. McWillie. Both Ruby and McWillie state the trip was purely social" (R 370). This covers up several facts which were known to the Commission: a 1959 police report called McWillie (whom Ruby "idolized," 5 H 201) a "gambler and murderer" (23 H 166); he was a former employee of big-time gambler Benny Binion, the power behind the Delois

Green gang who was now in Las Vegas (23 H 163,
CD 1193.249); in 1959 he was manager of the Tropicana Casino
in Havana, a syndicate operation (23 H 166); both in Havana
(The Capri) and in Las Vegas (The Thunderbird), McWillie
worked at casinos where a cut went to top Syndicate financier
Meyer Lansky.

Today this story of a Ruby involvement in Havana gambling
has a renewed interest, for in 1959 Castro's supervisor of gambling concessions is said to have been Watergate burglar Frank
Sturgis *alias* Fiorini, a gun-runner to Castro before the overthrow of Batista. The owner of the Havana Tropicana (where
McWillie worked and Ruby visited) was Norman Rothman, a
gun-runner to Castro who in 1959 was indicted on other charges
with *mafioso* Samuel Mannarino (another Havana gun-runner
and casino operator) and Giuseppe Cotroni, identified in the
Senate Narcotics Hearings (p. 1002) as "head of the largest and
most notorious narcotics syndicate on the North American con-
tinent."

Overlapping Conspiracies

In this dark area of gun-running to Cuba, the careers of
Sturgis, of Ruby, and of Oswald begin to overlap. First-hand
accounts linked Ruby himself to Cuban gun-running
(14 H 330-64), and to Robert McKeown, arrested in 1958 for
gun-running with his friend, former Cuban President Carlos Prio
Socarras. (Prio Socarras helped organize the Cuban exile demonstrations at the party conventions in 1972, when his Miami
office was only two doors away from Bernard Barker's.) And
Carlos Bringuier claimed he suspected Oswald of trying to infiltrate—as an informant either for Castro or for the FBI—the
Louisiana training camp of the Christian Democratic Movement,
a Miami-based exile group close to the DRE, which the Kennedy Administration was cracking down on in late 1963
(10 H 35, 43). Bringuier noted that five days before Oswald's
first contact with him, the FBI had raided an illicit arms depot
one mile from the camp. These arms were stashed in the home

of one of the McLaney brothers, prominent casino operators in Las Vegas, the Bahamas, and in pre-Castro Havana.

Since 1963, U.S. narcotics officials have referred to the existence in Miami of a small but tightly organized "Cuban Mafia" in narcotics, "for the most part previously little-known underworld members employed and trained in pre-Castro Cuba by the American Mafia, which then controlled gambling in Havana" (*New York Times*, February 1, 1970, p. 57). Certain U.S. business interests collaborated for decades with the narcotics-linked American Mafia in Cuba—as they did with similar criminal networks in China and later in Vietnam—for the Mafia supplied the necessary local intelligence, cash and muscle against the threat of communist take-over. Some of those Cuban-Americans recruited by the CIA (presumably from the Cuban-American Mafia) are now suspected by federal and city authorities to be "involved in everything from narcotics trafficking to extortion rackets and bombings" (*New York Times Magazine*, June 3, 1973, p. 46).

And behind the bureaucratic screens of "security" and "intelligence" there appear signs of a more sinister overlapping of conspiracies: in the gun-running and gambling background of Frank Sturgis and his allies, and the common responsibility for narcotics intelligence of E. Howard Hunt and John Caulfield in the White House, G. Gordon Liddy in the Treasury Department, and Egil Krogh (supervisor of the White House "plumbers") as Director in 1972 of the Cabinet Committee on International Narcotics Control.

The grey alliance in pre-Castro Cuba between business, intelligence and Mafia led to a central role in the post-war heroin traffic of the Havana connection, which later became the Miami connection. This Miami connection is typified by Bebe Rebozo's business associate "Big Al" Polizzi, who was named in the 1964 Senate Narcotics Hearings as "one of the most influential figures of the underworld in the United States" and "associated with international narcotic traffickers . . . and illicit gambling activities" (p. 1049). Polizzi and Rebozo collaborated in the construction of a Miami shopping center, where Rebozo also employed a former mayor of Havana under Batista who headed up "Cubans for Nixon" in 1968. In addition, Polizzi and the Rebozo family have been recorded as signing legal petitions in support of each other, in 1952, and again in 1965 (*Newsday,* October 7, 1971; *Village Voice,* August 31-September 6, 1973).

Another piece in the puzzle is provided by the Keyes Realty Company, a Miami business with underworld connections, which has helped both Rebozo and Nixon in various land deals, including the Winter White House. Keyes Realty and its lawyers were named in the Kefauver Crime Hearings (Part 1, p. 716) for their role on behalf of organized crime in bribing Dade County's Sheriff Sullivan to run Miami as a wide-open gambling town. In 1948, Keyes Realty, and its lawyers, with the help of a wealthy Cuban banker called Agustin Batista (no relation to the dictator), collaborated in the transfer of southern Key Biscayne to a shadowy Cuban investment group (the Ansan Corp.) in which an Internal Revenue investigator suspected the presence of funds belonging "to Luciano or other underworld characters" (IRS Report of Feb. 20, 1948, cited by Jeff Gerth in the November-December *Sundance,* p. 38). The visible partners were former Cuban President Prio's investment ally and Education Minister Jose Aleman, who had defrauded his government of tens of millions of dollars (*New York Times,* March 26, 1950, p. 92), his wife Elena Santiero, daughter of Luciano's Cuban attorney, and Batista's Finance Minister and investment ally, Anselmo Alliegro.

Later control of this Key Biscayne real estate passed to men near Hoffa and the Teamsters' Pension Fund, and Meyer Lansky's conduit, the Miami National Bank. In 1967, some of this land was sold at bargain rates to Nixon and Rebozo, by a man named Donald Berg; after Nixon became President, the Secret Service advised him to stop associating with Berg because of his background. Nixon delayed registering the purchase of one lot for four years, until the final payment had been made on a mortgage to Arthur Desser, associate of both Jimmy Hoffa and

Meyer Lansky.

Recently, Nixon's links with Desser, Keyes Realty et al. have been less prominent. But one of the Watergate burglars, Eugenio Martinez, was a vice-president of Keyes Realty until 1971, when he and Bernard Barker set up their own realty office, Ameritas, in the same office building. Some of Barker's real estate ventures, according to Jack Anderson's column (June 26, 1972), have also involved Bebe Rebozo. Funds for the Watergate operation were channeled through Barker's bank account in a Cuban-owned Miami bank, Republic National, whose president had formerly worked for Agustin Batista's bank in Cuba. (The first president of this bank had earlier chaired the board of the Miami National Bank and another director was from the law firm of Keyes Realty.)

In 1961, Agustin Batista and his brother Laureano, leader of the Cuban Christian Democratic Movement (CDM), employed Sturgis' friend Hans Tanner in the CDM's "Project 26"—yet another effort to assassinate Castro.* Tanner's account also describes how Nixon himself, out cruising in the Miami River, shouted "Good luck" to a boatload of CDM guerrillas training, supposedly in secrecy, for their diversionary role in the Bay of Pigs.† In 1965, Nixon intervened legally on behalf of the CDM's imprisoned political leader, Mario Garcio Kohly, who had been arrested by the Kennedy Administration for his anti-Castro activities in October 1963.

No congressional committee has fully explored the alleged illegal activities of Hunt and Sturgis over the last decade. Some congressional committee should learn more about these men's Cuban activities, such as those which in September 1963 brought strong U.S. government warnings to Sturgis and death to his friend Rorke. It is almost certain that a full inquiry in this direction would uncover past alliances between intelligence networks and organized crime for mutually advantageous opera-

---

* Tanner, op. cit., p. 143.

† Ibid., p. 2.

tions—including the attempts to assassinate Fidel Castro. And the disturbing evidence of a cover-up in Dallas suggests that such assassination efforts have not all been aimed abroad.

> *Anyone who opposes us, we'll destroy. As a matter of fact,*
> *anyone who doesn't support us we'll destroy.*
>
> —Egil Krogh, Director
> National Transportation Safety Board

Flight 553:

The Watergate Murder?

Barboura Morris Freed

December 8, 1972—Friday

It was far from the light-dress, short-sleeve, easy weather of a sultry Washington, D.C., summer. Seven months had passed since May of 1972, when E. Howard Hunt had, for the first time, attempted to reconnoiter the Watergate. The trees were bare now and it was cold.

Hunt and his wife Dorothy had left their rambling estate on River Road in Potomac, Maryland, which they had purchased in 1968 and Hunt had named "Witches Island." The Hunts were headed toward Washington's National Airport.

A little less than twenty-four years earlier, on September 7, 1949, the former Dorothy L. Wetzel from Dayton, Ohio, had become Mrs. Everette Howard Hunt, Jr. The CIA was only two

This essay is excerpted from *The Watergate Women*, a book in progress, by Barboura Morris Freed, edited by Donald Freed. © Citizens Research and Investigation Committee, 1974.

years old in 1949 when Hunt, calling himself a "State Department Reserve Officer" (in reality he was the blackest of "black"
clandestine operatives), appeared in Paris as liaison, for the Marshall Plan, between the American Embassy and the Economic
Cooperation Administration (a CIA tront). It was there that
Hunt met and married Dorothy Wetzel, who was also a func-
tionary in the Paris CIA station. Though something of a white
supremacist and certainly an elitist, he betrayed nothing when
she informed him that she was a full-blooded American Indian.

They were a "CIA couple" from the beginning, but over the
years of intelligence work and travel, they had made a life:
children, homes, books, plots and counter-plots in fiction and
for real.

The Hunts pulled into the airport. One result of E. Howard
Hunt's three-month-old indictment on six counts of conspiracy
was restricted travel. He could not leave the Washington area.
Since his September 15 indictment, Dorothy alone had made all
the trips with the money to keep the Cubans quiet. He had
thought about getting (and also contemplated disregarding) the
necessary court order and taking this flight, up to the last
minute. Then he had changed his mind.

Now six oblique and hectic months after the break-in at
Watergate, Dorothy and Howard Hunt were here, saying goodbye at Washington's number two airport. She was fifty-two and
felt it for the first time. She had made it clear to them all the
she was tired, wanted out, that this was the last trip.

Her husband was gone. Dorothy Hunt moved on through the
terminal. Was she thinking about Hunt's private papers—the
ones that he told her to say could "impeach the president ten
times over" if the White House ever tried to turn her down
financially? Time was about up on "the papers," the press was
digging out the "eight cartons," their life insurance.*

---

* Hunt's "eight cartons" of documents were removed from his White
House office and stored with a federal employee, Roy H. Sheppard. UPI
reported that "when no one asked for them" Sheppard burned them at the

Did Dorothy Hunt's luggage and handbag actually contain the most damaging from the collection of Hunt's papers and a three-page inventory of the rest, plus several different packets of monies and securities—as later unofficial investigators would claim—or simply the officially admitted $10,588 sum found in the plane's wreckage and prematurely designated as clean? Could there ever have been papers pertaining to plots in the work or future plans which would be damaging to Hunt's superiors? Howard's new novel, *Berlin Ending,* dealing with a West German leader exposed as a communist spy did prefigure the toppling (or set-up) of Willy Brandt.

The stubby twin-engine Boeing 737 jetliner, N9031U, United Airlines Flight 553, was scheduled to leave National Airport at 1:20 P.M. Eastern Standard Time, final destination Omaha, Nebraska, with one prior stop scheduled at the old Midway Airport in Chicago.

Dorothy Hunt's travel companion was Michelle Clark, a handsome black CBS news reporter. How much would she tell Ms. Clark this time?

Ms. Clark had learned from her inside sources that the Hunts might be getting ready to "blow the White House out of the water," and that before Howard Hunt was hung out to twist slowly in the breeze he would "bring down every tree in the forest." Hunt's co-conspirator James W. McCord would testify that matters were coming to a head early in December 1972. "Mrs. Hunt was unhappy with her job going all over the country to bribe defendants and witnesses in the bugging case. She wanted 'out.' " The talk, further, was that Hunt's "bottom line" price for silence was twofold: a confirmation of the promise that he was going to get Executive Clemency, and $2 million in negotiable securities.

What was to be the in-flight exchange from the "bag lady," as the press posthumously would dub her, to the CBS cor-

---

city dump in November 1972, but Jack Anderson reported that they were returned to Hunt in August 1972.

respondent, Michelle Clark?

In the summer of 1972, prior to any major revelations regarding Watergate, Ms. Clark had tried to pick the brains of Chicago Congressman George Collins, regarding the bugging of the Democratic National Headquarters. Now bound for home and moving along in the direction of United's Flight 553 in a stylish overcoat, attaché case in hand, was that same Congressman Collins, member of the House Committee on Government Operations and Public Works. Collins was a forty-seven-year-old black congressman from a black ward, the twenty-fourth, on Chicago's West Side: "The Champion of Lawndale."

With each opening of doors, cold air swept into the terminal. Out of these brisk, short shafts, other passengers had come, sixty-one in all, including two infants, five children, and six crew members, who were about to board the same Boeing 737. A muted voice announced: "All those boarding United Airlines Flight 553 please go to gate . . ."

Dorothy Hunt and Michelle Clark crossed the macadam in a swirl of sound and wind to where the plane was docked for departure, and boarded the cold metal stairway together.

The two women were seated side by side. At the very rear of the plane a man sat alone on the aisle, a man Dorothy Hunt, with her trained and sensitive eye, might have recognized—or if not, definitely suspected of something. He was Harold Metcalf, a thirty-four-year-old federal narcotics agent with DALE (Drug Abuse Law Enforcement), the president's newly commissioned super task force.

He had reported to the captain that he was federal narcotics and armed. He had sought one of the very last seats, near the food galley and close to the rear door in the tail of the plane, seat B17 (only the jump seat for stewardesses was behind him), being "fearful that some passenger might bump against him, feel the bulge of the weapon worn on his hip and perhaps mistake him for a hijacker."

There were other passengers with occupations and interests that converged on Watergate from another angle. They all sat in

the Muzak waiting for takeoff. These other Watergate passengers were probably unknown to Dorothy Hunt and Michelle
Clark. What a story it would have made for the star CBS reporter if she had only known.

That week there had been a gas-pipeline lobbyists' conference
held in conjunction with an American Bar Association meeting
in Washington, D.C. Among those attending were Ralph
Blodgett and James W. Kreuger, both attorneys for Northern
Natural Gas Company of Omaha, Nebraska. Other associates
with them on the plane were Lon Bayer, attorney for Kansas-
Nebraska Natural Gas Company, and Wilbur Erickson, president
of the Federal Land Bank of Omaha.

Three months prior to this Washington meeting, some officials of Northern Natural Gas Company and its subsidiaries,
including the mayor of Hammond, Indiana, and city officials of
East Chicago, Indiana, had come under federal criminal indictment in Omaha, Nebraska; Chicago, Illinois; and Hammond,
Indiana. The charge was bribery of local officials in northwest
Indiana and Illinois, for the purpose of securing contracts to put
through a multi-million-dollar pipeline system.

Their corporate destiny at stake, Northern fought back:
against the indictments they pitted the "Mitchell Papers." These
blackmail documents purported to reveal illegal acts of conspiracy between former Attorney General John Mitchell and the
Justice Department with Northern's fiercest competitor, El Paso
Natural Gas Company, along the lines of the ITT scandal.

In 1969, the Justice Department, then headed by Attorney
General Mitchell, had dropped pending anti-trust charges against
El Paso. And it was not until approximately three years after
this fact, in March 1973, that a spokesman for Mitchell be-
latedly claimed that Attorney General Mitchell had "disqualified" himself from that 1969 decision because, admittedly,
his law firm did represent El Paso Natural Gas Company. But
the main results, and collusion, of that 1969 decision had long
since transcended the belated, unsubstantiated Mitchell disclaimer:

1. The charges against El Paso had been dropped.
2. Almost simultaneously, John Mitchell, through a law partner as nominee, received stock interest in El Paso.
3. El Paso was later to contribute heavily to Mitchell's Committee to Re-Elect the President.
4. The favorable decision to drop anti-trust charges was worth an estimated $300 million to El Paso.*

Northern's legal hatchetmen boarded Flight 553, though they had previously been warned that they would never live to reach Chicago.

It was cold and overcast in Chicago on December 8, 1972. A thin fog, rain, and some snow had covered the area all day. Visibility was one to two miles with a variable cloud ceiling of four hundred to six hundred feet, some clouds as low as a hundred feet, and ground or surface winds mild at six nautical miles per hour.

United Airlines Flight 553 from Washington was now entering the area served by the Chicago Air Route Traffic Control Center. The twin-engine Boeing 737 jetliner was reportedly flying at ninety-five hundred feet at a point fifty-five nautical miles southeast of its intended destination, Midway Airport. It had been a routine flight, and Captain Wendell L. Whitehouse, forty-four, prepared for a routine instrument landing. Whitehouse was an experienced pilot, with eighteen thousand flying hours behind him. His colleagues and supervisors considered him "one of the best in the business," a strict disciplinarian who "flew by the book." "In the soup" over Chicago, Whitehouse would be flying IFR (instruments) on approach, as commercial pilots always do. He and his crew would be descending "visually blind" until such time as they broke the cloud cover. Until then, all those aloft would be wholly dependent on the proper functioning of the electronic and mechanical guidance systems on board and on the ground, as well as on the Chicago air controllers.

---

* See page 235 of this volume.

As the plane drew nearer to Midway, the Chicago Air Route Traffic Center yielded responsibility to the Chicago Approach Control Center, located at Chicago's main airport, O'Hare International. O'Hare assumed guidance for 553's initial pattern of descent and actively monitored radar tracking of the craft. According to the O'Hare Approach Controllers, they issued an initial speed directive to 553 to slow down to 180 knots, but after twenty-three sweeps of their Precision Arts III Radar (fifteen sweeps per minute) the Boeing was still doing 210 knots. This was too fast. Later they claimed they gave 553 a second speed directive. But from available evidence O'Hare never directly inquired as to 553's "deceleration lag," or warned her, as is their practice and duty, to correct.

O'Hare also failed to give the incoming flight a "Cleared to Approach." The Approach Controller "forgot," he later admitted. In the absence of "clearance," any experienced pilot would normally hold at some fix and maintain his last assigned altitude until necessarily assured by ground control that it was safe to descend. If need be, he might put into effect his alternate landing plan and head elsewhere. But officials maintain neither was the case for 553. The flight continued on its inbound course. [Nine months later, in the National Transportation Safety Board's Aircraft Accident Report number NTSB-AAR-77-16, the absent order giving permission to approach was insufficiently explained away as "understood," and no criticism was ever made of O'Hare's failed responsibility.]

Then O'Hare stopped watching, transferring all active monitoring and responsibility to the Approach Controllers at Midway Airport. Unofficial investigators (using unpublished official documentation) place the "hand-off" at 8.9 miles out from Midway; official reports place it at 5.3 nautical miles out. In either case it was too early and in violation of the letter of agreement between the up-to-date, precision O'Hare Center and the smaller Midway, whose guidance system lacked the precision radar needed to determine the altitude of an incoming aircraft. O'Hare Approach Control had made a premature hand-off, and from the evidence they did so without giving Midway any information on 553's excessive speed or other in-flight factors.

Within seconds the new Midway Approach Controllers issued two contradictory communiqués. They informed O'Hare that they were going to send 553 around for a second approach, while almost simultaneously they instructed 553 to continue inbound.

The flight crew of 553 was scheduled to land on Midway's runway 13-Right. Outdated and unsophisticated as Midway's equipment was, 13-R was the only runway with a "Glidescope" to give the height and angle of descent directly to an incoming plane, compensating in part for Midway's lack of precision radar. But, for some reason, 553 was redirected to runway 31-Left at the opposite end of the field. 553 would have to land without the Glidescope. [This redirection officials never adequately explained.] Surface winds are the usual reason for redirecting aircraft, yet that day they were nearly nil.

O'Hare Approach Control had already properly "cleared" a private Aero Commander to approach Midway's 31-L ahead of 553. The Aero Commander then declared a "missed approach," Midway responded affirmatively to the request for the "wave off," and the small private plane went around for a second approach. O'Hare and Midway had overlooked the possibility of a spacing problem arising between the two planes.

The flight crew in the Boeing were by now determining their flight path by reliance on the first intercepted and main electronic ground device known as the "localizer." Radio beams from the device would show 553's relative distance from the runway and its relationship to the runway's center line. As 553 was approaching on it, the localizer either stopped working or was somehow lost to the aircraft. "Is Kedzie Localizer off . . . Off the air, is that it" was a documented question asked by the captain of 553. [His query was never printed in subsequent post-crash news articles, nor did it appear nine months later in the Safety Board's final Accident Report.]

A second electronic signal, the "Kedzie Outer Marker," which would signal the plane when it passed over a point 3.3 nautical miles from the runway, giving the plane its exact position, was "turned off." This fact is buried in the fine print of the final NTSB Report, but was not deemed pertinent to crash cause and was left uninvestigated. No mention was made of the Outer Marker malfunction having any possible bearing on or relationship to the lost Localizer. It was at this safe Kedzie site, 3.3 nautical miles out, that the O'Hare-Midway "hand-off" should have occurred.

Was 553 closing in on the Aero Commander, which was coming in ahead for a perfect—if delayed—touchdown? According to Midway Approach Control, they ordered a missed approach for 553, waving off the flight just on that possibility. According to officials, the Boeing was then 3.3 nautical miles southeast of 31-L, when Midway exercised this precaution. Later the same officials would claim that the "wave off" came "just before 553 disappeared from view on Midway's radar screen." Officials consistently claimed controllers had exercised proper caution, since part of their job is to "expedite," and that the last-minute "wave off" was not relevant to crash cause.

The pilot of Flight 553 spoke to his passengers three times. At first, in a tone that revealed the uneventfulness of the routine flight, he advised all passengers that the aircraft would be a little late because of head winds. From the cockpit to the passengers came the second announcement: they were over Gary, Indiana, and would be landing in about five minutes. The last communiqué from Flight 553's flight deck to passengers was to let them know that they were at four thousand feet, that all was well and that they would be landing momentarily.

Now, overhead, 1.7 nautical miles from Midway Airport and far wide, to the right, of runway 31-L, United Airlines Flight 553 was beneath the cloud cover. Under the "friendly skies of United" visibility was one mile, cloud ceiling at five hundred feet. The overcast gone, the passengers saw the clear sky, the rooftops, the schools and churches, the wintry tops of trees.

The engines roared madly, as a stewardess screamed, "Get down in a crouch!"

The nose of the Boeing 737 "pitched up"; the engines wound laboriously; "spooling up," the aircraft "stalled," suspended in midair, shuddering in its death throes. Then Flight 553 plummeted to earth 1.5 nautical miles on the southeast course to Midway, in a working-class neighborhood of one-story bungalows.

Within two minutes, Chicago radio station WLS called Midway. When they asked if there had been a plane crash, Midway responded, "I don't know." Within four minutes, radio station WGN called and received the same answer: "I don't know." According to official reports, radio contact between Midway and 553 did not fail at any time in the course of the flight. Yet Midway's initial and final claim was that they had heard nothing at any time to indicate that Flight 553 was in any kind of trouble.

Just hours after the crash an anonymous call came into Bob and Betty Sanders' WBBM Chicago (CBS) talk show. The self-described "ham operator" claimed to have monitored ground control's communications with 553, and he reported a strangely tense exchange concerning gross control tower error or sabotage. But CBS, Michelle Clark's employer, did not see fit to notify or present this tape to authorities. No attempt was ever made to find the ham operator for testimony.

The plane crashed a block and a half from Queen of the Universe School and two blocks from Hurley Elementary, pancaking down belly first in the 3700 block of West 70th Place. As it smacked down, the United Boeing severed two power poles and sheared through the twelve-thousand-volt utility lines, causing a power blackout in five thousand homes over an area of two square miles. All electrical and telephone service stopped. It was an hour before repairmen restored even partial service.

Survivors and neighborhood residents gave consistent testimony to the almost immediate materialization of "police," using the easiest and most practical synonym for plainclothes official-looking strangers.

Witnesses living in the crash zone told of "FBI types" parked on side streets in unmarked cars, and of others arriving at the time of the crash. These "officials" were in the crash area before the Fire Department, which received a "3-11" call within one minute of the crash—even though all telephone lines in the area were down. And Midway Tower claimed that it knew nothing of the crash until five minutes after the aircraft had vanished from its radar screen.

Shortly after December 8, 1972, a remarkable and very unofficial body, the Citizens Committee to Clean Up the Courts (CCCC), stated that immediately after the "air disaster," two hundred FBI and Defense Intelligence Agency (DIA) operatives, all refusing to show their credentials, had flooded in and taken over the crash site. This charge was dismissed out of hand.

But six months later, on June 17, 1973, Chairman John Reed of the National Transportation Safety Board (the government body always entrusted with investigational *priority* in all such disasters) told the House Government Activities Subcommittee (headed by Jack Brooks, a Democratic congressman from Texas) that he himself had sent a letter to William Ruckelshaus at the FBI containing the following statements:

Dear Mr. Ruckelshaus:

As you may know, the National Transportation Safety Board is currently investigating the aircraft accident of the United Airlines Boeing 737, at Midway Airport, Chicago, on December 8, 1972. Our investigative team assigned to this accident discovered on the day following the accident that several FBI agents had taken a number of non-typical actions relating to this accident within the first few hours following the accident.

Included were: *for the first time in the memory of our staff* an FBI agent went to the control tower [Midway] and listened to the tower tapes before our investigators had done so; and *for the first time to our knowledge* in connection with an aircraft accident, an FBI agent interviewed witnesses to the crash, including flight attendants on the aircraft prior to the NTSB interviews. As I am sure you can understand, these actions particularly with respect to this flight on which Mrs. E. Howard Hunt was killed, have raised *innumerable questions* in the minds of those with legitimate interests in ascertaining the cause of this accident . . . [Emphasis added.]

Previously, the FBI had told the NTSB that no more than a "dozen agents" had participated in the crash investigation. In replying to Reed's letter, Ruckelshaus admitted that "approximately fifty FBI agents responded to the scene." According to Ruckelshaus, the agents conducted twenty-six interviews and handed their records over to the NTSB within twenty hours of the crash. Ruckelshaus conceded that his agents had committed unprecedented actions by listening to voice tapes of transmissions to and from Flight 553 at the Midway Control Tower, and by interviewing the stewardesses and other witnesses, in both cases before NTSB investigators arrived on the scene. But he justified his agents' conduct, according to the *Washington Post* of June 14, 1973, by saying that, *in cases of possible sabotage,* the FBI has "primary investigative jurisdiction." [Emphasis added.]

This rather amazing statement by the former Acting Director of the FBI concerning his agents' conduct with regard to the Midway crash surely raises many more questions than it answers. It seems to suggest that the FBI—then under L. Patrick Gray's control—was responding to information it had received *prior to the crash* that Flight 553 was to be sabotaged. But Ruckelshaus's statement has never been further elaborated or explained in any public forum.

The nearest FBI office is forty minutes from the crash site, and since the Bureau insists that agents work out in the field rather than in the office waiting for calls, there are never fifty agents available at once without prior warning. Yet local authorities and police, who were initially no more than half a minute away, found the FBI already at the crash when they arrived. The local authorities contend that the FBI sought no help from them in the investigation, but sent them at once to the outskirts of the crash site to handle transportation problems and the increasing traffic jam.

The FBI's immediate appearance in such large numbers was unheard of, as well as their astounding subsequent behavior. One FBI agent proceeded into Midway's control tower and confiscated the tape containing information only second in evidentiary import to 553's own two recording devices. No permission was asked. The FBI did this before the NTSB could act—a unique and illegal intervention.

At the disaster site itself the FBI agents interfered with rescue operations. They kept a medical team away from the plane, even though a member of the team swore that he had heard someone in the crash screaming. The FBI had the least injured persons evacuated from the crash area first, contrary to established practice of speeding the most injured to possible life-saving medical treatment. FBI agents, not medics, separated the dead from the living and stripped the dead of all belongings and identification. They swept through the plane's twisted aisles and compartments, taking their confiscated findings somewhere other than to the hospitals and morgue. They permitted only FBI interrogations and searches, barring even inspectors from the Federal Aviation Administration, which was authorized by law to investigate the accident.

The FBI cordon was complete, but one man managed to penetrate it—an executive aide to black Congressman George W. Collins, one of the passengers. The aide happened to have some old military ID papers on him. Once on the inside, he claims that he saw a man in coveralls climbing out of the split fuselage of the Boeing 737. The aide recognized the man as an operative of the CIA. Other witnesses claimed to see operatives of the Defense Intelligence Agency.

The 737 had vanished from Midway's tower radar at 2:28 P.M. Central Time, according to a Federal Aviation Administration official, and crashed at 2:29 P.M., when all clocks in that area stopped. From 2:30 P.M. until the next morning, Saturday, December 9, the FBI was in complete charge for the first time in air-crash history.

What did Dorothy Hunt think? The veteran CIA spy, the dedicated horsewoman, the wife, the mother who alone related to the pair's four children, the American Indian, the literary critic, the secretary, the translator, the bag lady (code named "Chris"), the witch of "Witches Island," the woman, the person who now at fifty-two would be the victim—did she picture in her mind's eye, in the last vertiginous seconds, the Operation Gemstone charts that her husband and G. Gordon Liddy had designed—the charts that diagrammed the illegal manipulation of flight communications and electronic signals. Perhaps she thought of Howard's plan for "trace" spy planes to follow Democratic campaign jets and electronically eavesdrop aloft. Did she think of the other Watergate women victims and what had happened to them: Martha Mitchell, drugged, kicked and held captive beyond even the control of her powerful husband; and Dita Beard, kidnaped and drugged by Liddy, and interrogated for hours on end by Howard. Poor Dita Beard, who had suffered a "heart attack" on another United Airlines flight between Dulles and Denver.

Howard Hunt claimed that he learned of the crash from his son. It was Friday evening and he was sitting at his typewriter making the final changes Dorothy had suggested in his new novel. Hunt secured permission and late that night "flew to arrange for his wife's funeral," and then returned home.

Dorothy's cousin by marriage, Howard C. Carlstead, learned of the crash at Midway Airport, where he was expecting to meet her. The following day he would be identified by the press as having been among those waiting. Carlstead, a Chicago CPA, did his accounting and tax work for businesses owned by organized crime in the Chicago area. He also operated two Holiday Inns, one a hangout for gangsters and dope traffickers like "Cool" Freddie Smith, Grover Barnes, and the late Sam De Stefano. As he acknowledged publicly some days later, it was he who identified Dorothy's body. She was not among the twenty-five so disfigured that extra time was needed for physical identification.

Not until Sunday, December 10, did the morning news carry the first brief bleeps about Dorothy Hunt: "Wife of indicted Watergate figure dies in December 8 plane crash of Boeing 737 in Chicago . . ."

Dorothy Hunt was head. But the big play in the press was on Howard Hunt, Watergate, and money: "LINKED TO WATERGATE FIGURE," "$10,000 FOUND IN JET WRECKAGE."

In Chicago, the first news accounts reported that the police had found ten thousand dollars in one-hundred-dollar bills in Mrs. Hunt's purse, which had been found inside a piece of luggage. The *New York Times* reported that the police had found ten thousand dollars in Mrs. Hunt's purse while "sifting through the rubble," suggesting that the purse had been loose and not in the luggage. The accounts also differed on whether Mrs. Hunt had an additional $385 or $585 and where it was found. Neither mentioned the FBI agents who had monopolized the initial search, let alone what they had found originally and what they had taken away. On Friday Carlstead and Hunt immediately identified and requested the "bag she was carrying."

Later, from his home in Maryland, Howard Hunt spoke of Dorothy's "purse," explaining that his wife was taking ten thousand dollars for Carlstead to invest. He said that the money had no connection to the Watergate incident, and that the "planned" investment had been under discussion for a "long period of time." *

The FBI investigated and the Chicago police announced on Wednesday, December 13, that Dorothy Hunt's monies were clean, "because the money found in Mrs. Hunt's purse was old and none of the bills had sequential serial numbers, while the

---

* Hunt implied that he was facing poverty because of his recent "unemployment," although his author's royalties alone assured him a reasonable standard of living. And after the crash a quarter of a million dollars would be available from air travel insurance taken out on Dorothy Hunt's life.

hundred-dollar bills traced to Watergate suspects were new and numbered in sequence." The serial numbers on Bernard Barker's bills began with a different letter, but much later it became public knowledge that the Barker hundreds were only a small part of the laundered slush fund of Operation Gemstone.

The announcement that the money was clean was by no means the only piece of official premature investigatory disclosure regarding elements in the 553 disaster. The technique prevailed. One bill had piqued the interest of "investigators," said the *Chicago Tribune*. It was a "C"-coded note, with the inscription "Good Luck F.S." written across its face. "Good Luck Frank Sturgis." But was the good luck expression from or *to* the notorious CIA sharpshooter?

If early news accounts slighted Dorothy Hunt, they ignored a second Watergate figure altogether, one who would come to play a significant role in the continuing drama of Flight 553— Egil "Bud" Krogh, Jr.,* since jailed for directing the burglary of the office of Daniel Ellsberg's psychiatrist. On December 9, 1972, one day after the crash, President Nixon appointed Krogh Undersecretary of Transportation. This put Krogh in a position to supervise the National Transportation Safety Board and the Federal Aviation Administration—the quasi-independent agencies authorized to investigate airline crashes. Krogh's appointment did not make the big news or the back page. No photographs for Dorothy or Krogh, and for Krogh no headlines or kickers.

Krogh would hold his new post in Transportation until May 9, 1973, when the Watergate scandal forced him to resign. Two weeks later, witnesses before the Senate Commerce Committee

---

* A devout Christian Scientist, Krogh had been John Ehrlichman's chief deputy in the White House and a member of Ehrlichman's law firm in Seattle. Krogh specialized in narcotics and security. He had run the Plumbers Unit, participated in an AID-sponsored (CIA) study on "Vietnamese Land Reform" at the Stanford Research Institute in 1968, and traveled to Southeast Asia on a "narcotics-related" intelligence mission for the White House in July 1971.

would testify that Krogh played a leading role in at least one attempt to intimidate members of the National Transportation Safety Board during the time they were investigating the Midway crash.*

Egil Krogh was only the first of the Watergate personalities to move into a post from which he could oversee the investigation. The second was Alexander P. Butterfield, "ex" CIA, Secretary to the Cabinet, the White House aide in charge of secretly taping presidential conversations and telephone calls, and the one who revealed the existence of those secret tapes to the Senate Watergate Committee. On December 19, 1972, President Nixon named Butterfield to head the Federal Aviation Administration.

The third Watergate figure to shift jobs soon after the crash was Dwight L. Chapin, appointments secretary to the president and the man who "ran" Donald Segretti and his network of provocateurs in the president's re-election campaign. In January 1973 Chapin was named an executive in the home office of United Airlines in Chicago.

Chapin had no previous business experience, but he was well qualified for his new job. In February 1973, he appeared at the first public 553 crash-cause hearing. According to consumer advocates there, he warned the media to steer clear of any question of foul play in the crash or any hint of a cover-up by the NTSB, FAA, Boeing Aircraft, Pratt-Whitney (the engine manufacturer), or United Airlines. If the newsmen failed to obey, Chapin threatened to use Nixon's communications czar Clay Whitehead to break up the networks. United had already prohibited its own employees from talking and had refused immediately after the crash to release information or even to dis-

---

* The general manager of the NTSB, Richard Spears (a former assistant to Republican Senator George Murphy of California), was also charged with adversely affecting the quality of NTSB reports in early 1973. He fired the head of the NTSB's Bureau of Aviation Safety, C. O. Miller, who supervised the early investigation of 553, and directed later investigators to take less time, make fewer recommendations, and redefine "probable cause."

close the home addresses of its crew members.

The president's personal attorney and Gemstone "bagman" Herbert W. Kalmbach had served as an attorney for United Airlines even before the crash. He was also attorney for the Marriott Corporation, which catered in-flight food and drink service. Marriott's executive vice president was the president's brother, Donald Nixon.

First the FBI. Then Egil Krogh, Alexander Butterfield, and Dwight Chapin. From start to finish the supervision of the investigation of the crash of Flight 553 was in dubious hands.

FAA officials had been on the scene from the day of the crash, though outnumbered, outflanked, and illegally outranked by the FBI agents. The NTSB had sent a team the following day, headed by William A. Haley.

The NTSB team included experts on aircraft engines, air frames, electrical and hydraulic systems, flight operations, interrogation of witnesses, air traffic control, meteorology, and human factors. According to a spokesman the investigators would require autopsies on the three dead crew members; they would remain at the crash site until December 14; they would take as long as a month to determine the probable "cause of crash."

Chief investigator William W. Lamb announced that the NTSB would hold public hearings in January with more than forty witnesses expected to testify. Among those already interrogated for a second time was Harold Metcalf, the narcotics agent.

Daily reportage made it look like a long, careful examination of all possible factors was in progress. But from the outset the investigation had its conclusion: "pilot error." Captain Whitehouse and his two co-pilots were to blame. Their mishandling of the plane had caused the crash.

"Experts with the NTSB now are inclined to believe mishandling of the United Airlines 737 jetliner contributed to its crash and fiery destruction," began the lead story in the December 14 *Chicago Tribune*. And "the Safety Board is convinced that the difficulty was confined to the United airplane." In no way did information within the article clarify this official statement. In fact, the NTSB did not know exactly what had happened. To fill the gap three main and sharply different scenarios were put forth regarding flight events immediately preceding the crash. Two of these accounts mentioned an application of power just prior to crash. First day accounts from stewardesses and passengers had attested to a major application of power. Yet the NTSB Report oddly claimed, when finally citing probable cause, that no power had been applied at the last and also that some power had been applied but it was insufficient to recover from a "stall," which they were finally to claim occurred in level flight. In the *Tribune* article, there was no mention of Whitehouse's reputation as a pilot—"the best in the business"—nor any mention of his earlier experience as a stunt pilot.

The headlines of the NTSB's summarizing account suggested that the experts had listened to the tape from 553's Cockpit Voice Recorder: "ALL ROUTINE: VOICES SHOW NO ALARM . . . LAST WORDS OF CRASH CREW TOLD." The implication was that at last NTSB, after comparative study, had knowledge of all pre-crash events. As the story explained:

> No vocal or other indication was received from United's three-man flight crew that an emergency had developed aboard. Instead, the voice of 2nd Officer, B. J. Elder, 31, was almost languid as he responded to Midway Tower's instruction to "Take it around again; you are too close to the Aero Commander ahead."
>
> Elder, who was believed to be handling radio communications, said, "Okay, Tower, if that's what you want us to do."

At this point NTSB was still pushing their main theory of a failed ascendancy on aborted approach, and stall. But whether 553 had been 1) failing on final descent and attempting a braking reconfiguring action or 2) strangely entering a stall regime in level flight and making an improper response or no response at all for recovery as NTSB finally maintained or 3) facing a hopeless task of attempting to survive sabotage, it is hard to believe that voices showed "no alarm" or "pressure," as was reported in the *Tribune* article.

The fact that not even one word was in evidence on the cockpit voice tape, referring to trouble in the final moments, is harder yet to believe. Especially if NTSB's final case for probable cause were valid. On entry into a stall regime there are unmistakable warning alarms that go off in the cockpit leaving time to act before the stall become fatally irreversible.

Even with the drag produced by having the landing gear and the flaps down, and flight spoilers deployed, an application of full power and the aircraft's nose rotated downward assure recovery even at low altitudes.

NTSB never reconciled their own final evidentiary claim that 553's final nose attitude was high, not low. Full throttles and nose rotated up is the attitude for an aborted approach.

From Midway's "take it around again," it would seem that 553 had already been around, possibly circling one and a half times as the crew shifted approach from runway 13-R to 31-L. From Midway's "you are too close to the Aero Commander ahead," it seemed that 553 might be closing the mileage gap on the Aero Commander and threatening a collision. But from Second Officer Elder's languid reply, it seemed more likely that 553 and the Aero Commander were too close together in time— not in space—and that the Aero Commander was "ahead" only in having priority to land.

Midway itself wasn't sure whether it had "waved off" 553 at 3.3 or 1.7 nautical miles out. Perhaps Midway had "waved off the Boeing twice, with the languid exchange taking place the first time. According to "experts," the voice recorder had been "filled with hydraulic oil when recovered from the wreckage, and some four days were required in the laboratory to clean the tape sufficiently for it to be played back to Safety Board listeners." Were the crash crew's "last words" only the last understandable words? Had the tape been broadly edited and left purposely incomplete? Only an exact picture of 553's flight path, a fix on the time of each recorded exchange, and a full transcript of Midway's instructions from live and taped testimony could clear up the confusion, and all were missing from the initial accounts.

Further news on the fourteenth concerned the tape from the Tail Flight Recorder, which could give a complete picture of 553's final movements—speed, direction, altitude, time, and acceleration loadings. According to the *Tribune,* officials in Washington would shockingly disclose that there had been nothing to read, that the Tail Flight Recorder had stopped recording fourteen minutes prior to crash. The most valuable piece of evidence turned up blank. All official disclosures regarding 553's two all-important tapes left much to be desired.

According to earlier news accounts, the Commissioner of Streets and Sanitation had handed over the "two flight recorders . . . recovered from the wreckage" to the newly arriving NTSB team. But it was hardly possible that the well-made, highly insulated, tightly secured instruments—built to survive far worse crashes—had been loose, just lying in the street to be swept up by custodians. Had the Commissioner gotten them from someone else, possibly the FBI? Again the initial accounts didn't say.

There were more disturbing notes. At first, the press had suggested that United would fly 553's engines to its Maintenance Headquarters in San Francisco. "They may hold the key," the Safety Board explained. United then decided against flying the engines, fearing that lifting them into the plane might irreparably jar them. Instead, United would ship them all the way across country *by truck!* All the while, Pratt-Whitney, the makers of the engines and no doubt most qualified to assist the NTSB in an investigation, were close at hand in Connecticut.

Almost hypnotically, the Safety Board, through the media, conveyed their message: We are the professionals, we have the proof, we are inclined to believe, we suggest, we are convinced. The inquiry is "far from complete," our proof is limited and flawed and not conclusive, but we are inclined to believe nonetheless; we are convinced . . .

One controversial independent investigator, Sherman Skolnick of the Chicago-based Citizens Committee to Clean Up the Courts, was not convinced.

One week after the crash the telephone rang in Skolnick's apartment/office. He picked up the receiver: "I'm calling you from Midway airport. Flight 553 was sabotaged. I'm risking my life to tell you . . . you better get your group working on this—people were murdered."

This call—from an FAA employee—launched a continuing CCCC investigation that was to unearth an entirely new edition of remarkable facts and questions never touched on or made public by the NTSB.

Sherman Skolnick attempted to offer his findings as an alternative to the official view at the NTSB hearings. Denied the right to testify at the first hearing, the ubiquitous gadfly went to federal court to force the NTSB to re-open the public hearings. In June, Skolnick—a peripatetic paraplegic and muckraker with credentials—wheeled into the banquet room of the Airport Hotel, ready to face the media, officials from Washington, United Airlines executives, and various law enforcement observers.

Forced to play to the gallery, Skolnick pointed out the possibility that Flight 553 had been sabotaged electrically at National Airport (Washington) during the ten to fifteen minute delay before takeoff. A skilled technician who knew the plane could easily strip down the "bus bar" and insert a "filament" that would short out the electrical system on descent, he explained.

It was Skolnick who first enumerated the long list of blunders, malfunctions, and failures which the official investigation had down-played, ignored, or simply deleted. He quoted from some thirteen hundred pages of *official* Flight 553 crash documentation that he claimed he had *stolen* from the NTSB files. (Did the CCCC take responsibility for the stolen documents in order to protect their FAA informant? In any case, the government made no move to prosecute Skolnick or any of his thirty-six volunteer investigators.)

Skolnick's accusations continued. He cited involvement with Watergate of those aboard 553. He pointed out that the body of Captain Whitehouse had contained incredibly high counts of cyanide, as did at least five of the passengers. The post-crash fire might have produced part of the cyanide, he admitted. But the bodies had contained four times more than could have come from the fire, or "nine whiffs too many." He claimed that this was why CBS had demanded Michelle Clark's body for immediate cremation. He claimed that Captain Whitehouse was not at the controls during the last minutes of flight. He demanded to know why.

Skolnick's charge of cyanide poisoning forced the NTSB to counter with its own expert, Dr. Paul W. Smith, Chief of the Aviation Toxicology Laboratory of the Civil Aeromedical Institute, Oklahoma City. Dr. Smith and the NTSB claimed that the Cook County coroner had made a mistake and that the cyanide count in the blood of the pilot was only 3.9 micrograms per milliliter. But Dr. Smith admitted that this *was the highest blood cyanide reading he had ever recorded in a crash victim.*

In Skolnick's view, Flight 553 was sabotaged. The relentless investigator also alleged that the Joseph Sarelli mob, a highly sophisticated gang of former aircraft technicians and "fences" who specialized in stealing securities and other valuables from the baggage compartments of airplanes in flight, was involved. CCCC's staff investigator, Alex J. Bottos, and his friend, Joseph Zale, had infiltrated the Sarelli mob, purporting to be fences. At the time 553 crashed, the two were working in deep cover in coordination with the Justice Department Strike Force—poised to prosecute the gang for a $2.1 million securities' theft perpetrated in August 1972.

Two days after the crash they had seen samples of items taken from the plane. Bottos was stunned to see the "Mitchell Papers" taken from James Kreuger's suitcase, as well as an additional forty thousand dollars in cash he was told had been in the possession of Dorothy Hunt.

He claimed also to have seen $2 million in American Express money orders, traveler's checks, and postal money orders, drawn on the National City Bank of New York. Also, invaluable written evidence of executive "high crimes" abstracted from Howard Hunt's eight cartons of "White House Horrors," that included *pre*-Watergate complicity in assassinations in both North and South America and plans for future Gemstone operations. Bottos was not allowed to testify to any of this at the crash-cause hearing.

Bottos and CCCC were also prepared to claim that Carlstead and Hunt had issued a fake cover story regarding what Dorothy Hunt had carried in what bag, in a bid for time to recover the more "negotiable" luggage. Was it Hunt and Carlstead who had given the Sarelli mob a post-crash contract to get the "Hunt Papers" and valuables?

This combined Hunt-"Mitchell Papers" package was rumored to have gone on the crime underground market. Further, it was rumored that this "package" was successfully fenced for no less than $5 million. If so, who bought? The White House and/or El Paso?

Bottos (code named "Doyle" for the government's Strike Force) had first brought his explosive information about the theft and what he had seen to the Justice Department. They froze their investigation of the Sarelli mob and postponed all prosecution. Bottos then went to the CCCC and gave them the information. This, combined with the other startling new facts, led to the two circus-like "public hearings" played out before a hostile and intimidated Chicago media.

After little success at the first hearing, investigator Sherman Skolnick began suit for a second hearing. He also started to leak his information from the unnamed FAA informant and Bottos. The government reacted by arresting their own agent and now ex-star witness Bottos and shipped him off *in secret* to a federal prison hospital in Springfield, Missouri, which journalist Jack Anderson labeled a "political prison" on April 9, 1973. Skolnick blasted open this scandal. Public pressure and angry inquiries from Bottos's former employer, the Indiana Crime Commission, secured the double agent's release some forty days later. His "sanity" had been certified by three psychiatrists, three psychologists and six social workers. On April 23, 1973, the Indiana Crime Commission took the extraordinary step of calling a press conference to accuse the Federal Strike Force of fraud for silencing its own star witness.

It was Bottos who had questioned the narcotics agent Harold Metcalf for CCCC. (CCCC was to learn later that this chief narcotics agent in the Midwest for DALE had practically no knowledge of drugs.) A few days after the crash Bottos stood facing Metcalf in a secret subterranean room in Hammond, Indiana, which Metcalf used to interview DALE informants. Bottos knew about this "safe house" because he had also worked undercover for DALE. In response to Bottos's question, "Did you know the plane was sabotaged?" Metcalf blurted out half a sentence—"It was not supposed to . . ." Turning purple, he stalked from the room.

Skolnick's hard-hitting scatter of allegations may have been hard for some to believe, but no harder than the NTSB's Final Report.

The Final NTSB Blue Book Report appeared in late September 1973—nine months after the crash. It contained some surprises. But none regarding the "probable cause" of the air disaster. It was still "pilot error." Still "the Captain's failure to exercise positive flight management," though it continued now to read ". . . during the execution of a non-precision approach, which culminated in a critical deterioration of airspeed into the stall regime where level flight could no longer be maintained." Still, in the body of the report, NTSB could not decide whether or not 553 was attempting a missed approach at the last. In the fast-brush booklet, there was still no mention of malfunctions in the aircraft, engines, flight controls, pertinent ground instrument failures, or ground guidance errors, "nor . . . any evidence of any sabotage or foul play."

Erroneously claiming a complete picture of Flight 553's final movements, the Board ruled that Whitehouse had made only a single approach, starting out "too high" rather than "too low." The Board placed 553 at twenty-two hundred feet above sea level (or twenty-two hundred m.s.l.) as the plane passed over the site of the Kedzie Outer Marker. The prescribed minimum for this site, 3.3 nautical miles out from Runway 31-L, is fifteen hundred m.s.l. Their final claim positioned the Boeing seven hundred feet too high. NTSB did not explain, nor did it claim to have investigated, this error.

The Board's final statement regarding 553's altitude at the Kedzie site totally contradicted its earlier one—presented in public testimony by its star altitude witness, William J. Simonini. Simonini claimed that he had observed 553 from the Kedzie ground site—fifty feet beneath the five hundred foot cloud ceiling, or four hundred fifty feet above ground level (four hundred fifty a.g.l.). Aeronautical terminology always uses sea level as a base referent. Sea level at the Kedzie site is approximately 619 feet. When comparing NTSB's early and late claims for 553's altitude over the Kedzie Outer Marker, in above-sea-level terms, an eleven hundred foot differential appears. *Had* 553 made two separate approaches? Had Simonini lied? Was the final statement fact or an integral part of a cover-up? And what body is to separate our national facts from fictions?

The Report also blamed Whitehouse for flying too low, too slow, and for having the aircraft poorly configured just before impact. The booklet explained that "The plane's Captain had called for the First and Second Officers to read a checklist while the plane was approaching the runway" and that this meant the First Officer could not make "any of the required altitude call-outs, . . . nor does it appear he was monitoring air speed and rate of descent."

NTSB claimed this poor flying triggered the onset of the "stickshaker stall warning signal"—a clamorous bell and shaking control pedestals—and then, the stall itself. And in response, the pilot acted as if he were trying to reconfigure the aircraft to maintain level flight. The charge was improbable. According to the Blue Book, Midway issued the "wave off" simultaneous with the first sound of the stickshaker stall warning. And that after a seven second interval 553 responded affirmatively to Midway's order for the missed approach, making no comment, then, about the stall warning nor in the remaining eleven seconds before impact.

Even if 553's speed had been sufficiently slow over a period of time long enough to trigger the onset of the stickshaker stall warning, the pilots could not fail to respond. The signals are so startling that only the unconscious could miss them. For all their "simulated tests" . . . "transcriptions of tapes" . . . "derivations of Flight Profile" . . . and "Studies," in lieu of hard evidence, NTSB could not prove that enough time had elapsed for 553's entry into a stall regime in level flight.

Whether at 3.3 or 1.7 nautical miles out and even at a four-hundred-fifty-foot height, if Whitehouse had visibility, no mechanical failure and just one functioning guidance instrument—the Boeing's Air Speed Indicator—he could have aborted safely.

Five days after the crash Chicago's O'Hare Traffic Control commented, in response to complaints about low-flying aircraft, "There is nothing dangerous about flying that low [five hundred feet] unless there is a malfunction. Then we've got a serious problem."

Quite possibly, 553 had suffered aircraft malfunction or sabotage while still up in the cloud cover, and then rapidly descended, disoriented and imbalanced. What ground witnesses and passengers described as a "climb and stall" at 1.7 nautical miles out might have been only the end result of trouble—the doomed twin-engine aircraft making a brief rally for control and balance before continuing its fall to the ground.

Equally possibly, 553 could have suffered mechanical malfunction or sabotage after emerging below the clouds. But if all were well and its brief climb characteristic of an ascent from an untroubled final approach, why did its nose tip up so steeply?

Why did its engines wind "laboriously"? Why did the missed approach maneuver not succeed? And why was 553 fourteen blocks far wide to the right of runway 31-L when "wave-off" instructions for a missed approach from 31-L call for a left turn to 180° and a climb to two thousand feet.

Undercurrents of sabotage haunted the nine-month period of official investigation. There were first-day accounts which petered out, reappeared in the form of a disclaimer, and finally disappeared altogether: *"Witnesses said they heard a thunderous roar and saw a flash of flame as the aircraft plowed into houses."* From the *Chicago Tribune* of December 12: *"Earlier reports that Thomas Togas, 27, saw one of the plane's engines ablaze were incorrect. Togas said, 'I saw sparks and smoke after it [the plane] hit the power line.'"*

On what basis four days later had Togas changed his testimony? Why was he sought out to make a second statement that was pointedly publicized? Many people had heard a "boom." And Thomas Togas was clear in his first account: *"I heard a boom, looked into the sky, and saw the plane with one engine apparently ablaze. It was about 200 feet high at the time and had not yet hit any buildings or trees. I recognized it as a 737. I used to fuel those planes at Midway."*

With the spectre of sabotage not laid to rest, notices like the one appearing in the *Chicago Tribune* on December 9, 1972 tend to catch the widened eye more readily:

TEST IS PASSED BY A SPRINT MISSILE—Washington, Dec. 8, UPI. A sprint missile . . . "destroyed" an ICBM nose cone . . . the Pentagon announced. The test was designed to check out the special radar and computer that launch and guide the Sprint to destroy incoming missiles at close range. . . .

In May 1974, the *Los Angeles Times* reported:

FEARED BLAST: PILOT TELLS HOW HE GOT VESCO'S JET.
The pilot was reported as saying: ". . . he became worried that the craft's former operators might have planted explosives on the jet. There was a fear that pressure detonators had been placed in the plane . . ."

A pressure detonator triggers a blast when pressure is applied or released. The sophisticated pilot knew how easily a plane could be sabotaged. He also knew that it is done, he said.

Like so many reports on major tragedies, the NTSB Accident Report offered answers, but left only questions. The chairman, John. H. Reed, refused to sign the report though his name was boldly visible on the bottom of the report's last page. The Board placed Reed's three-page Safety Recommendation, with his signature, at the book's end, giving a look of official credibility for the casual reader. Commercial pilots and aeronautical experts laughed at the accident report. The Airline Pilots' Association filed a complaint to the effect that the ground computer fed misinformation to the 553 crew. The public suspected it, even as they had suspected the crash itself once having heard that Dorothy Hunt had been on board, loaded with hundred-dollar bills.

No one has yet proved sabotage. *No one can,* no matter with how much evidence, *without subpoena power.* There was certainly a cover-up; Congressman Brooks proved that. Can there be a cover-up without a crime?

On June 24, 1974, the *Washington Post* rang the alarm bells along the whole corridor from Dallas to the Watergate. The *Post* revealed that President Nixon perceived himself as a virtual prisoner, in his oval office, of the Central Intelligence Agency. The source was the highest—Charles W. Colson. And Colson told *Time* magazine, *"I think they killed Dorothy Hunt."*

Nixon was upset and suspicious to find out that "Robert W. Mullen, founder of the public relations firm, complained that former CIA Director Richard M. Helms 'twisted my arm hard' to hire Hunt." And he was convinced that the Midway 553 event deserved *"a closer look at the circumstances of the plane crash that killed Hunt's wife, Dorothy, in December 1972."* [Emphasis added]

The NTSB Aircraft Accident Report came out of the cloud cover, firing off assertions.

It is astounding to realize that in all of the final official NTSB report and news accounts there never *once* appeared a single question mark. Had the mark itself been deleted or simply relegated to the sports section and the gossip columns, where it is *fun* to be lively, *safe* to conjecture, and *easy* to speculate? This is a form of invisible propaganda; this is hypnosis, the attempt to suppress the most lively and hopeful of all human symbols. Is this suppression of the interrogatory not the most profound sign of official *hubris?*

Setting aside the pattern of violence done to "aggressive" women in the Gemstone affair—Martha Mitchell, Dita Beard, and Dorothy Hunt—the horrible deaths of forty-five men, women and children in the Flight 553 crash cry out for a genuine investigation. The American people cannot stand an "investigation" that is, after all the lies and contradictions, only a body count.

There must be an accounting, a new investigation, totally free from the taint of White House-Gemstone agents like Egil Krogh, Alexander Butterfield, Dwight Chapin, Herbert Kalmbach and all the other king's men—who will never put those forty-five passengers and United Flight 553 back together again.

The sources for this article, in addition to all major media and the transcripts of congressional hearings, include: NTSB transcripts and Accident Report; Donald Freed and the Citizens Research and Investigation Committee; Gordon St. Dietrich for CRIC; Sherman Skolnick and the Citizens Committee to Clean Up the Courts; Alexander Bottos for CCCC; Carl Oglesby and the *Boston Phoenix;* Martin Goldsmith, author and pilot; the Black Panther Intercommunal News Service; Jack Kimbrough, author and researcher; Tom Matthews, commercial airline pilot and member of the Airline Pilots' Association; Robert Burney, former member of the United States Air Force; Lance Yellowhand, Creek Indian and worker for the American Indian Movement; Air Controller, California's Clover Field; and informants, from United Airlines Pilots' Association and other aeronautical associations, who specifically wish to remain nameless.

A special note of thanks to Donald Freed, whose help and encouragement were of paramount value, as editor, researcher and dear husband; and to Martin Goldsmith, without whose unstinting friendship and aeronautical informational aid the piece essentially could not have been done; along with deep thanks in this department to Tom Matthews and Jack Kimbrough. A special note of gratitude to Sherman Skolnick, Alexander Bottos and CCCC who bravely followed through their leads and were magnanimous in sharing their first, hard-won investigatory finds. Thanks to Gordon St. Dietrich, whose additional research was a major contribution to CRIC. Many thanks to Sherry Swanhuyser and Arlene Freedman for difficult manuscript preparation. And to the many unnamed sources in whose concern lies some of the hopes for truth in government.

Now this is the kind of thing you expect under a person like Hitler.

George McGovern

What really hurts in matters of this sort is not the fact that they occur, because overzealous people in campaigns do things that are wrong.
What really hurts is if you try to cover it up.

Richard Nixon

Stop McGovern

Editors of NACLA

Americans tend to view politics as a contest between individual politicians or, at most, between the Republican and Democratic parties. Even with the break-in at Watergate, the view remains. Nixon was the overeager politico; the Republicans were out to bug the Democrats. The same game; the same players.

The original version of this essay, entitled "Opening the Watergate," appeared in NACLA's *Latin America & Empire Report*, October 1972. Reprinted by permission of NACLA.

If we look at the significant connections of the Watergate personalities, however, a new reality emerges. Ever since World War II, a bipartisan business coalition had effectively controlled both major parties. Then, in the weeks before the Watergate break-in, George McGovern began to win primary after primary in the Democratic Party. He was rousing youth, blacks, Chicanos, peace people and women—the insurgents whom the Nixon years had quieted, downgraded, impoverished and repressed. He was putting together an impressive grassroots organization which operated outside the established party structures and which raised issues outside the established limits of party politics. He had the support of the Kennedy machine *and* he was defeating candidates whom the bipartisan coalition found acceptable—Humphrey, Muskie and Jackson. The coalition responded by giving its sanction—and its money—to a covert counter-campaign of political espionage and sabotage. Politics as it is, and not as most Americans believe it to be.

The Kennedy Menace

Conflict in U.S. party politics, over the last decade, has centered on the ambitious Kennedy organization. Nurtured by an independent fortune and utilizing charismatic figures, the Kennedy machine has repeatedly threatened the political hegemony of established business groups. It successfully challenged the power of these groups first *inside* the Democratic Party and then secured a run for the presidency. Since the political process is the medium through which business controls the government, the Kennedy organization was able to challenge established business control of the White House, that vital command post for regulating the national and international economies. The groups who benefited from Nixon's leadership are in no mood to put up with another threat from the Kennedy machine.

To counter just such insurgent threats, the established business groups organized themselves long ago into a *bipartisan coalition.* The groups agreed to place their common economic necessity to control the White House ahead of party loyalty. Unity behind their representatives in both parties would guarantee their dominance and limit the power of insurgents backed by the independently wealthy. If by chance such a maverick should secure the nomination in one party, the coalition members would cross party lines in order to win the election.

Nixon was the overwhelming choice of this coalition for the 1972 election. He had served its interests faithfully and "deserved" another term. To insure his victory, the coalition would engineer the nomination of a phantom opponent in the Democratic Party. Nixon would then sail through the election and the myth of the two-party system would be sustained.

Inside the Democratic Party, the coalition front-man most favored was Hubert Humphrey. Humphrey (of whom LBJ had said, "Boys, I've got Hubert's balls in my pocket") had proven his loyalty to the business groups as LBJ's VP. He had defended the commitment to the war in Vietnam. Humphrey was financially dependent on contributions from the Minneapolis, Texas and Jewish banking groups (all part of the coalition); he was entirely predictable, despite his liberal image. In 1968, he owed his political life to Johnson and his nomination to RFK's assassination. *He even offered the vice-presidential slot on his ticket to the rock-ribbed Republican, Nelson Rockefeller.* His backers knew a Rockefeller would swing GOP coalition members behind HHH and sew up the election. But the Rockefeller-led coalition stayed with Nixon. Humphrey went down to defeat.

In 1972, the power of the bipartisan coalition inside the Democratic Party was seriously weakened by rule changes coupled with a concerted Kennedy-McGovern drive for the presidential nomination. Anxious Nixon backers set about hatching an elaborate set of contingency plans to stop the growing insurgent effort.

Their principal source of anxiety was Senator Edward Kennedy. In the event of his nomination (or anyone equally as formidable) it appears very drastic action was contemplated. A nine-year Los Angeles undercover agent, Louis Tackwood, de-

scribes the formation of "Squad 19" by the LA police Criminal
Conspiracy Section and the FBI.*

> The plan entailed planting a number of agent provocateurs both
> inside and outside the 1972 (San Diego) Republican Convention.
> Agents were to infiltrate the groups planning demonstrations against
> the war and poverty. At the time of the demonstrations, these agents
> were to provoke street battles with police surrounding the conven-
> tion hall. Meanwhile, agents inside the convention hall were to plant
> explosives timed to blow up coincidental with the riots in the
> streets. The purpose is to kill a number of delegates.
>
> The result would be to create a nationwide hysteria that would
> then provide President Nixon with the popular support necessary to
> declare a state of National Emergency.
>
> Nixon would then arrest all militants and left-wing revolutionaries
> and cancel the 1972 elections. He could invoke special emergency
> powers leading to the detention of political activists. Martial law
> would be achieved.

By May, the Nixon staff realized Kennedy wasn't going to
run. At the same time primary results showed George
McGovern, Kennedy's less menacing ally, overtaking the coalition's Democratic Party representative, Humphrey. To bolster
HHH's chances, the Nixon staff activated a less drastic contingency, intelligence gathering. They were bent on securing embarrassing material on McGovern through less public sources
and more sinister means—espionage. Any ultra-sensitive operation like this would require the sanction of the bipartisan
coalition—Democrats as well as Republicans. The details were
left to the operatives but the idea of using political espionage
had to be approved.

The trick was to gather support for such clandestine operations from Humphreyites without jeopardizing pre-convention

---

* Louis Tackwood, *The Glass House Tapes,* as quoted in Mae Brussel,
"Why Was Martha Mitchell Kidnapped?" *The Realist,* August 1972. There
were also rumors circulating in 1969 of a secret RAND Corporation study
on various ways of canceling elections during times of social unrest.

power inside the Democratic Party. More than simple embarrassment was at stake. Exposure of the Nixon-Humphrey complicity to stop McGovern would certainly doom HHH's chances, weaken Nixon, and reveal that the financial strength of this business coalition was so overwhelming as to make a mockery out of the two-party system. Exposure would also reveal that the Democratic Party's commitment to social change, however gradual, was not only a farce, but was being abandoned. There was obviously another fear: that, in fact, the perceived interest of the majority of the electorate lay with McGovern.

Faced with this problem, the Nixon staff might have reasoned that if Humphrey backers were willing to finance the espionage, their loyalty as well as absolute silence would be guaranteed. A ready-made vehicle for accomplishing this delicate task existed in the form of a super-secret Nixon slush fund.* One purpose of the slush fund was to hide the names of contributors. It could cover other secrets as well. Among the donors were the traditional fat-cat Republicans paying their dues for past business favors or future promises. The ITT handout is typical of such deals which, if exposed, cause much embarrassing publicity.

The fund was put together in late 1971 when Congress passed a new Federal Election Campaign Act requiring the full disclosure of donations in excess of a hundred dollars. This act, however, was not to take effect until April 7, 1972, providing the Committee for the Re-Election of the President with a convenient opportunity to rake in large untraceable sums. A high-powered White House team, composed of staunchly conservative, fully trustworthy Republicans, was put to work specifically for this purpose under the leadership of White House hatchet-man Charles W. Colson, Attorney General John

---

* The slush fund, an old U.S. political institution, is composed of secret contributions from fat cats given to a particular candidate for past and/or future business favors involving government regulations and contracts. This untraceable money is then used for shady activities, including pay-offs and planted publicity to aid the victory of the candidate.

Mitchell and Commerce Secretary Maurice Stans. The immediate operations officers were recruited from a White House intelligence team of so-called "plumbers," originally used by the administration to plug leaks to the media.

For four months, from December 1971 through March 1972, this special fund-raising intelligence squad collected at least ten million dollars in secret contributions, an enormous slush fund similar to those other ventures so characteristic of Nixon's career. The squad set up one discreet operation under the cover of a small Washington public relations firm, Robert R. Mullen & Co. Its offices are conveniently located across the street from the White House and down the block from CREEP.

Hand-picked to run this quasi-public make-shift slush fund operation was E. Howard Hunt, Jr., a leading CIA spook. Hunt painstakingly erected seventy-five to ninety secret conduits with such Nixonian-fantasy names as "Supporters of the American Dream." This whole set-up resembled a classic CIA structure, from the use of a public relations outfit as a front to the channeling of untraceable funds through fly-by-night conduits.

Certainly, in choosing Hunt the White House had selected not any old CIA agent, but an embodiment par excellence of the spook generation.* Since 1949, he had climbed up through the ranks of the CIA. He specialized in super-secret covert operations in Latin America. His advancement ran parallel to the expansion of the Agency and its development into the most powerful weapon for constructing the U.S. empire. It appears

---

* Hunt was born in 1918 and received his A.B. from Brown University in 1940. During World War II, he served in the OSS in China, for which he won a presidential citation and the China Star. His career continued with a screen-writing stint in Hollywood until one of his stories, published in the *New Yorker*, caught the eye of Alfred Friendly. In 1948, Friendly hired Hunt to work in Paris in the Public Information Office of the Economic Cooperation Administration (ECA)—at that time, under the direction of Averell Harriman. Hunt left to join the CIA in 1949, moving on to stations in a number of locations, including Paris, Vienna, Mexico City and Montevideo. Years later, Friendly (who had since become a managing editor of

likely that Hunt's rapid rise slowed down after the 1961 Bay of Pigs invasion of Cuba, that massive CIA failure for which he served as chief operations officer under the code name, "Eduardo." President Kennedy's refusal to save the mercenaries by sending in U.S. troops infuriated the invasion's organizers and aggressive supporters, who included the former vice president, Richard Milhous Nixon. From this point on, it appears that Hunt and Nixon's careers were inextricably entwined.

It is important not to be bemused by the more covert and glamorous aspects of the intelligence community, particularly the CIA. U.S. intelligence operations really came into their own after the outbreak of World War II, when the business groups needed a coordinating and tactical agency *directly* under their control to secure and maintain a world empire. Other established agencies (like the FBI or military intelligence) were not able to fulfill this function because of lack of direct corporate control, provincial bureaucracies and congressional scrutiny. So the business groups built the Office of Strategic Services, which evolved into the CIA, and staffed it, at the top, with scions from the business groups.

In 1970, Hunt reputedly "left" the Agency. He surfaced in 1971 as a part-time hundred-dollar-a-day White House consultant to Charles W. Colson. "One of the original back-room boys," Colson handled the Nixon Administration's most sensitive ultra-secret business and political assignments. He worked with Peter Flanigan, better known as "Mr. Fix-it," and the ubiquitous Murray M. Chotiner in the "dirty tricks" department (intelligence parlance for covert action). Hunt's tasks included work on "Operation Intercept" (an anti-marijuana campaign

---

the *Washington Post*) saw Hunt "in the lobby of the National Press Building where he blandly denied his identity." (*Washington Post*, June 22, 1972)

The government bureaucracy being a fairly small world, in 1949 it happened that Friendly served in the same ECA information department as Robert R. Mullen, founder of the Washington PR firm which Hunt used as a fundraising front.

along the Mexican border that increased the use of heroin) and "declassification" of documents following the Pentagon Papers revelation. He also spent some time in Henry Kissinger's office on international narcotics traffic, a subject in which he is a reputed expert.

The other key slush fund organizer, G. Gordon Liddy, operated in a more public capacity as finance counsel to CREEP. A former FBI agent, he was originally hired in 1969 by the Assistant Secretary of the Treasury, Eugene Rossides. In late 1971, Liddy was shipped over to the White House to work on Operation Intercept (alongside Hunt). When probing the publication of the Pentagon Papers, Liddy reportedly asked Justice Department attorneys to bug the *New York Times*'s offices to discover who had slipped the secret documents to the newspaper.

According to the *Washington Post* of September 3, 1972, Liddy "was the chief adviser to the Nixon campaign staff on the new Congressional statute requiring stricter reporting of campaign contributions. In the eyes of some people on the campaign staff and others close to the investigation of the Watergate incident, Liddy was probably the second-ranking policy-maker in the Nixon fund-raising effort, next to finance chairman Maurice Stans." In effect, a division of labor existed among Hunt, Liddy and Stans limiting possible embarrassment to high Nixon officials in case of public exposure. The dirtiest and most controversial contributions passed through Hunt's conduits; Liddy tried to coordinate this activity with Stans' more public collections.

With this intricate structure at their command, Hunt and Liddy went after Humphrey backers to finance anti-McGovern political espionage. The fund provided a means through which they could secretly contribute to the Nixon effort, solidifying their membership in the bipartisan coalition, while simultaneously preserving their power inside the Democratic Party.

Key Humphrey fat cats from Minneapolis and Texas were quietly approached by slush fund agents and simply asked to demonstrate their loyalty to the plan in the form of cold cash.

Dwayne Andreas, the Minneapolis soybean magnate and the most important financial power in Humphrey's career, forked over twenty-five thousand dollars.* Another eighty-nine thousand dollars was collected from four Texas Democrats and was laundered through the bank account of a Mexican lawyer with a big U.S. corporate clientele. Simply enough, as demonstrated in Robert Winter-Berger's *Washington Payoff;* you pay for what you want and everything is for sale, so long as it is not in conflict with the overriding interests and priorities of the dominant and senior members of the bipartisan business coalition.

The cash traveled through the secret fund to the Miami bank account of Bernard L. Barker, an old CIA side-kick of E. Howard Hunt, Jr. A Cuban-born Florida real-estate broker, Barker served as paymaster in the Bay of Pigs invasion under the code name, "Macho." Together, the two spooks have invested in unsuccessful real estate ventures in Nicaragua, Puerto Rico and the Dominican Republic. This was all part of the murky CIA-business-right-wing network deeply penetrating the Caribbean. Barker's other business associate is Miguel A. Suarez, another *gusano*† lawyer, who represented the exile community (which includes Nixon's business pal, Bebe Rebozo) in its dealings with former Florida GOP Governor Claude Kirk, Jr.

In Miami, Barker recruited a three-man commando team from the well-heeled part of the Cuban exile community. Each of its members had participated in the Bay of Pigs invasion and maintained close CIA connections.

An acquaintance of Barker's for eleven years, self-styled soldier of fortune Frank Sturgis joined Fidel Castro's Rebel Army in 1958, according to an FBI report, at the behest of Batista's military intelligence. Sturgis defected from the Revolution in

---

* The twenty-five thousand dollars in cash was passed on April 8 to Kenneth H. Dahlberg, a Minneapolis hearing aid manufacturer and regional finance chairman. Andreas, head of Archer-Daniels—Midland Company, also donated at least seventy-five thousand dollars to Humphrey's primary campaign. See *New York Times,* August 25, 1972.

† Literally meaning worm, a derogatory term used by the Cuban government to describe those who left their country after the Revolution.

1960, getting his U.S. citizenship back with the help of the then-Florida Senator George Smathers (dubbed the "Cuban Senator" during the 1950s). Under various aliases, Sturgis has been associated with many Cuban exile groups. Using money collected from right-wing Texas and California businessmen, he organized several counterrevolutionary exile invasions against Cuba. For example, in 1962, he trained a twenty-three-man invasion force in Guatemala which landed east of Havana only to be wiped out.

Eugenio R. Martinez, an employee of Barker's real estate firm, was brought in. He had operated a weapons shuttle to Cuba and, with Barker, at various times was active in undercover work for the Defense Intelligence Agency and the CIA.

Associated with both Martinez and Barker was a Miami locksmith, Virgilio R. Gonzales. As a friend of Angel Ferrer, president of the Cuban exile group, Ex-Combatientes de Fort Jackson, Gonzales moved freely within the CIA-backed counterrevolutionary network.*

Rounding out the raider quintet was Washingtonian James W. McCord, full-time security chief for CREEP and the Republican National Committee. A former Air Force Lieutenant, McCord was employed by the CIA since 1951. He was in charge of security at the CIA's super-secret Langley headquarters. "Retiring" in 1970, he founded his own Maryland-based security consulting firm, McCord Associates, Inc. (His retirement date closely parallels that of our other leading spook, E. Howard Hunt, Jr.) It turns out that his firm's only "clients" were CREEP and the RNC. Like other members of the Watergate team, he participated in the Bay of Pigs invasion and maintained associations with exile groups which desperately needed a McGovern defeat to survive.

McCord's close ties to CREEP and the RNC immediately

---

* Ferrer was also registered at the Watergate the night of June 17. An added note of interest—four days earlier, a class of Ex-Combatientes graduated from a refresher commando paratroop course in Florida (*El Tiempo,* June 14, 1972).

distinguished him from the other members of the Watergate Five. His strategic position, in charge of security for the Republican Convention, makes it highly likely he was programmed for the more drastic contingency plans described by Tackwood, such as the major convention disruptions. Another important piece of evidence also suggests his involvement in these plans. As a member of a special sixteen-man Military Reserve unit under the President's Office of Emergency Planning & Preparedness, McCord dealt with the specific steps for rounding up radicals in a national emergency. In all likelihood, when disruption plans were placed on the back burner, he was switched to the espionage operation.

The commando team might have carried out its first job across the street from the Watergate. On May 16, someone broke into the law office of McGovern's eventual running mate, R. Sargent Shriver, and the Democratic Party's credentials committee chief, Patricia Harris. Nothing was stolen, but documents might have been photographed and the office bugged.

Ten days later, five men checked in at the Watergate Hotel for the Memorial Day Holiday under now famous aliases. During that time, there were two attempted break-ins at the Democratic National Committee (DNC) headquarters and, according to Lawrence O'Brien, an aborted attempt to plant an eavesdropping device in Senator McGovern's pre-convention headquarters. Film processed in a Miami photo shop on June 10 for Barker and Sturgis showed correspondence bearing the DNC letterhead and the signature of Lawrence O'Brien.

McGovern's chances vastly improved on June 6 when he won the winner-take-all California primary. Another wave of anxiety must have passed through the bipartisan business coalition. The CREEP, through Hunt and Liddy, stepped up its effort to get the goods on the senator from South Dakota.

The June 17 break-in reads like a pulp mystery novel by Hunt, a prolific writer of just such material. After several secret meetings and telephone calls as well as the acquisition of money and espionage equipment, the four Miamians flew to Washing-

ton on that day and, with McCord, registered at the elegant
Watergate Hotel, all using aliases out of Hunt's books.*

Finishing off a hearty lobster dinner, they proceeded to
break in to the DNC headquarters to repair already-planted bugging devices and rummage the files to photograph key documents. The group was equipped with walkie-talkies set for fre-
quencies assigned to McCord by the FCC and transmitting to
Hunt and Liddy, reported to be somewhere inside the Watergate
complex (across the street, a suite of rooms in a Howard Johnson's motel had been rented to serve as a listening post). But, an
alert Watergate guard, spotting tape on the doors, notified the
police who, at gunpoint, apprehended the Watergate Five inside
the DNC headquarters. Hunt and Liddy, forewarned in time by
a lookout, fled into the night.

The cover-up began almost immediately when a lawyer friend
of Hunt's, Douglas Caddy, showed up at the jail.† However, the
Five's cover aliases were quickly blown and the unraveling of
their connections to the top Republican leadership began. Address books of two defendants listed Hunt's name along with
the notations "W.H." and "W. House." McCord's employment
by the CREEP and the RNC definitely blew the whistle. Need-
less to say, he was fired immediately. A large amount of cash in

---

* The capital's most *in* address, the Watergate complex was erected by
Italy's largest real estate firm, *Societa Generale Imobiliare.* The Vatican
owned 15 percent of Imobiliare, which it sold to Michele Sindona in 1969.
Watergate's tenants include former Attorney General John Mitchell,
Madame Anna Chan Chennault (hostess-queen of the China Lobby and
head of Asians for Nixon) and several other prominent Nixonites.

† Caddy was the first executive director of the ultra-reactionary Young
Americans for Freedom and a former leader of the Youth for Goldwater
movement. With the Washington law firm of Gall, Lane, Powell & Kil-
cullen, Caddy served as liaison between Robert R. Mullen & Co. and its
client, General Foods. At this PR firm, Caddy shared an office with Hunt.
Nixonites seem to have a real propensity for General Foods. In September,
Attorney General Kleindienst, campaigning for Nixon, gave a major address at General Foods's Westchester, New York, plant.

consecutively numbered hundred-dollar bills was traced first to Barker's Miami bank account, then to CREEP fund-raisers, including finance chairman, Maurice Stans, and from there to Democratic fat cats.

More firings and resignations ensued. Liddy came next— dropped by Mitchell on June 28 for failing to answer questions from his former employer, the FBI. Martha Mitchell freaked out, apparently over her husband's role in Watergate and his less than gentlemanly associates. On June 22, she phoned a UPI reporter saying, "Politics is nothing but a cops and robbers game," "I saw dirty things," and "I am not going to stand for those *dirty tricks* that go on." John resigned on July 1, for "personal reasons;" more likely, he needed an excuse to step down from a high public position before a full disclosure unmasked his role. In searching Hunt's abandoned White House desk, FBI agents found a loaded pistol and a walkie-talkie.

With the arrests, the battle against McGovern shifted to the credentials committee of the Democratic Party and to the courts, where the pro-Humphrey forces tried to take away McGovern delegates from California, Illinois and several other states. But McGovern beat back the challenge, and after the early floor votes at the Democratic Convention, it was clear that Humphrey would lose.

The bipartisan business coalition now had only one course of action. They had lost control of the Democratic Party, at least temporarily, and now they would have to put all their eggs in one basket. On August 10, John B. Connally announced formation of Democrats for Nixon. The oil company lawyer and protégé of Lyndon Johnson was breaking party ranks, and behind him came the big business Democrats who had pledged their fortune to Richard Nixon even as they were publicly backed Hubert Humphrey. The list of "turn coats" was impressive, but two stand out as particularly interesting: the Committee's vice-chairman Jeno F. Paulucci, a long time campaign organizer from Minneapolis, and Johnson-Humphrey fundraiser John M. Loeb, unofficial overseer of several New York banking houses

(Lehman Brothers; Goldman, Sachs; Lazard Frères; and Loeb, Rhoades). It was an enormous concentration of business power. With this financial and political muscle, Nixon badly beat McGovern. The coalition had kept control of the White House and, with the election of Texas attorney Robert Strauss as National Chairman, took back the Democratic Party from the McGovern forces. The victory was key. Had McGovern become president, and put through his program of reform, he might not have changed the system in any fundamental fashion. But he certainly would have threatened the political hold of the bipartisan business coalition.

Watergate and the War

Harry Magdoff and Paul Sweezy

The Watergate scandal has broken wide open at a time when U.S. capitalism is in as deep trouble as at any time in its entire history. Appearances may seem to contradict this judgment, for it is undoubtedly true that the economy is in a strong cyclical upswing, with profits at an all-time high and officially counted unemployment down to "only" 5 percent. Inflation, especially in the area of food prices, has made a strong impact on all strata of society and has imposed extreme hardship on some, but establishment spokesmen are quick to point out that consumption of both durables and nondurables is running higher than ever before, hardly a symptom of imminent crisis.

But these appearances are misleading. U.S. capitalism's troubles *at this stage* are most acute in the international arena. These are less visible, in fact to ordinary citizens may be quite invisible, but they are neither less real nor less ominous for the future on that account. The once almighty dollar has had to be devalued twice in less than two years. According to orthodox

The original version of this essay, entitled "Watergate and Indochina," © 1973, appeared in *Monthly Review*, June 1973. Reprinted by permission of the authors.

neoclassical economic theory, these devaluations of the dollar should have remedied, or at least begun the process of remedying, the underlying deficit in the U.S. balance of payments which has kept the capitalist world's monetary system in a state of turmoil for more than half a decade now. And yet, as we argued before,* the balance-of-payments deficit reached enormous proportions in 1972 and gives every indication of remaining high for the visible future. This is quite simply not a tenable situation. If present trends were to continue, a profound crisis with most far-reaching international and domestic implications would be inevitable. This is why we stated at the outset that U.S. capitalism is in as deep trouble as at any time in its history.

From the point of view of U.S. capitalism the responsibility for taking action to meet this menacing situation rests in the first instance with the federal government, now headed by President Richard M. Nixon. What is the Nixon administration doing to discharge this responsibility?

It is already waging a trade war against the other major capitalist powers and is preparing to wage a much bigger one. This probably has the support of most of the U.S. ruling class, though the full implications for many of the country's giant multinational corporations are still far from clear. It is also maneuvering to expand trade with the Soviet Union and China and to fortify the U.S. international power position by improving relations with these largest of noncapitalist countries, and ruling-class opposition to this course appears to be negligible. But there is one area in which the policy of the Nixon administration is, to say the least, a great deal more controversial—Indochina.

There has long been a conflict in the American ruling class over the right policy to follow in Southeast Asia. Not that any significant section or group ever doubted the desirability, or even the great importance, of keeping the region in the "free world," i.e., open to penetration by capitalist business: as long as this goal seemed to be attainable at a reasonable cost (com-

---

* See "Review of the Month," *Monthly Review*, May 1973.

parable, for example, to the cost involved in maintaining a neo-colony in South Korea), there was virtual unanimity on South-east Asia policy in ruling-class circles. But as the Vietnam war dragged on and its costs in lives, in the effectiveness of U.S. armed forces, in dollars, and in damage to the balance of payments continued to mount, this unanimity dissolved. Some came to the conclusion that the war could not be won at any cost, others that even if it could be won the cost would be unacceptably high. The first showdown in this intra–ruling-class conflict came after the 1968 Tet offensive of the Vietnamese liberation forces. The military demanded a huge increase in the commitment of U.S. soldiers to Vietnam. Johnson's civilian ad-visers, including some of the ruling class's anointed wise men from outside the government, balked. This marked the end of the escalation of U.S. military involvement dating back to the early 1960s, and also the end of Lyndon Johnson's political career.

Nixon took office in January 1969 understanding that a new course would have to be plotted in Southeast Asia. One possi-bility would have been to get out on the best terms available, but he rejected this alternative (if indeed he considered it at all). The other possibility was to prolong U.S. involvement in the war while reducing the cost sufficiently to defuse domestic op-position. Nixon chose this course. Its two basic features were "Vietnamization," i.e., an enormous build-up of puppet forces, and the withdrawal of U.S. ground troops. Domestically, the strategem worked well, taking most of the pressure off Nixon and giving him time to try to win the victory which had eluded his predecessors. But in Indochina the policy suffered a series of disastrous defeats. The incursion into Cambodia in the spring of 1970 spread the war to another country which has been almost entirely "lost" in the short space of three years to a new, rapidly maturing, national liberation movement. The Saigon offensive into Laos the following winter was routed despite massive U.S. air support. And finally the spring 1972 offensive of the Viet-namese liberation forces all but delivered a knockout blow to the Thieu regime. It took the heaviest aerial bombing and naval shelling campaign in history to keep the Saigon dictatorship from total collapse.

When serious cease-fire talks finally got under way in October 1972, it seemed to many, ourselves included, that Nixon had finally come to the conclusion that the two-decades-old U.S. objective of maintaining a neocolonial regime in South Vietnam was unattainable and that he had decided to get out while saving as much face as possible. On this interpretation, the section of the ruling class favoring this course, which had been growing as the war dragged on, had at long last prevailed. Not only would it be possible to effect an immediate and important reduction in the costs of empire, but also the stage would be set for a serious longer-run effort to solve the interrelated balance-of-payments and dollar problems. There was never any chance, of course, that the basic goal of U.S. imperialism—to keep as much of the world as possible open to U.S. corporate business—would be changed. But it did seem for a while that long and bitter experience had finally convinced even hawks like Nixon and Kissinger that their conception of what was, and is, possible would have to be revised.

Now, however, more than three months after the signing of the cease-fire at the end of January 1973, it is harder and harder to accept this interpretation of Nixon's intentions.*

Confronted with this situation, the PRG and Hanoi are obviously defending themselves and making active preparations for the increasingly likely eventuality of a resumption of full-scale fighting. For this they are accused by the Nixon administration (and a press which certainly knows better) of "totally" violating the agreements and threatened with the resumption of U.S. bombing. Meanwhile, U.S. actions in Cambodia reveal more clearly than anything else the depth of Nixon's resolve to hang on in Indochina, come what may. For in Cambodia upwards of

---

* See, for example, "Indochina After the 'Cease-fire,' " by Noam Chomsky, which appeared in the April 13, 1973 mimeographed newsletter number 71 of *Resist*.

four fifths of the country is in the hands of the liberation forces, and the Lon Nol regime in Phnom Penh is in a state of virtual collapse. Only a very long-term effort with heavy direct U.S. participation could hold out any hope of creating a situation in Cambodia similar even to that in South Vietnam. Under the circumstances we must assume that this is exactly what Nixon has in mind.

So it looks increasingly as though Nixon, in negotiating and signing the cease-fire, was simply playing for still more time, tranquilizing domestic opposition to the war by withdrawing remaining combat troops and getting the POWs back, but still pursuing the chimera of a stabilized neocolonialism in the greater part of Indochina. No one should be under any illusions about what this implies. Not only will the costs of empire in that part of the world remain high; even more important, they are bound to increase without assignable limit as revolutionary national liberation struggles, inspired by the example set by the Vietnamese, the Laotians, and now the Cambodians, spread to nearby areas both on the mainland and in the island archipelagos which are essentially extensions of Southeast Asia. Cambodia has shown how rapidly a supposedly lethargic people can move into decisive action once sufficiently aroused by aggression combined with oppression. This is a story which will be repeated again and again, regardless of the calculations and efforts of Nixon, Kissinger, and the Pentagon, none of whom has apparently learned anything from failures and frustrations of the nearly two decades since French rule in Indochina was overthrown.

What we are saying is that historically Southeast Asia is in an irreversible state of revolutionary upsurge. U.S. imperialism can either accept this fact, as it finally had to accept the facts of the Russian and Chinese revolutions, or it can blunder in deeper and deeper, progressively exacerbating an already incipient global crisis and making any future efforts to avoid the threatened catastrophe less and less likely to succeed.

It seems to us that it is in this particular setting that Watergate takes on its greatest immediate significance.* Two questions immediately present themselves: (1) Have Nixon's Indochina policies had anything to do with the way the Watergate case has been handled? And (2) is it likely that Watergate will play an important role in determining the future U.S. course in that part of the world?

So far as we know, there is no firm evidence on the first question. C. L. Sulzberger begins one of his "Foreign Affairs" columns in the *New York Times* (May 6, 1973) with the statement: "The Watergate scandal isn't even remotely concerned with United States foreign policy." Maybe that is true. And yet it wouldn't surprise us to find that there is indeed such a link, albeit of a rather subtle kind. Nixon and his White House gang obviously thought the whole affair would soon blow over: all that would be needed were a suitable pay-off for those caught in the act and a cover-up story to protect the higher-ups. But it didn't work out that way, thanks largely to the efforts of a certain section of the press and of the judge who presided at the Watergate trial. How can one explain the persistence of these efforts in the face of what must have been very strong pressure from Nixon and company when they were still riding high?

One possibility of course is that the press, and especially the *Washington Post* and the *New York Times,* were glad of an opportunity to get back at Nixon for his administration's long-standing and vicious campaign against the media, and were determined to make the most of it. As for Judge Sirica, he may simply be a conscientious man who felt he was only doing his

---

* To avoid misunderstanding it should be added that Watergate can of course also be placed in various other settings, all of which are bound to overlap and interact, at least to some extent. One such setting, which for obvious reasons figures prominently in current discussion of Watergate, is the long sweep of political and constitutional history of the United States. There is good reason to believe that Nixon and his accomplices have been engaged in an operation which can be accurately described as an attempt to subvert the traditional U.S. system of bourgeois democracy. But this is a subject which requires full treatment in its own right.

duty. On the other hand, there are additional facts that should be considered. For one thing, the *Post* and the *Times* have all along been spokesmen for the anti-Vietnam-war wing of the ruling class, and were the ones primarily responsible for publishing the Pentagon Papers. And for another, as we now know, Watergate and the Ellsberg trial were much more closely linked than anyone could have suspected at the outset, and both newspapers had an obvious stake in the outcome of the trial. Furthermore, we have the impression—which, to be sure, a careful review of the record might not sustain—that there was a lull in reporting about Watergate from some time before last fall's election to the opening of the Watergate trial, i.e., during the period when it seemed possible that Nixon was really trying to pull out of Indochina. In any event the case only broke wide open when it became increasingly probable that he was maneuvering to stay in, rather than get out of, Indochina.

Against this background, it is at least plausible that Watergate was kept alive and eventually built up to its present formidable proportions as a means of weakening Nixon's ability to continue pursuing a policy which an increasing section of the U.S. ruling class had come to see as potentially disastrous. But whether or not this is true, there can be no doubt that this has been the *effect* of Watergate. The first, but certainly not the last, indication of this was the 219-to-188 vote in the House of Representatives on May 10, 1973, aimed at stopping the bombing in Cambodia. This was the first time the House had voted against the administration's Indochina policies, and it clearly resulted from a combination of two factors. In a news analysis article in the *New York Times* of May 12, 1973, James Naughton, after quoting a number of Republicans who were deserting the president, wrote:

> The anti-bombing vote was attributable as much to what members described as a desire to get out of Indochina. But one antiwar lobbyist said after the vote that it would never have been a majority view had it not been for Watergate.

"The sad thing," he said, "is that it came out of Nixon's weakness instead of Congressional strength. But maybe this will be a watershed. Nixon is essentially crippled for three more years."

One of the big questions now is whether Nixon really is crippled for three more years. Another, closely related, is what his opponents can and/or will do to take advantage of his present predicament.

Here again, it seems to us that any speculation on these questions which fails to recognize the centrality of Indochina, and indirectly of the profound crisis which threatens U.S. capitalism, is worse than useless. If Watergate is looked upon merely as a scandal, however monstrous and extensive it may turn out to be, there is no reason to attribute earth-shaking importance to it. In this respect, the example of Teapot Dome is instructive. That too was a major scandal which took place under a Republican administration, and it produced huge streamer headlines, heavy moralizing, highly publicized investigations, court trials, and prison sentences. And yet its lasting effect was just about nil: the Republicans didn't even lose the next election. The reason of course was that American capitalism was enjoying its greatest period of prosperity. Not only was the Great Depression several years in the future; even more important, no one—at least no one who amounted to anything—could see anything but fair weather ahead. Under the circumstances, the U.S. ruling class was united in its satisfaction with things as they were. Teapot Dome could even be considered to be a good thing. It was first-rate entertainment that helped to take people's minds off their ever present private troubles; and it showed how the great American system could not only survive evildoing but actually purify and justify itself in the process.

Nixon and his supporters are counting on a repeat performance, and it would be foolish to think that their calculation has no basis. The American people are not about to rise up in their wrath and demand that Nixon be cast into the outer darkness. As his critics never tire of pointing out, Watergate fits perfectly into the pattern of his behavior since the very beginning of his political career, and still he was elected president twice, the second time by a very large majority. It is sometimes said that Americans are cynical, and there is certainly some truth to it. But what appears to be cynicism is often simple realism. "All politicians are crooks" is not a cynical remark, it is a fact of life. But it is also a fact that politicians are pikers compared to businessmen who are currently ripping off American working people to the tune of some $57 billion a year.* In a system where such things are not only possible but inevitable (since anti-human behavior is virtually forced on people as the price of survival), morality is synonymous with hypocrisy, and the distinction between legitimate and illegitimate behavior is at best shadowy and at worst nonexistent. The American people are of course aware of this condition, they live it every day of their lives, and they are hardly likely to get greatly excited by revelations of scandalous behavior in the White House or anywhere else. Nixon knows this better than anyone else, and it is what lies at the bottom of his confidence that he will survive this crisis as he has previous ones in his checkered political career. "I do not stand here tonight as a loser," he told a gathering of Republican faithfuls on May 9, 1973. "We stand here tonight as winners, and we are going to win again." He undoubtedly believes it.

But things may be different this time. By far the greatest number of crimes are never prosecuted, either because the perpetrator is not known, or because the responsible prosecuting authority chooses not to act. But if the perpetrator is known and if the prosecutor wants to "get" him, then a situation is set up in which one of the two has power over the other. This power may be used to try and in case of conviction punish the

---

* This was the annual rate of corporate profits after taxes in the last quarter of 1972, the latest available figure at the time of writing. Actually, of course, this is far from the total amount of surplus value squeezed out of workers and appropriated by capitalists and a host of other parasitical beneficiaries of the monopoly capitalist system. But it will do for illustrative purposes.

criminal, or it may be used in one way or another to force him
into the service of the prosecutor (for example, he may be let
off lightly on condition that he agrees to act as an informer).

The analogy is not perfect, but it can help us to diagnose the
present situation. Nixon has been caught in clearly actionable
behavior.* The question is whether those with the power to
prosecute have the will to proceed against him. If they do, the
way is clear; there should be no legal or constitutional obstacles.
And they could either attempt to press the case through to its
ultimate conclusion, i.e., his removal from the presidency, or
they could seek to use their position to gain control over his
policies and actions during the remainder of his term.

Who, then, are those with the power to prosecute? Formally,
the House of Representatives, which can impeach by majority
vote (the case then goes to the Senate, which can convict by a
vote of two thirds of those present). But in reality of course
power is not in the House (or the Senate), still less in the hands
of the people whom the congressmen are supposed to represent. Real power is in the ruling class, i.e., those who own
and/or control (hence benefit from) the country's means of
production and other forms of wealth. The politicians are their
agents and normally carry out policies which most of the ruling
class approves. As long as this is the case, the politicians are
given a pretty free hand to do things their own way, which of
course includes using their offices or their influence to accumu-
late enough wealth to become *bona fide* members of the ruling
class in their own right. Actionable behavior, which could perhaps be found in most cases if it were diligently sought out, is
overlooked or ignored, and no question of using the power to
prosecute ever arises.

Our argument, sketched out above, is that this is *not* the

---

* It must be kept in mind that impeachment is not necessarily for crimes
as defined by law but can also be for misconduct in office, a much wider
concept. Nor, under the U.S. Constitution, does a successful impeachment
result in any punishment other than removal from office and ineligibility
to hold office again. A criminal trial may, but does not have to, follow.

situation that exists at the present time. There is a real split in the ruling class over an issue of profound importance for the whole future of the system itself. Unfortunately we don't know much about the line-up of the two sides—ruling classes are not in the habit of calling meetings and publishing minutes—or whether recent events in Indochina have materially affected the balance between them. But we do know that those who oppose the Nixon/Kissinger policy of continuing military involvement in Indochina now have a golden opportunity to put Nixon on the spot and either throw him out of the White House or (perhaps more likely) force him to toe their line. That is, of course, if they are strong enough and bold enough to mobilize the necessary forces in the House and the Senate. We should be finding out in the not too distant future.

C. Arnholt Smith
and the San Diego Connection

Lowell Bergman and Maxwell Robach

Richard Nixon's fondness for San Diego reaches back to the early beginnings of his political career. Ever since his first campaign for the Senate in 1950 it has voted for him overwhelmingly each time he ran for office. Its local establishment boasts some of his oldest friends and backers who have personally raised and donated the millions which helped him climb to his succession of political offices. In 1966 San Diego sprouted the country's first Nixon-for-President committee, two years before he declared himself a candidate. And after the 1968 election he made his first stop in the city, staying at the home of Ogden Armour, a major stockholder in San Diego's Yellow Cab Company.

As Nixon relaxed at the Armour residence, a frequent visitor was a seventy-year-old, tanned and silvery-haired local tycoon who had risen from high school dropout, box boy and bank clerk to become Southern California's living legend of success.

The original version of this essay, entitled "Nixon's 'Lucky City': C. Arnholt Smith and the San Diego Connection," © 1973, appeared in *Ramparts*, October 1973. Reprinted by permission of the authors.

Like Nixon, he was a "self-made" man and they had known each other a long time. The visitor was the perennial chairman of the San Diego County Republican Finance Committee; he was also a member of the exclusive Lincoln Club of Orange County, a millionaire right-wing Republican coven, whose other members included Herbert Kalmbach, Nixon's personal lawyer, GOP arm-twister and fundraiser. In 1968 Nixon's visitor was reported to have brought in more than $1 million for the candidate's election campaign; four years later he set about to raise more than $3 million for the Nixon campaign chest. At the 1968 Republican convention in Miami his hands were the first of some five thousand Nixon would shake during the reception for party delegates; a few months later he was at Nixon's Waldorf Astoria Towers suite in New York, watching the election results; and not long after Nixon went to the White House, rumors surfaced briefly in San Diego that he would be the next Secretary of the Navy. He had the face of a sunbitten terrier. His smile cracked like a persimmon, slightly awry. "Arnie Smith," Pat Nixon once confided gratefully, "was one of our first supporters."

The Beige Kingdom

The favorite color of C. (Conrad) Arnholt Smith is beige. His suits are beige, he drives a beige car, even his wife's hair is beige. Beige is also the color of his major holding, the U.S. National Bank, with more than $1 billion in assets and some sixty-five branches. Beige suits Smith; it is a soothing tone and for years it provided a neutral coat to the spongier underside of his empire as it spread to soak up much of San Diego's police department and mayor's office; the City Council, Planning Commission, and County Supervisors; judges, DA's, U.S. Attorneys, congressmen and a corner of Richard Nixon's presidential seal. Simultaneously, Smith filled out Westgate-California, his other major holding, with electronics, insurance and fund management companies; with a commuter airline, advertising agency, Yellow Cabs and the San Diego Padres; with real estate, agribusiness, the world's third largest packer of canned tuna and the "plush-est hotel anywhere." Westgate-California comprises a $215 mil-lion conglomerate; aimless and shapeless like much of Southern California, its interests run restless and eclectic from fishing and truck fleets to olives and dog racing.

C. Arnholt Smith's personal worth could go as high as $50 million. He began his career in a grocery store, moved up to clerk at the Bank of Italy (now Bank of America), and in the early thirties made it to vice president at the U.S. National Bank, a small hometown institution run by a conservative banker, James R. Russell. Within a few short years Russell had been shouldered out—with an assist from C. Arnholt's brother, "Black Jack" Smith, who had gotten into banking and oil in Los Angeles. "Smith promised to see that my property rights were fully protected," Russell protested ruefully in a deposition years later while suing to get his bank back; but he died of a stroke before the case got to court, and as Arnie Smith devel-oped his political contacts he parlayed a holding in National Iron Works (now National Steel and Shipbuilding), into a gold mine of government contracts during the Second World War. National Steel and Shipbuilding has been sold since, as Smith's enterprises sank into deeper furrows, producing quicker, hardier yields.

C. Arnholt Smith has done well by San Diego. And San Diego likes to think it has done well by C. Arnholt Smith. He con-tributed much of the money that helped rebuild the downtown area in the early sixties, for which the city reciprocated with a ringing accolade, naming him "Mr. San Diego of the Century." In this, as in any other honors involving Smith or his lieu-tenants, the fanfare was sounded by San Diego's war hawk and press baron, James Copley, an old friend of Nixon's and owner of the city's only two dailies, the *San Diego Union* and *Evening Tribune*. Copley's fears of revolutionaries, especially black ones, fits the San Diego mood. Three years ago his presses steamed at San Diego's Black Panther Party and "Marxist" professor Her-bert Marcuse; they cooled down only after three Panthers were murdered and Marcuse was "retired."

Smith himself has not been above dashing off an editorial for Copley, and until recently neither of San Diego's dailies would print a word to criticize him or his associates. When in the beginning of 1970 a local underground paper ran a series of exposés on Smith and his means to power, it quickly became the target of firebombs, vigilante terrorism, police infiltration, arrests and harassment. "I wish there was a way to bomb them clear to the other side of the Coronadoes," Smith fumed to stockholders about the radical "street people" running the exposés.

Eventually, even Copley's papers had to print the facts. Watergate had burst. Smith's donation of fifty thousand dollars in checks to the Nixon campaign was returned in March 1972, as three different government investigations (prompted by an article in *Life* magazine) began turning over the rocks on his well-appointed grounds. With government investigators moving in from all sides, Smith resigned as president of Westgate-California, though remaining chairman of the Board of Directors. Likewise he stepped down as head of U.S. National Bank. On May 31, 1973 an SEC suit charged Smith with misappropriation of funds from both Westgate and the bank. On August 3 the IRS filed a $22.8 million dollar income tax lien on Smith's 1969 income—reportedly the largest claim ever levied against an individual for a single tax year. Meanwhile the FBI was peering into his conduits of campaign funds and political payoffs. His onetime protegé and business partner of more than forty years had just gotten out of jail. Two of his other associates were named along with him in the SEC suit. Still others were being indicted or sued in different courts. And as the plumb line sank deeper into Smith's affairs it touched upon the hidden layers of his power base—an accretion of "front men" and shady business deals, interrelated with union bosses, gangsters, politics and the Nixon connection.

The Self-Dealing Tycoon

As his empire grew, Smith's favorite story about himself was meant to show that he was not in it for the money; there were years, he claimed, when as chairman and president of his two corporations he would refrain even from taking a salary. But broaching the wrap of his business operations in the spring of 1969, the *Wall Street Journal* discovered that Smith had other ways of rewarding himself and friends—primarily as a "self-dealing tycoon" who used "publicly-owned firms to aid private ventures." The yield from this arrangement more than made up for his paycheck; the chairman took his pickings from inside—at the expense of the shareholders.

For close to a decade the key to Smith's wealth and that of his allies has been the intimate relationship between the U.S. National Bank, Westgate-California and the various front corporations controlled by Smith and associates. For instance, Smith would lend Westgate assets to his privately owned front corporations free of interest. These front companies would then use these assets as collateral for loans they would receive from the U.S. National Bank. Meanwhile, other Smith front operations were buying Westgate assets at fantastically low prices, and selling other properties to Westgate for handsome profits. In order to hide these operations from Westgate stockholders, Smith manufactured over $17 million in false Westgate profits through dummy sales of Westgate properties at inflated prices, which were financed by the U.S. National Bank. While this "self-dealing" enabled Smith and his front men to reap a bonanza of "large and sometimes quick profits," the *Wall Street Journal* pointed out that "the earnings performance of Mr. Smith's publicly owned firms has been less than spectacular."

The SEC indictment of Smith cited USNB for misappropriating funds, making false statements to the investing public, and generally exploiting Westgate and USNB for the benefit of the chairman and his friends. Since 1970 stockholders have been fighting back with a growing number of suits, while the SEC asked for the appointment of a receiver for Westgate-California, as well as a preliminary injunction prohibiting Smith from holding office in any public company.

The Rise of Big John

Smith's resignation as president of Westgate-California followed by two years the departure of another member of the board—that of "Big John" Alessio, reputed boss of San Diego's underworld and owner of horse and dog tracks on both sides of the border. Alessio resigned his Westgate seat to begin serving a three-year sentence first at Terminal Island Federal Penitentiary, then at Lompoc, California, and finally at McNeil Island in Washington State. His failure to report $1.2 million to the IRS was one of the bigger tax evasion cases on record. But Alessio had a few consolations; the honors and awards that decorate his office overwhelm the visitor. Alessio was "Mr. San Diego of 1964," as well as "Mr. Coronado." He has been "Man of the Year in Racing," a recipient of the "Book of Golden Deeds" from the local Exchange Club, and of an honorary Doctor of Laws degree from the University of California.

The son of an Italian immigrant coal miner from Virginia, Alessio grew up in San Diego. His rise to fortune began in 1929 when C. Arnholt Smith, then a sharp-eyed exec with the Bank of Italy, took young Alessio away from his downtown shoeshine stand and got him a job *al otro lado,* as a messenger with the Banco del Pacifico in Tijuana. Thirty-five years later, their relationship came full circle: in 1965, John D. Alessio, stocky now with thick earnest glasses and silk tailored suit, opened a block-long twelve-story office building in San Diego's business district—not far from the very spot where he used to shine the shoes of C. Arnholt Smith.

In the intervening years he had risen quickly at the Banco Del Pacifico; his interests were fluid, the bank gave him a cushion, his Mexican contacts clicked—he picked up Hollywood's fabled pleasure dome of the thirties, Tijuana's Hippodromo with its Aqua Caliente race track. It marked the beginning of a fabulously lucrative bookmaking operation, mainly to serve U.S. bettors. Run by his three brothers, joined later by his son-in-law, Caliente in its heyday was reported to be doing a business of $75 million a year.

From Tijuana, Alessio's money spilled north in a complex of San Diego holdings, including banking, real estate and hotel interests. For a long time the take was simply trucked past deferential guards across the line into the U.S.; hot lunches would often descend on the border officials, compliments of the Alessio brothers. But as the Alessio Corporation grew, the brothers managed to funnel the Mexican money through the fifteen corporations owned by Alessio in Mexico; an Alessio Trucking firm in San Diego, for instance, would sell equipment to an Alessio company in Mexico—at inflated prices. Once in San Diego the "skim" from Caliente often appeared transfigured in properites of prestige: in the early sixties Alessio bought and renovated the venerable Hotel del Coronado, a massive Victorian pile on an island in San Diego harbor that was to serve as the set for *Some Like It Hot*; he also picked up the swank Kona Kai Club and opened another race track in Juarez, Mexico, soon to become known as a "major lay-off book for the United States." In 1964 the Alessio Corporation merged with Smith's Westgate-California, increasing the number of musical chairs.

San Diego's hospitality to the operations of its two favorite sons remained tolerant to a fault—largely because the names of C. Arnholt Smith and John Alessio carried the aura of a special enshrinement; their images were fused into that of one formidable patron, unique in the manner of its benefactions. Smith's impulse in charity would be unpredictable, a sudden spasm of generosity: "Go buy some presents for the kids in Southeast," he once ordered, stuffing a bank officer's hands with two thousand dollars and hurrying him on to the black ghetto; one black employee of the bank, a guard with an alcohol problem, was dried out at a local sanatorium at Smith's expense, including chauffered delivery and pickup. Alessio, on the other hand, enjoyed the drama behind benevolence; he liked to build schools in Mexico, especially the ribbon-snipping part of completion, before a shaded grandstand, fluttering flags, brass bands, Mexican generals and dignitaries, an American congressman or two, the governor of California, speeches, his face in the papers—until the Mexican government objected that he was naming the schools after himself.

In San Diego such grumbling went unnoticed. "Alessio is a driving ambitious tycoon of the first magnitude and a sort of father-saint to Mexican children," wrote Copley's *Evening Tribune* seven years ago—at a time when government investigators were clasping the links on John Alessio's connections with gambling and police corruption in San Diego.

Conviction and Jail

The case against Alessio had been moving in fits and starts since 1966 when federal agents began looking into his ties to organized crime; they knew that U.S. gangsters were using his operations as a "layoff book"—a method of covering bets by transferring funds to another bookie so that heavy betting on a local favorite can be balanced by wagering on the opponent. The probe took five years that ran like an obstacle course over Justice Department, White House and local judiciary interventions. It was a frantic effort, *Life* magazine wrote in March 1972 "to keep San Diego's law-abiding veneer from being washed away."

During this period, a local radical newspaper, and later the *L.A. Times,* reported that C. Arnholt Smith took a trip. In the early spring of 1970 he traveled to Washington and talked to Nixon directly. He was hoping that the Grand Jury report could be held off until the statute of limitations on Alessio's tax problem had run out. Smith had an under-the-counter stake at Caliente, but this was not his main concern: the investigations had spilled over into the County office, threatening a raw dissection of the San Diego government, the city council, the mayor, the police department; State Attorney General Lynch had been prodded into action; and the Federal Crime Strike Force investigating Alessio was zeroing in on Smith for illegal contributions to Nixon's 1968 campaign.

Not long after Smith's return from Washington, the IRS special agent in San Diego, David Stutz, heard from Nixon's domestic affairs chief: John Ehrlichman wanted Stutz to come to Washington for a talk. *Life* magazine said that the man who passed on this message was Jack Caulfield, special assistant to Nixon's counsel John Dean and later the White House contact man with James McCord. "We can't let this ever get out," Caulfield warned Stutz about the White House request that he circumvent the IRS commissioner and deliver the tax records on Alessio, a breach of federal regulations. Stutz refused—Alessio went to Terminal Island Federal Prison and from there to more congenial Lompoc.

Alessio's time in prison was almost as busy and eventful as his life on the other side of the wall. From the moment the gates shut behind him at Terminal Island his cell became an executive office from which directives and advice went out to his brothers and sons in the operation of the family business. There was also time for diversion. At Lompoc he went hunting with the guards and kept assignations in a motel with a movie starlet. On Thanksgiving he put on a catered dinner for twenty-four relatives and friends in the prison's main visiting room. Smith flew up loyally once a week; Los Angeles Mayor Sam Yorty stopped by, as did former California Governor Pat Brown and San Diego Congressman Bob Wilson, who talked to the supervisors at Lompoc and promised Alessio an early parole. The guards and administrators liked their amiable, generous inmate. John Alessio's word was enough to stand them free dinner and entertainment at the Kona Kai; one earned a big discount on a trailer he bought from Alessio's trucking firm; others tasted the salt spray on the deck of C. Arnholt's yacht as it took them cruising around the bay.

But John Alessio never got his parole. A fellow prisoner got angry at the persistent attentions Alessio paid to his visiting daughter and squealed. The *Los Angeles Times* picked up the story and the Justice Department's Organized Crime and Racketeering Section began in investigation into John Alessio's free-wheeling prison life. After nine months three sets of indictments were handed down by a Federal Grand Jury in Los Angeles. Alessio spent his remaining year in prison at less hospitable McNeil Island in Washington.

The Politics of Corruption

The union of the Alessio and Westgate-California corporations in 1964 formalized more than a long-standing business engagement. For years the partners had practiced the principles of "lay off" betting in their political choices—until recently Alessio backed the Democrats, while Smith covered the Republican side. Alessio, for instance, developed a most rewarding relationship with Democratic Governor Pat Brown.

Smith, meanwhile, kept his eye on up-and-coming young Republicans, such as a young congressman from Whittier he spotted in the late forties. As Nixon pursued Alger Hiss with all the harpies of his cold-sweat American Dream, the GOP moneymen of Southern California took notice. The Republican manager of Whittier's Bank of America had first opened the door to a political career. And it was a Republican banker in San Diego who became one of Nixon's first, most loyal backers. C. Arnholt Smith knew how to nudge the shoals of self-doubt, insecurity, smalltown prejudice and resentment in the plain, plodding congressman. Often he and Nixon would meet and trade advice at a popular downtown San Diego delicatessen. And less than two decades later Smith's faith was rewarded as his new wife breathlessly recounted their conversation with the 1968 GOP candidate for president: "They were telling us, " she recalled at the delegates' conclave in Miami, "that we would be their first guests in the White House."

As Nixon progressed to senator, vice-president, wealthy Wall Street lawyer and president, Smith solidified his control over

San Diego's Republican machine. The city and county fell agreeably in line. Smith's GOP loyalty, though, was never blind —it had a way of dissipating when it clashed with more important matters. In 1958 he backed Democrat Bert Betts for state controller. And after Betts got into office, Smith had a modest explanation for the sudden jump from $813,000 to $15.6 million in state deposits held by the USNB: "He appreciated what we had done for him and he reciprocated." Betts's thoughtfulness made USNB California's second largest depository of state funds. Alessio, too, faced by the "tax problem" switched political horses in 1968, contributing twenty-six thousand dollars to Nixon's campaign and raising many thousands more—an act of faith that earned him an invitation to attend the Inaugural Ball in Washington as a privileged guest.

Smith and his politician friends have pulled through some close legal scrapes together, such as the Yellow Cab scandal. In 1970 a San Diego County Grand Jury indicted San Diego Mayor Curran and practically all of the city council for taking bribes in exchange for a big boost in taxi fares. At the same time David Stutz, the IRS special agent, sought prosecution of Smith and the president of Smith-controlled Yellow Cab, as well as of Frank Thornton, vice president of the Smith-owned Barnes/Champ advertising agency. Stutz accused Smith and Thornton of making false corporate tax returns, and conspiring to violate the Corrupt Practices Act.

The evidence showed that Barnes/Champ was the tap and Thornton the spigot which sent money and favors lapping around the San Diego Police Department, local public officials and Richard Nixon. Charlie Pratt, the president of Yellow Cab, testified that he had given Curran thirty-five hundred dollars to get the fare increase. Pratt explained how he would receive the money from Thornton and deposit it in a trust account held by a former San Diego Democratic Party wheel, John Donnelley; in turn, Donnelley would make out the checks for Pratt on request. Barnes/Champ, it was shown, would send bills for fictitious services to a number of other firmed owned by Smith—the bills would be paid, the books balanced, the money went into the Nixon campaign kitty.

Because of the problems of the Alessio brothers, Nixon's election had been more than an excursion of sentiment; the seepage from the Justice-IRS investigations into the County and State Attorney General's office could be damped only by a friendly Republican U.S. Attorney. And the man Nixon appointed shortly after his election was Harry Steward, a zealous GOP fundraiser in San Diego who had worked closely during the previous presidential campaign with Smith's *alter ego,* Frank Thornton. As the new U.S. Attorney, Steward was soon faced with the question of a subpoena for Thornton concerning his part in the illegal fundraising scheme. But after pleading in vain with IRS agent Stutz to leave Barnes/Champ alone, Steward refused to serve it. And when he was subsequently charged with obstructing justice, Deputy Attorney General Richard Kleindienst quickly "evaluated the matter"—to the satisfaction of Steward, Smith and Thornton. The long arm reached out from Washington again in the trial of Mayor Curran and his city council members; it took a letter from John Dean invoking "executive privilege" to keep agent Stutz from testifying to the bribery charges. Curran was acquitted, and amidst the jubilation at City Hall came a call from San Clemente. Nixon sympathized with Curran, then president of the National League of Cities. "We in public life," Nixon complained, "take a lot of knocks."

Gangster Hospitality

By 1964 huge amounts of cash were flowing into Northern San Diego County. A land boom got under way, much of it fed by Syndicate loans from the Teamster Pension Fund. Morris "Moe" Dalitz, longtime head of the Cleveland Syndicate and owner of Las Vegas' Desert Inn, moved into the swank, exclusive Rancho LaCosta, a cluster of hightone, natural-wood condominium hotels nestled in the hills just off Highway 5 between San Diego and San Clemente.

Among Rancho LaCosta's charter members were John Alessio and publisher James Copley. As Dalitz continued to expand his development with at least $46 million in Teamster money, Rancho LaCosta became the choice site for hush-hush cabals, a secluded compound where the new-money satraps could pace in private and mull over their concerns. Their foregatherings were discreet, but an unusual cross-section of guests, even for Dalitz's domain, was seen moving over LaCosta's in-house security screens during the weekend of February 10, 1973—the shaded projections of Teamster boss Frank Fitzsimmons, a clutch of Syndicate wheels, John Ehrlichman, Bob Haldeman and John Dean; Fitzsimmons could be seen talking at the bar to a man thought to be a national crime syndicate representative while Ehrlichman, Haldeman and Dean were in a room nearby, thrashing out the Watergate cover-up. Afterwards, Fitzsimmons moved out of sight to nearby San Clemente, flying back East with Richard Nixon aboard Air Force One.

The conjunction of mafiosos and Teamster leaders in the neighborhood of the Western White House followed a path that had been well trod elsewhere in the U.S., particularly along the rim of Sunbelt states from Southern California to Florida. Teamster money has long since moved close on the heels of the Syndicate chiefs; the union's Central and Southwest States Pension Fund goes where the smart money goes—author Hank Messick (*Lansky, John Edgar Hoover*) calls it the "Reconstruction Finance Corporation of Organized Crime."

Originally the creation of Chicago union racketeer "Red" Paul Dorfman, the Pension Fund reached its present form under the guidance of Jimmy Hoffa and "Red's" son, Allen. Teamster Pension Fund money has financed the building of casinos in Las Vegas and the Bahamas and thrown up acres of real estate in Southern Florida. In San Diego an estimated $250 million in Teamster loans has gone to local builder and casino owner Irvin Kahn, the man behind University City and Los Penasquitos, one of the largest real estate developments in the country which will house more than a hundred fifty thousand people.

Locally, Kahn obtained the services of John A. Donnelley, who was Dalitz's local legal whiz and administered the pay-offs in the Barnes/Champ scandal. Donnelley had sailed out of local Democratic Party politics a decade earlier to become Secretary-Treasurer at the Desert Inn in Las Vegas; he returned to the legal affairs of Meo Dalitz and the LaCosta group, as well as of Hughes' Air West and Kahn's huge University City development. And in July 1973, Donnelley was appointed to the board of none other than C. Arnholt Smith's Westgate-California corporation.

A Friend of the Working Man

Smith's own rapport with the local Syndicate chiefs has been wrapped in discretion; his relations with Teamster leaders have been less disguised. With interests in ground transportation through cab and truck fleets, in real estate and in banking, his friendship with the union bosses has been a matter of ardent cultivation. In *The Fall and Rise of Jimmy Hoffa,* author Walter Sheridan quotes an intermediary in the attempt to get Hoffa out of jail, boasting about his access to Nixon through C. Arnholt Smith and Treasury Secretary John Connally. Hoffa's successor, Frank Fitzsimmons, enjoys a similar esteem from San Diego's number one citizen. Smith's U.S. National Bank has reportedly handled at least $10 million of Fitzsimmon's Central States Pension Fund, although bank officials deny this.

Fitzsimmons' Teamster Pension Fund business frequently takes him to the San Diego area, where his comminglings are confined to the same circuits as those traveled by the city's ruling elite. On May 4, 1973 he and C. Arnholt Smith shared a fifty-dollars-a-plate dinner platform for Fitzsimmons's favorite charity, the Children's Asthma Research Institute. In the plush-padded lap of the Kona Kai, where the function was held, Fitzsimmons spoke and C. Arnholt Smith, the charity's honorary chairman, listened. Among those in the audience were Dave Beck, the former West Coast racketeer and Teamster president who was recently relieved from having to pay the government $1.4 million in back taxes, and Irvin Kahn, casino owner and local builder who builds with Teamster Pension Fund money. The glow of bonhommie that surrounded the fifty-dollar plates at the Kona Kai made a contrast to the angry gathering outside, a demonstration of United Farm Workers members against Teamster union-busting in the San Joaquin Valley. The pickets rattling against Teamster goons and bosses concerned Smith, as well as Fitzsimmons. The largest non-corporate landholder in the San Joaquin Valley was the hundred-thirty-thousand-acre Roberts Farms, employing a total of twenty-five hundred workers on its major holdings near Delano and on others ranged throughout the area. Smith's stake in this spread came via Hollis Roberts, a rotund Dust Bowl native with an unlimited line of credit at the USNB. Near bankruptcy in 1965, Roberts Farms was put back on its feet as part of a variety of Smith land-syndicates valued at a net worth of $125 million. The surge of UFW power in 1970 forced Roberts to sign up with Cesar Chavez, but he recently went back with the Teamsters—whose Pension Fund money has been well-seeded through the USNB accounts.

Through Roberts, Smith's voice ran quietly beneath the battle clamor in the Valley where the other landholders remember how he and Thornton organized the campaign which won Proposition 7, the issue of State Bonds to pipe water from Northern California to the San Joaquin. The reluctance of California Attorney General Evelle Younger to deal with the strongarm Teamster harassment of the Farm Workers has been no mystery to Smith; almost all of Younger's 1971 campaign money from San Diego County —close to forty thousand dollars—came from the special tap at Barnes/Champ. With Younger becalmed in Sacramento, one other flank of the San Joaquin Valley was covered when Nixon appointed Hollis Roberts to the Agricultural Advisory Board—upon the recommendation of C. Arnholt Smith.

The Front Men

Hollis Roberts was one of the "front men" in the small platoon that has brought Smith a wealth of corporate and political plums. Another redoubtable member of this squad was the Master of Ceremonies at Fitzsimmons' charity gala on May 4, who also happened to own the Kona Kai Club where the function was held; a well-known figure to Teamster honchos and a frequent visitor at Rancho LaCosta, a vice-president of USNB, a former bookie and delicatessen operator, Lew Lipton was also the lieutenant who handled all of Smith's financial dealings with the Teamsters; Lipton was Kahn's contact man and Smith's plenipotentiary in Syndicate relations.

Lew Lipton has been a "character" on the San Diego scene since well before World War II; convicted in 1938 under the alias of Felix Aguilar, it was Lipton's name, along with Alessio's, that Federal crime fighters kept stumbling over each time they ventured a foray on the West Coast. Lipton's Delicatessen in downtown San Diego boasted a motley crew while it lasted— gamblers, gangsters, cops, judges, lawyers, bookies, goons, bank execs, hotshot entrepreneurs, a fraternal conclave on neutral grounds of those serving the law and those beyond it. C. Arnholt Smith introduced Nixon to the place; the young congressman would eat open-eyed and watch the shakers and movers.

Smith liked the way Lipton operated. An agreement was reached. Lipton clearly recalls what he knew about banking at the time of his recruitment by Smith: "I never done it, and he put me at a desk and didn't introduce me. He said, 'Stay there' . . . And they made me an assistant vice-president, and then in five months, vice-president. . . ."

The informality of his appointment carried over in Lipton's style of banking. It was breezy, he took things as they came. His area of expertise, "Business Development," was wide enough to confound definition of his connections in the underworld and with labor racketeers. Lipton was busy outside the bank as well;

in 1966 he occupied a strategic position on the 22nd Agricultural Board, which had jurisdiction over the Del Mar Race
Track, and he helped swing John Alessio's short-lived lease on
the property. The Attorney General's report which finally rejected the bid and took the lease away quoted Lipton as wor-
shipping "Mr. Alessio's Midas Touch."

And then there is M. J. "Mike" Coen of Kansas City. In the
avalanche of stockholders' suits and SEC indictments that has
descended on Westgate and USNB, C. Arnholt Smith is mentioned most commonly in conjunction with Coen, a big, strap-
ping, backslapping Midwesterner with longstanding ties to the
Dallas oil group of Clint Murchison, Jr. Coen and his First California Corporation have been named in at least two civil suits as
well as in the May 31, 1971 SEC action against Smith. But in
Kansas City the magic of his name and the wonder of his doings
die hard; Coen's troubles, the *Kansas City Star* spoke up bit-
terly, are "all C. Arnholt Smith's fault."

Coen's favorite activity was raiding corporations, selling
stocks, juggling assets, buying, dissolving, merging, cleaning up—
with a platoon of accountants and lawyers standing by to make
it all look good on paper. But despite the wide range of his
activities, Coen has always stayed close to C. Arnholt Smith;
since 1962 he has been involved in some two dozen transactions
with Westgate-California and the United States National Bank.
The rudiments of the operation involved an arrangement of
front men selling assets and buying them with loans from the
United States National Bank. At one time or another, Coen has
alternately owned himself, or through subsidiaries, part or all of
Smith's tuna fleets, Yellow Cabs, Aero Commuter (later Golden
West Airlines), Barnes/Champ Advertising, Golconda Corporation (silver mining, restaurant equipment, pressure valves), San
Luis Rey Estates (a luxury housing development bordering
Rancho LaCosta), and a handful of other assets from Smith's
private cookie jar. With ownership alternating inside a closed
group of "self-dealers," the same companies have at other times
been in the hands of "Black Jack" Smith, Alessio, C. Arnholt,

Hollis Roberts, relatives and trusted friends. Since almost all of the companies being passed around were stock-issuing public corporations, the operations of this charmed circle served to leach profits which would have normally surfaced in increased shareholders' dividends.

"Self-dealing" represents the final levitation of capitalism from its material base, the ultimate divorce of product from profit. The civil suits and SEC indictment of Smith and associates list over thirty-five such deals, involving well over fifty different corporations and an estimated $20 million in "misappropriated" funds. In one of the "paper" deals cited, Coen bought a tuna fleet from Westgate, then turned it back to the same corporation for a cool $5 million profit. It was a neat scheme, and it netted a fortune for Smith and his business associates. But those days are over now.

The Chickens Come Home . . .

When John Alessio was released from prison in May 1973, he found his ancient business partner beset by the ague of a grizzled pirate. The time had come. It was dog eat dog. In the end the System played no favorites, there were no rules, and the behemoths that had grown fat on the turf of others would be devoured in turn. Nixon was whirling in the sluices of the Watergate. And by August, C. Arnholt Smith was moaning, "The people who have supported the President the last eight years are targeted and singled out by those damn bureaucratic agencies." Just as Nixon's troubles had been brought on by the inner destructive drive of the System, so the indictments and suits that had been loosed against Smith were the instruments by which new powers were raised to take his place. The System was getting a change of oil, a fresh lubricant that would grind the gears even faster.

The SEC action had caught Smith "short," the stakes to his treasure scattered: the myriad deals with Coen, Roberts, Lipton and other fronts had left him with an unknown amount of cash on "loan" without collateral. The racket of selling assets and buying them with USNB loans could involve far more than the estimated $20 million, as much as $100 million. Blinds were being drawn in the house of many rooms. There were rumbles in the ranks and Lew Lipton, the vice president of Business Development, had a punchout in the bank's coffee room with the vice president of Marketing who had said he was leaving the "sinking ship."

For a while the SEC had suspended Smith from trading stock in Westgate and its affiliates. In the spring Smith was scrambling to cover himself. Without success he tried to withdraw $50 million from an account at Barclay's Bank in London. Through Hollis Roberts he managed to unload thirty thousand acres of land for some $44 million. He arranged to sell the Padres to a Washington, D.C. group for $12.5 million, although that may be delayed by Smith's legal troubles. He removed himself from the official positions in the bank and Westgate, filling them with handpicked veterans of the old "self-dealing" days. And he engaged Mudge, Rose, Guthrie and Alexander, Nixon's former New York law firm.

C. Arnholt Smith was seventy-four, and fledgling tycoons with newer, crispier money were rattling the gates. The noise reached him, but he was powerless. The city machinery was slipping from his hands. The new contenders were two fast-food entrepreneurs, Bob Peterson and Richard Silberman, reform Democrats, who would blunt Smith's rough edges and ingratiate their power more subtly; they had made their fortune with Jack-in-the-Box drive-ins and now controlled Southern California's First National Bank, San Diego's second largest. There was a new mayor, a new D.A., and soon a new U.S. Attorney. Smith had no institutionalized wealth like the Rockefellers or the Mellons. He had come up scavenging, and it seemed that he would leave the same way. The IRS saw the straws in the wind and heard the rumors that he was salvaging what he could to live out his life in self-banishment abroad. In an effort to keep hold of him, the agency slapped him with a huge tax lien. A year before, he could have avoided such humiliation. But now his Washington benefactors, caught in the Watergate spotlight, were beyond helping him.

For years, Smith had controlled his turf. He had been the fastest gun in Southern California, fighting off federal agents and young upstarts alike. But the frontier fights a losing battle against the encroaching larger society, and C. Arnholt Smith is condemned to live out his days in constant defense of his reputation and his gains. Whatever the outcome—and Smith has survived some tough scrapes before—he leaves his mark on San Diego: the place where Richard Nixon wanted the 1972 convention because it was, he said, "my lucky city."

The Moneymen

Stu Bishop and Bert Knorr

Over the years Richard Nixon has suffered more than his share of political crises. But the old pro has bounced back, secure in the continuing support of powerful groups within the ruling class. Their favor—and their money—have kept Nixon afloat, at least until Watergate.

To keep the dollars coming, Nixon has relied heavily on one man, Maurice Stans, the GOP's leading fundraiser and finance chairman of the 1972 Committee to Re-elect the President.

According to Republican insiders, Maurice Stans was one of four Republicans to establish the Nixon for President Committee in 1967. The other key individuals were: Robert C. Hill, former director of the United Fruit Company and one of the engineers of the overthrow of the Arbenz government in Guatemala in 1954, as well as Eisenhower's ambassador to Mexico; John Davis Lodge, Eisenhower's ambassador to Spain and former governor of Connecticut; and Fred Seaton, Eisenhower's

The original version of this essay, entitled "Stans: He Fixed the Books," appeared in NACLA's *Latin America & Empire Report,* November 1973. Reprinted by permission of NACLA.

Secretary of the Interior and GOP senator from Nebraska.*

To be a successful political fundraiser for a major U.S. party, one must have direct ties to the powerful businesss interests that finance the electoral campaigns. Maurice Stans had those ties. He has been the president of a major western bank (Western Bancorporation), the head of a New York investment banking house (Glore Forgan), a director of six corporations in five different states, and a senior partner in one of the nation's leading accounting firms (Alexander Grant and Company of Chicago). In the 1950s Stans won several awards for being the nation's top accountant, and in 1960 he was elected to the American Accounting Hall of Fame.

Stans the Investment Banker

Stans's most important corporate affiliation was his presidency of Glore Forgan from 1965 until 1969, when he became Secretary of Commerce under Nixon. Later part of the Dupont Walston firm, Glore Forgan was formed after a merger in 1965 between the Los Angeles firm of William R. Staats and Glore Forgan. An investment banking house, like a law firm, is one of the less visible mechanisms in the overall capitalist structure. It is a strategic link between those who need capital (corporations) and those that can provide it (e.g., banks). Investment banks raise money for corporations by underwriting and selling issues of stocks, bonds and other corporate securities. Investment banking houses also act as financial advisers to corporations and coordinate mergers and acquisitions.

The Forgan in Glore Forgan's name is *James Russell Forgan,* one of the original partners. His activities illustrate how an investment bank is more a coordinating center for implementing the political and economic objectives of the bourgeois interest groups than a mere financing institution. During the latter years of World War II, Forgan was a commander of European opera-

---

* Stephen Hess and David Broder, *The Republican Establishment* (New York: Harper & Row, 1967), pp. 185-86.

tions for the OSS, the predecessor of the CIA. When he stepped down in 1946, he recommended that his close friend, Allen Dulles, take over his post, thus providing Dulles with a key stepping-stone to his eventual directorship of the CIA (1953-1961). Forgan had close ties to European capital. His board position on a large Italian corporation, "Italian Superpower," for example, was of use when the OSS was attempting to protect the company from Nazi saboteurs retreating from Italy. After the war, he and his firm founded the Eurofund, the first investment fund of its kind, to buy up holdings in European companies. The directors of the fund were such powerful men as Philip Reed, chairman of General Electric; Bankers Trust chairman S. Sloan Colt; mining magnate and apartheid supporter Charles Englehard (the original "Goldfinger"); and first Assistant Director of the CIA Kingman Douglas.

Another Glore Forgan partner with extensive CIA ties was *William Jackson*. Before joining Glore Forgan in 1953, Jackson had served on the commission that drew up the plans for the formation of the CIA in 1947 and had been a Deputy Director of the CIA and a member of Eisenhower's committee charting the psychological warfare strategy and covert operations for the Cold War. Also a director of Bankers Trust and the Great Northern Railroad, Jackson was partner in one of Wall Street's most important law firms—Carter, Ledyard and Milburn.

Stans's other partners at Glore Forgan included Richard Millar, a director of Northrop Aircraft (a major client of Herbert Kalmbach's West Coast law firm), and Charles Hodge, Glore Forgan's key intermediary to the Penn Central Railroad.

Glore Forgan's business interests included several important corporations, including Wynn Oil, Commonwealth Edison, Universal Oil, and the Interstate United Corporation. But one of its biggest accounts was the Penn Central. Partner Hodge was (1) principal investment adviser to Penn Central; (2) investment adviser to and broker for the Penn Central Supplementary Pension Fund and the Contingent Compensation Fund; (3) investment banker for three Penn Central subsidiaries—Tropical Gas,

Great Southwest, and Kaneb Pipeline; (4) director of Great Southwest, Arvida, and Tropical Gas; and (5) holder of investment in the above corporations. With these conflicting interests, Glore Forgan played a major part in diverting assets into non-railroad investments, leading to the eventual bankruptcy of the Penn Central.

Hodge and Penn Central chief David Bevan, a close friend, initiated part of the diversification program in 1962 by establishing an investment firm called Penphil. According to the House Banking Committee, this firm was one of the primary culprits in the wreck of the rail firm. An example of how the Penn Central was "looted" is provided by Penphil's investment in Executive Jet Aviation. Hodge and Bevan dumped $21 million of the railroad's money into the firm—money that was supposed to be utilized by the railroad for its own growth, not for jet planes. Even though the investment proved a severe loss for Penn Central, Stans's Glore Forgan made a fortune from the Executive Jet Aviation transactions. The Senate Commerce Committee, which also conducted investigations into the bankruptcy, charged that Penn Central's investment bankers (Glore Forgan), in collusion with top directors and officers, must also share in the responsibility.

As House Banking Committee Chairman Wright Patman pointed out:

> How could Charles Hodge give sound, objective investment advice to Glore Forgan's clients concerning their investments while being so personally involved in the management and control of these significant corporations? Similar questions can be raised for other people involved with the Penphil-Penn Central-Glore Forgan complex.*

Stans also profited personally from Glore Forgan's relationship with the Penn Central. As a finder's fee for helping the Central buy into Great Southwest, Stans and several other Glore Forgan partners each received thirty-eight thousand shares of

---

* Staff Report of House Banking and Currency Committee, Part 3, "Penphil: The Misuse of Corporate Power" (Note 10).

Great Southwest (a real estate firm) stock. Before he took office as Secretary of Commerce, Stans's shares in the Great Southwest were worth more than half a million dollars. However, like all cabinet officers, Stans pledged to place the holdings in a "blind trust" while he served as Commerce Secretary.

When the Penn Central went bankrupt, the Nixon administration's highest aides, including Stans, began discussing whether to bail out the firm with government loans. It was disclosed during this time that Stans had failed to report his Great Southwest holdings at the time of his confirmation as Commerce Secretary. In short, Stans was involved in discussions about how to save the parent company of a corporation in which he held a large interest. In an obvious admission as to how blind his trust was, Stans disqualified himself from later meetings, saying his presence raised too many questions about possible conflicts of interest!

Who suffered from the wreck of the Penn Central? Not Glore Forgan or Maurice Stans. It was rather the thousands of Penn Central workers who were laid off, and the seven thousand who had their savings in the company's pension fund, which Hodge and Bevan had used to help loot the Penn Central.

Stans the Corporate Director

Besides serving as president of Glore Forgan, Stans held important positions in three other firms. From 1963 to 1969 he was a director of the Fluor Corporation, one of the two or three leading refinery engineering and construction firms in the country. J. Robert Fluor, president of the company, was the 1964 Los Angeles County Republican finance chairman and now heads the powerful Lincoln Club, a right-wing Southern California power base located in Newport Beach. Fluor has long been a supporter of the GOP's right wing and gave at least thirty thousand dollars illegally to the 1964 Goldwater campaign, a contribution Stans most likely arranged.* Another Fluor direc-

* See Morton Mintz and Jerry Cohen, *America Inc.* (New York: Bell, 1972), pp. 211-212.

tor, Thomas Pike, a former Assistant Secretary of Defense under Eisenhower, was one of Stans's CREEP-West lieutenants. Fluor directors also sit on the major California firms: Crown Zellerbach, Wells Fargo Bank, Hewlett-Packard, and the United Financial Corporation of California.

Stans was also a director of the Oglesby Norton Corporation, a Midwestern firm tied into the strategic iron and steel industries. His fellow board members included such Cleveland powers as George Karch of Cleveland Trust and Firestone Tire and Rubber, and Courtney Burton, former head of the Ohio Republican Finance Committee and an Assistant Coordinator for Inter-American Affairs under Nelson Rockefeller in the 1940s.

Earlier, after leaving his post as Budget Director under Eisenhower in 1961, Stans became the head of the Los Angeles-based Western Bancorporation, a holding company for twenty-four banks in eleven Western states. Among its holdings is the large United California Bank. During Stans's presidency at Western Bancorporation (1961-63), the board included John McCone, past CIA director, ITT board member, and Standard Oil of California director; and Sherman Hazeltine, Nixon's former law partner in the Los Angeles firm of Adams, Duque and Hazeltine.

Stans the Fundraiser

With this background in big business, Maurice Stans was just the man to raise big money for political purposes, and in 1972 he masterminded the collection of $60 million to re-elect President Nixon, the most successful presidential fundraising campaign ever—and probably the most corrupt. The bill of particulars against Stans which has emerged from the Watergate investigations to date includes the following:

1. Stans was one of the links in the "laundering" of dollars that found their way into the Nixon political war chests. To cite the best documented example: the eighty-nine thousand dollars that started in the hands of Midwest soybean king Dwayne

Andreas was channeled to Gulf Resources and Chemical chairman Robert Allen in Texas, then to shady lawyer Manuel Ogarrio in Mexico City, to Stans in Washington, and finally to the Miami bank account of former CIA agent Bernard Barker—one of the Republican spies caught breaking into the Watergate Democratic Party office.

2. Stans kept a secret safe in his CREEP office containing three hundred fifty thousand dollars; this money was utilized by Bernard Barker to finance various missions against Nixon opponents.

3. Stans bribed G. Bradford Cook at the time the latter was Chief Counsel to the Securities and Exchange Commission Investigative Unit. While goose hunting in Texas, Stans told Cook that if Cook would halt an SEC investigation into Robert Vesco's business affairs, Stans would "put in the good word" to Nixon for Cook to receive the position he wanted: the SEC chairmanship. Nixon eventually named Cook SEC chairman, but he had to resign in the wake of the Vesco-Stans-Mitchell indictments. Vesco illegally dumped over two hundred thousand dollars into the Nixon campaign coffers in an attempt to stop the investigations into his financial affairs.

4. Stans ordered CREEP treasurer Hugh Sloan and Herbert Kalmbach, head of CREEP-West, to destroy all records of incoming contributions. This was a blatant attempt to hide the identities of all Nixon donors both before and after the April 7, 1972 deadline requiring disclosure of all donations.

5. Stans utilized numerous ploys in amassing $60 million for the Nixon re-election campaign—the largest amount ever raised for a U.S. political race. His tricks included the establishment of hundreds of "dummy" committees, including such gems as "Active Friends of a Balanced Society" and "The Committee for the Preservation of the American Dream," whereby a donor could circumvent the required gift tax on contributions of three thousand dollars or more.

6. Stans squeezed funds from reluctant donors. For example, while Commerce Secretary, Stans would approach potential

donors threatening that if they did not contribute the desired sum, he would initiate unfavorable pollution action against their corporations. He would take this action, he said, through the Pollution Council he helped establish at the Commerce Department. The scope of Stans's fundraising operations while he was still Nixon's Secretary of Commerce was revealed recently by two oil company executives. They told the Senate Watergate committee that a hundred-thousand-dollar contribution was expected from all large corporations. Though corporate contributions to national political campaigns are illegal, Gulf Oil executive Claude Wild, Jr., told the committee the practice is not unusual. He said that in his post as vice president for government affairs he had also given in previous campaigns to Democrats but observed, "the Republicans always cost you twice as much as the Democrats."

Kalmbach the Bagman

Stans's number two man in the fundraising effort was Herbert Kalmbach, Richard Nixon's personal attorney and one of the central figures in the Watergate affair. Ever since 1968, Kalmbach has been entrusted with the secretive and sensitive duties that Nixon's financial dealings require. For example, he personally supervised the purchase and renovation of the San Clemente estate. This urbane, mysterious "Mr. Moneybags" of the cover-up was also deputy chairman of the Nixon 1968 and 1972 campaign finance committees under Maurice Stans. He has been credited with raising $6 million for the 1968 campaign (out of a total $35 million), much of it from Nixon's friends in the Lincoln Club. The Kalmbach-Stans fundraising was so successful that $1.7 million was left over after the 1968 campaign. And this money was the basis of Kalmbach's deep Watergate involvement.

Kalmbach distributed the extra campaign funds into numerous bank accounts he controlled with two other men: Francis M. Raine, Jr., (H. R. Haldeman's brother-in-law), and Thomas W. Evans (a Nixon law partner). By 1972 only half a million dollars of the $1.7 million was left. A full account of what happened to the remaining $1.2 million remains to be given. Significant chunks were utilized in a program of political sabotage against Nixon enemies. For instance, two to four hundred thousand dollars was funneled to Albert Brewer, who opposed George Wallace in the 1970 Alabama gubernatorial race—an obvious attempt to sabotage Wallace's 1972 presidential aspirations and remove him as a threat to Nixon's reelection. Kalmbach gave some forty thousand dollars to Los Angeles lawyer Donald Segretti to finance a campaign of political sabotage against Democratic front-runners, primarily Edmund Muskie. Kalmbach had hired Segretti on the advice of presidential assistant Dwight Chapin.

Prior to April 7, 1972, the date set by the new campaign financing law for beginning to report donations, Kalmbach solicited millions of dollars from such groups as the dairy industry and numerous large corporations. Since he destroyed all his campaign finance records once the heat was on, we have no complete record of the secret donors.

After the Watergate "plumbers" were caught in June 1972, Nixon and his most trusted aides moved quickly to hush their hired operatives. Kalmbach, with his considerable acumen for behind-the-scenes financial deals, took on the sensitive job of collecting and distributing the hush-money. He gathered up to half a million dollars for the Watergate defendants from various sources. Some of it was again money left over from 1968 campaign funds; some three hundred fifty thousand dollars was CREEP money that had been transferred to Haldeman's White House safe and then funneled to Kalmbach; seventy-five thousand dollars was from Thomas V. Jones, chairman of the Northrop Corporation, a large defense contractor and a client of Kalmbach's law firm.

The hush money was too little, too late, and the Watergate burst open. But, dealing to the end, Kalmbach arranged to plead guilty to only one count of soliciting illegal campaign contributions.

Kalmbach's association with Nixon grew out of his friendship with Robert Finch, Secretary of Health, Education and Welfare in Nixon's first administration, and a classmate of Kalmbach's at the University of Southern California Law School. In 1958 Finch had enlisted Kalmbach's aid as Orange County chairman of his successful campaign for lieutenant governor of California. Up to that time, Kalmbach had been a vice president of the Security Title Insurance Company in Los Angeles. In the late fifties and early sixties, Kalmbach practiced law in Newport Beach, California, except for a brief stint in Arizona where he was the president of the Arizona Title and Insurance Company. In 1962 he worked in Nixon's unsuccessful California gubernatorial bid against Pat Brown. From 1964-67 he served as vice president and director of the Macco Realty Corporation, a firm which eventually merged into Great Southwest Corporation—the Penn Central subsidiary.

Kalmbach the Lawyer

In 1967, Kalmbach joined a group of lawyers in establishing the Newport Beach, California, firm of Kalmbach, DeMarco, Knapp and Chillingworth. It is clear from the following list of clients that Kalmbach's new firm received numerous lucrative accounts as a result of his relationship with Nixon. Much of the business of the firm's clients is dependent on the rulings of federal regulatory agencies. This raises obvious conflict-of-interest situations for a lawyer whose clients include the president of the United States as well as some of the nation's largest corporations which are regulated by the federal bureaucracy he oversees. Among the firm's numerous clients listed in *Martindale-Hubbell Law Directory* for the years 1969-72 appear the following names:

1969:

Atlantic Richfield (ARCO): Donald Kendall, a close Nixon friend and chairman of Pepsico, is an ARCO director and gave the Nixon campaign sixty thousand dollars in 1972.

Coldwell Banker: this real estate firm had a suit charging them with barring blacks from their housing dropped by the Justice Department.

Great Southwest Corporation: this giant real estate firm was a subsidiary of Penn Central.

Glore Forgan-Staats: the New York investment bank headed by Stans.

1970:

Flying Tiger Line: according to *Business Week* (May 22, 1971), "The reason that Tiger has done so well is that in August 1969 it began flying a new route across the Pacific which it won through skillful maneuvering in Washington. . . . Mrs. Chennault (Tiger VP for International Affairs) is not only a formidable member of the top Republican social set in Washington, but she retains a lot of clout in the Orient. . . . Mrs. Chennault is extremely close to the present regime in Saigon. . . . This was a key to Tiger's surge to profitability."

Nixon Foundation: Kalmbach is secretary of the board of trustees. The foundation plans to build a presidential library adjacent to Nixon's San Clemente estate.

1971:

Dart Industries: including Rexall Drugs, headed by Nixon Foundation trustee Justin Dart.

Marriott Corporation: this firm's president, J. Willard Marriott, has been close to every GOP president since Hoover; he headed both of Nixon's inaugural committees; he employs the president's brother, Donald Nixon, as international representative of the hotel and food firm; and he has contributed a hundred fifty thousand dollars to Nixon's last two campaigns.

MCA (Music Corporation of America): its president, Taft Schreiber, served on CREEP's Finance Committee, gave five thousand dollars to Nixon's 1972 campaign, and is a trustee of the Nixon Foundation.

United Airlines: Kalmbach received a hefty one-hundred-twelve-thousand-dollar retainer from this firm when it was fighting the merger of Western and American Airlines. One of

United's newest officers is Nixon's former aide, Dwight Chapin. Justin Dart (see above) sits on the United board.

1972:

Morrison-Knudsen: this firm, a member of the four-company consortium which contracted for the bulk of all U.S. war-effort construction in South Vietnam, now controls 40 percent of the construction market there.

Other clients of Kalmbach's firm include such corporate giants as Travelers Insurance, Pacific Lighting, Western Bancorporation, and Northrop Corporation, a prime defense contractor.

Fatcats and Fundraisers

Along with Kalmbach and Stans, the Nixon finance committee also attracted other Republican money men, among them:

Thomas A. Pappas: The key supporter of the fascist Greek junta is reported worth $200 million and has long been a GOP fundraiser. Pappas was one of Eisenhower's fundraisers in 1956, and nominated fellow Greek-American Spiro Agnew for the vice-presidency in Miami in 1968, and is reported to have made twelve CREEP trips to Greece during the 1972 campaign, returning with hundreds of thousands in cash for the Nixon cause. In addition, he chipped in seventy-one thousand dollars of his own. Pappas is a leading investor in Greece through his large stake in Coca-Cola Bottling of Greece and was instrumental in bringing Standard Oil (New Jersey) to Greece in 1962. His other large holding is the giant Hellenic Steel Corporation. Pappas has proudly admitted to collaborating with the CIA, and has gladly loaned his three foundations as CIA conduits for secretly funding cultural and educational institutions abroad, particularly in Latin America.*

Leonard K. Firestone: One of twenty-six trustees of the

---

* *Pan Hellenic Liberation Newsletter,* June 1973. Andreas Papandreou, "Greece: Neocolonialism and Revolution," *Monthly Review,* December

Richard M. Nixon Foundation, Firestone runs the giant Firestone Tire & Rubber empire, the thirty-fourth largest U.S. industrial company. Firestone has been a director of the Wells
Fargo Bank and Western Airlines. To understand his vast contacts among the wealthy and powerful, look at the men with
whom he shares a campsite at the exclusive Bohemian Club of
California: John McCone (former CIA director and now an ITT
director), Henry Kaiser (Kaiser Industries), Stephen Bechtel
(Bechtel Construction), and George Ducommun (Ducommun
Engines). Three members of the Firestone family—Leonard,
Harvey, and Ray—gave a total of $211,000 to Nixon's campaign
in 1972.

Gustav L. Levy: His position in one of Wall Street's most
powerful Jewish banking houses—Goldman Sachs—affords Levy
a wide range of corporate and financial contacts. He is a financial adviser not only to individuals such as Ambassador Walter
Annenberg (who entrusted his millions to Levy when Nixon
appointed him ambassador to Great Britain) but also to governments, including Panama.* Goldman Sachs partners often sit on
the boards of the corporations they help finance; hence Levy's
directorships include Hunt Foods, Braniff Airlines, Ling-Temco-
Vought, Keebler, and Deltec Panamerica. Like all wise bankers,
Levy has contacts with both the Democratic as well as the
Republican party. One of his recently recruited partners is
former Secretary of the Treasury (under President Johnson)
Henry Fowler. Levy gave seventy thousand dollars to Nixon's

1972. See also "Agnew's Junta Ties Disturb NATO," in Jack Anderson
column of November 1, 1968, and "A Bostonian Pappas Means ESSO in
Greece," *New York Times,* May 4, 1969.
* "The Honorable Mr. Annenberg," *Parade* magazine, *Washington Post,*
August 16, 1970. Annenberg's late father, Moe, was a famous bootlegger
of the Prohibition Era. Walter heads Triangle Publications, publisher of
Seventeen and *TV Guide.* Annenberg held one hundred eighty thousand
shares of Penn Central stock that he unloaded when he saw the firm was in
trouble. See *New York Times,* October 11, 1970, for an advertisement
about Goldman Sachs being financial adviser to Panama.

1972 campaign.

Daniel Hofgren: At age thirty-three, he is the second Goldman Sachs partner to turn up on the CREEP Finance Committee. Hofgren's recent biography helps illustrate how the corporate sector interacts with the government: In 1969, Nixon appointed Hofgren a Special Aide in charge of securities industry matters at the White House. In the spring of 1970, Nixon sent Hofgren to Panama as special U.S. representative for interoceanic canal negotiations. While negotiating the U.S. position in Panama, Hofgren was still a White House aide on securities matters and was a member of Charles Colson's three-man staff. In the fall of 1970, Hofgren resigned his White House post and became a vice president of Goldman Sachs, the financial adviser to the Panamanian government. Hofgren left Goldman Sachs in 1972 to join the CREEP Finance Committee. It was Hofgren who "just happened to run into" a key Vesco aide in Europe while on a plane and solicited the now infamous two-hundred-thousand-dollar Vesco contribution. Hofgren and Levy were among five Goldman Sachs partners that contributed heavily to Nixon's 1972 campaign.

Harold Helm: One of the most important bankers in the nation, Helm is the chairman of the Rockefeller-affiliated Chemical Bank of New York. A heavy contributor to GOP causes, he is a director of several multinational corporations, including Bethlehem Steel, Ralston Purina, Cummins Engine, Western Electric, Corn Products Company, Uniroyal, F. W. Woolworth, and Colgate Palmolive.

These are the men who raised the millions for Nixon. They have already received millions in return. The multinational banks and corporations which they and their associates head are among the chief beneficiaries of U.S. government policies: the subsidies, quotas, contracts, depletion allowances, and loans at home, as well as the creation and support of repressive governments abroad to maintain "favorable investment climates." By any fair standard, these men would rate above Gordon Liddy and Jeb Magruder as the real criminals in Watergate.

The Lawyers

Jon Frappier

Five years ago, long before the Watergates opened, Richard
Nixon and John Mitchell were partners in a Wall Street law
firm—Nixon, Mudge, Rose, Guthrie, Alexander & Mitchell. By
now they may wish that they had never left—not because they
had to change their way of doing business when they got to
Washington, but because they got caught doing in public what
many of their colleagues on Wall Street continue to do in private. Such are the risks when representatives of the powerful
economic interest groups take positions in government.

The Nixon-Mitchell law firm was one of probably less than a
hundred firms which handle the legal work for the nation's
leading financial and industrial corporations. The firms are relatively small, tight-knit organizations, whose lawyers branch out
into all important aspects of economic and political life. The
partners are primarily products of Harvard, Yale, and Columbia
law schools. They belong to the same social clubs as the top
corporate executives and often are members of America's

The original version of this essay, entitled "Invisible Power Brokers: The
Nixon-Mitchell Law Firm," appeared in NACLA's *Latin America & Empire Report,* November 1973. Reprinted by permission of NACLA.

wealthy families with access to extraordinary political power.

A highly specialized cadre, the lawyers in these select firms work largely behind the scenes. As lawyers they ply their trade under the cloak of secrecy and the mantle of law, safeguarded from public scrutiny by the privilege of the attorney-client relationship and the privacy of a partnership in whose decisions no outsider may participate. As legal counsel and corporate directors, they advise and assist in developing overall corporate policy at home and abroad. As government officials, both elected and appointed, they draft legislation, negotiate treaties, chair advisory commissions and administer the bureaucracies—often in the interest of the financial groups for which their law firms continue to work.

Wall Street lawyers have also participated extensively in the formation and direction of the Central Intelligence Agency, starting at the top with longtime director Allen Dulles, a partner in the powerful firm of Sullivan & Cromwell. The transition from corporate lawyer to intelligence agent is not difficult, since both jobs require covert operations and the gathering of intelligence.

Above all, the top corporate lawyers have the freedom and flexibility to move quickly from one important post to another. As Arthur Dean (Sullivan & Cromwell) explained it, "Lawyers can more readily than most executives effect temporary total or partial withdrawal from the daily routine to attend to public affairs or matters of personal interest."*

Nixon, Mudge, Rose . . .

Until 1963, Mudge, Stern, Baldwin & Todd was a stodgy old Wall Street law firm. It had its established clients, but needed some new blood if it was to keep up with the Wall Street giants. One of its oldest clients was Warner-Lambert Pharmaceuticals, whose chairman, vitamin king Elmer Bobst, had a personal stake in finding a job for his old friend Richard Nixon. And in 1963

---

* Arthur Dean, *William Nelson Cromwell*, p. 75.

Nixon definitely needed help.

After his defeat by Kennedy in 1960, Nixon had returned to California, where he became a counsel with the Los Angeles firm of Adams, Duque and Hazeltine. He then decided to challenge Edmund Brown for the 1962 governor's race. Eastern Republicans had convinced Nixon that to stay alive politically he needed a base of operations which could serve as a sanctuary in 1964 and a platform in 1968. But Nixon's home state refused to back him by three hundred thousand votes. With his political career at its lowest point, Nixon swore never again to run for public office.

In spite of these successive defeats, Nixon's four years in Congress and eight years as vice president had won him powerful connections and influence. Not to exploit these advantages would, by his standards, have been the sign of a defeated man. The decision he faced, then, was how best to capitalize on this position. He liked New York; it was the center of financial power and thus a stronghold of political power. Nixon called it the "fast track" and the fastest track of all was Wall Street.

Since he had been trained as a lawyer, a Wall Street law firm seemed like the best institution in which to advance. He had to choose an established and respected firm, but one whose partners would not overshadow him. An opening was finally arranged by Bobst, who convinced the partners at Mudge, Stern, Baldwin, & Todd that Nixon's presence would bring in new clients and boost its fees. The first new client was Pepsi-Cola International, brought in by Nixon's friend Donald M. Kendall.*

Nixon joined the firm in mid-1963 and on January 1, 1964, the name became Nixon, Mudge, Rose, Guthrie & Alexander.

---

* Kendall was indebted to Vice President Nixon for getting Khrushchev to drink Pepsi at a trade pavillion in Moscow in 1959. Pepsi-Cola was having trouble competing with Coke, but after the Khrushchev incident Pepsi sales increased. In 1972, with Nixon in the White House, Pepsi was awarded the sole franchise to distribute U.S. soft drinks in the Soviet Union.

When questioned at the time about his role in the firm, Nixon announced, "I shall engage in matters relating to the Washington and Paris offices of the firm," implying continued interest in politics and foreign policy. Nixon wanted to expand the firm into the area of international law and trade, where his contacts abroad could be best utilized. His first trip in 1963 included the Middle East, where, according to the *London Jewish Telegraph*, Nixon met with Egyptian President Nasser and offered his legal services for a two-million-dollar fee. Nixon held a press conference in Cairo in which he praised Nasser's sound and admirable policies (indicating a softening of his policy toward the Soviet Union). He emphasized that Egypt "is free to obtain technical assistance from any country, be it the United States, the Soviet Union, or any other country." There is no record, however, that Nasser ever retained Nixon's law firm.

Another international legal problem arose in 1966, when the illegitimate sons of assassinated Dominican Republic dictator Rafael Trujillo tried to get part of the fortune their father had plundered. Nixon, who had known and admired the dictator's anticommunism, was retained to force the oldest son, Ramfis, to share the loot he had deposited in secret Swiss bank accounts. Much of Nixon's international travel involved politicking: during his efforts to expand the Pepsi-Cola empire overseas, Nixon met with Ambassador Henry Cabot Lodge in Saigon, General Chiang Kai-shek in Taiwan, and many other heads of state to maintain his political contacts and public visibility through foreign policy statements.

The law firm's overseas activities were accompanied by expansion into other areas. In 1963, it absorbed the Wall Street firm of Dorr, Hand, Whittaker, and Weston, which represented railroad interests, and the Washington, D.C., firm, Becker and Greenwald, which specialized in admiralty law. Then, in 1966, John Mitchell's firm, Caldwell, Trumble and Mitchell, merged with Nixon's firm. Mitchell's specialty was municipal bond law. In the five years that Nixon was on Wall Street, the number of lawyers in the firm swelled from fifty-seven to one hundred five, placing it among the nation's ten largest in size. When Nixon and Mitchell moved into government, the law firm's name was changed again to Mudge, Rose, Guthrie and Alexander.

Law Partners as Corporate Directors

It is common for lawyers to become corporate directors, though the reasons vary—from the corporation's desire to have its legal counsel in closer contact with the company's activities, to a law firm's intent to control a corporation either on its own or a client's behalf. According to one study reported in *Business Week* (July 22, 1973), while partners of Mudge, Rose, Guthrie and Alexander held directorships in ten client companies, the firm received $1.6 million in fees from those companies.

Nixon was one of the more active partners in the corporate board room. By 1968, he had become a director of six companies, allowing him close contact with the corporate elite. The Nixon name and contacts were good public relations for the companies, some of which became new clients for the law firm.

In December 1964, Nixon became a director of four large Minneapolis-based mutual funds (Investors Mutual, Inc.; Investor Stock Funds, Inc.; Investors Variable Payment Fund, Inc.; Investors Selective Fund, Inc.) whose combined assets totaled $6.1 billion in 1968. The funds are controlled by Investors Diversified Services, Inc. (IDS), the nation's largest investment adviser and mutual fund distributor. IDS, in turn is controlled by the Alleghany Corporation, a gigantic holding company whose other interests included the New York Central, Missouri Pacific and Baltimore & Ohio railroads. The Allegheny Corporation, controlled by one of the nation's wealthiest men, Allan P. Kirby, found itself in a fierce economic interest group battle in the mid-1950s and early sixties when the Murchison brothers from Dallas decided to move some of their Texas oil money into Eastern investments. It took nearly a decade of proxy fights, court suits and management purges before Kirby sent Murchison back to Texas, though in the process IDS had suffered a severe identity crisis.

In search of a new image, IDS Vice President George MacKinnon went to his old friend Richard Nixon. They had met in the Navy and served together in the 80th Congress. MacKinnon had been a speechwriter for Nixon in the 1952 campaign. Director Nixon was perfect for IDS public relations since their customers tended to be Midwesterners with moderate incomes.

However, the most interesting aspects of Nixon's relationship with the mutual funds occurred after he left the directorships to begin his campaign for the White House. In April 1968, when Nixon announced he would not stand for re-election to the board of directors, his longtime friend and Pepsi-Cola president Donald Kendall replaced him as director of the four mutual funds. In September 1968, presidential candidate Nixon sent a confidential letter to three thousand of the Wall Street elite in which he attacked the Johnson administration bureaucrats who "sought wide-sweeping new regulatory powers over the mutual fund industry . . ." The Nixon aide who helped draft the letter was with the Washington law firm, Gadsby and Hannah, IDS's registered lobbyist. The partner's name was Charles W. Colson.

When Nixon took office, he replaced the reforming chairman of the Securities and Exchange Commission, Manuel Cohen, with his old-time friend Homer H. Budge. Cohen had tried to place minimal controls on the mutual fund industry to prevent its bilking of naive and isolated investors. Nixon reversed this policy and specifically favored IDS by allowing it to de-register as an investment company which exempted it from SEC regulations concerning capital structure and acquisitions in related financial fields. IDS interests were further served when Nixon ordered the Justice Department to file a supporting brief with IDS before the SEC, arguing that financial institutions be allowed to join the New York Stock Exchange, thereby saving commissions on their stock transactions that would normally go to the brokerage firms. The Internal Revenue Service put the icing on the cake with a new ruling allowing the mutual funds to go after the $250 billion pension fund market. So George

MacKinnon and IDS gave themselves a pat on the back for choosing Nixon. On April 23, 1969, Nixon appointed MacKinnon to the Washington, D.C., circuit of the U.S. Court of Appeals.

Nixon served on two other corporate boards. One was the Mutual Life Insurance Company of New York (MONY's 1972 assets were $4.1 billion, ranking it eleventh in size), where he sat at the board table with representatives from the major New York banks, investment houses, law firms and industrial corporations. Also on the board of directors was Arthur F. Burns, whom Nixon later appointed chairman of the Federal Reserve System.

Nixon also was a director of the Harsco Corporation, a metal fabricating and construction company with annual sales reaching $300 million. The company's Bower-McLaughlin-York Division in York, Pennsylvania, is a leading supplier of heavy vehicle (tank, gun and missile) equipment to the Department of Defense. This division currently holds a $50 million contract to modify and re-equip the tank arsenal of Iran. Harsco overseas operations are rapidly expanding with new plants in Mexico, Puerto Rico, Venezuela, India, and South Africa. The legal work for all these operations is done by Mudge, Rose, Guthrie and Alexander.

Nixon seems to have befriended Harsco's finance committee chairman, Richard J. Buck, who—besides contributing twenty-five thousand dollars to Nixon's 1968 campaign—offered to sell him a two-acre tract at Estate Blue Mountain, located next to David and Laurence Rockefeller's golf course on the Caribbean Island of St. Croix. Buck also did fundraising for Nixon in St. Croix and San Juan, Puerto Rico.

Nixon was not the only Mudge, Rose partner to serve as a corporate director. *Bliss Ansnes* is a board member of the General Cigar Company, whose brand names include Robert Burns, White Owl and Tiparillo. (General Cigar had large operations in Cuba until they were seized by the revolutionary government in 1960.) *Milton C. Rose,* the semi-retired senior part-

ner specializing in trusts and estates, was very active outside the
law firm. He was president and director of Straight Enterprises,
Inc., and a director of the client Warner-Lambert Pharmaceutical Company. He was also a director or trustee of numerous
foundations and colleges—among them the Farfield Foundation,
which served as a conduit for Central Intelligence Agency funding of favored projects. Rose was secretary and director of
Acción International, a "self-help" program for Latin America's
urban slums sponsored by U.S. corporations to counter communist propaganda. Senior partner and tax specialist *John H. Alexander* is a director of the law firm's client Stone & Webster, a
large construction and financial concern.

South Carolinian *Randolph Guthrie,* a descendant of the
Randolphs of Virginia, was the closest partner to Nixon until
Mitchell's arrival. Guthrie handles the corporate accounts and
was the chief architect behind the firm's rapid expansion in the
1960s.* Guthrie is the most active partner in outside corporate
activities. He does not merely attend annual board meetings,
but in two cases he is a board chairman—a key policy-making
position for these corporations. Besides his directorship on
Mercedes-Benz of North America and Iroquois Industries,
Guthrie was chairman of the board of Studebaker-Worthington
from 1963 to 1971 and chairman of the executive committee
from 1971 to the present. In 1963, Guthrie led the company
out of the money-losing auto business and, along with Gerald
Ruttenberg (now chairman), built up the production of auto
parts, gas turbines, garden tractors, valve pumps, compressors,
generators and STP into annual sales of $879 million (1972).
Through the company's 52-percent-controlled Pasco, Inc., an
investment firm (formerly Pan American Sulphur Company),
Studebaker-Worthington in January 1973 bought eighteen hundred former Sinclair service stations plus oil reserves and pipe-
lines from Atlantic Richfield Company for $157 million.

In June 1971, Guthrie and Ruttenberg became directors and

---

* See Paul Hoffman, *Lions in the Street: The Inside Story of the Great
Wall Street Law Firms* (Saturday Review Press, 1973), p. 109.

took control of the financially troubled Susquehanna Corporation, whose interests include rock wool insulation, plastic plumbing pipes, uranium mining and defense work. Susquehanna had been plundered by management before the Studebaker-Worthington takeover, and consequently major lawsuits were filed by Susquehanna shareholders. In response to a shareholder's concern over legal fees at the 1973 Susquehanna annual meeting, Guthrie answered, "They [Susquehanna] have got more litigation than any company I ever saw in forty-two years of business." Of the nine hundred thousand dollars in legal fees for 1972, not surprisingly seven hundred thousand dollars went to Mudge, Rose, Guthrie and Alexander.

Naturally, the workers who produce the corporate profits for Guthrie and others were not involved in making decisions that affect the company's future. In 1973, the elite who control and manage the corporate property threatened seven hundred fifty striking workers at Susquehanna's R. & G. Sloane Manufacturing plant in Sun Valley, California, with unilateral implementation of their "last and final offer" of a forty-two-dollar average decrease in weekly wages.

Guthrie is also chairman of the board of UMC Industries, Inc.; and another law partner and Guthrie protegé, *H. Ridgely Bullock,* is president and director of the company. Bullock is also chairman of the board of Eastern Air Devices and a director of First Washington Securities Corporation and Trend Exploration Ltd. in Denver.

The Moneymen Need a Lawyer

Capitalist expansion often requires corporations to raise new capital through the issuing of securities (stocks, bonds and other IOU's). Corporations rely on investment houses to underwrite this financing and distribute the securities to other investment houses and brokerage firms who in turn sell them to their institutional and individual customers. Once the investment house agrees to underwrite the securities, it obtains the capital required by the corporation through a short-term loan from the commercial bank or insurance company with which it has a working relationship. Like most of the big corporate law firms, Mudge, Rose plays an important role in the process, providing legal advice and expertise to several financial clients. These included two commercial banks (Irving Trust Company and Banque de Paris et des Pays-Bas) and three investment houses (Salomon Brothers; Hornblower and Weeks-Hemphill, Noyes; and Stone and Webster Securities).

Irving Trust Company of New York, the fourteenth largest U.S. bank with assets of $7.4 billion (1972), is controlled by the multi-bank holding company, Charter New York Corporation. Irving Trust deals primarily in large corporate accounts and it services its multinational clients through offices in the capitalist world's principal financial centers. According to a *New York Times* article (January 17, 1970) about Nixon's New York City inner circle, George A. Murphy, chairman of Irving Trust, said, "I'm an admirer—I like to think of him as a friend." The two had met during Navy basic training courses, but their friendship did not blossom until Nixon came to Wall Street in 1963.

Banque de Paris et des Pays-Bas (Suisse) is the Geneva subsidiary of Paribas, France's largest privately owned bank (assets of $2.4 billion in 1973). Paribas representatives sit on the boards of two hundred fifty French and foreign companies with investments in Africa and Southeast Asia. In 1965, Banque de Paris joined the Anglo-American Corporation of South Africa to create two jointly-owned investment companies with a portfolio of French and South African stocks valued at $15 million. Among the Banque's most important customers are the U.S. multinational companies who need financing from the European and Asian money market. Recently, Paribas established an international partnership arrangement with the Bank of America in which both banks operate together in the Eurodollar bond market in Europe and the Asian dollar market in Singapore.

Salomon Brothers underwrites and trades stocks and bonds

for major corporate clients.* It does not deal with the general public; rather it buys and sells gigantic blocks of bonds and stocks for institutional clients and for its own account. Salomon Brothers also acts as a financial adviser on mergers and other corporate transactions. All this requires legal counsel and Mudge, Rose provides a good share of it. According to William R. Salomon, managing partner of the firm, during an average day in fiscal year 1972, their inventory totaled $2.4 billion, and their total annual volume of purchases and sales was $201 billion.

Salomon Brothers' earnings for 1972 were $37 million, second only to Merrill, Lynch, Pierce, Fenner and Smith within the securities industry. While most Wall Street firms were retrenching due to a stagnating stock market, Salomon Brothers was moving into its ultra-modern $8 million headquarters at One New York Plaza. Their new trading room contains the largest bond quotation board in the world, rows of open cubicles for one hundred eighty-six traders and salesmen and the newest electronic communications systems. Recently, Salomon Brothers became involved in litigation relating to the biggest scandal in the financial world—the collapse of the fraud-ridden Equity Funding Corporation of America, a California-based mutual funds and insurance concern.†

---

* Salomon Brothers is the largest bond dealer and underwriter in the world. In recent years, their greatest increase in earnings has come from U.S. government, municipal and corporate bonds, and not the stock market. John Mitchell was a municipal bond lawyer and after he went to Washington, Mudge, Rose brought in new bond lawyers to maintain their expertise.

† Salomon Brothers filed an $8.3 million suit against the investment group Boston Company and its two subsidiaries, John W. Bristol Company and Boston Company Institutional Investors, charging that the defendants had prior knowledge of fraud at Equity Funding when they placed orders for sale of Equity Funding securities with Salomon Brothers. The Boston groups had placed an order for sale of four hundred fifty-six thousand shares on March 26, 1973 (at seventeen dollars and fifty cents per share).

Salomon Brothers has a pragmatic and self-serving interest in New York University. They made a "gift" of $3 million for an education and research center relating to financial organizations and institutions. According to New York University President James H. Hester, "Its primary objectives will be to help develop new capacities for professional management, to explore new approaches for effective self-regulation and self-discipline in the industry and to improve the strength and resiliency of financial markets." Other Mudge, Rose clients have an interest in New York University. Former chairman of Irving Trust, George A. Murphy is a trustee. Elmer Bobst, of Warner-Lambert, is not only a trustee, but also gave $11 million to New York University's newly dedicated Elmer H. Bobst Library.

What are Salomon Brothers' Washington connections? During President Nixon's re-election campaign, seventeen Salomon Brothers partners contributed a total of a hundred thousand dollars and one of those partners was forty-six-year-old millionaire William Edward Simon, who alone gave fifteen thousand dollars. Simon joined Salomon Brothers in 1964 when he began playing a key role in the firm's expansion. In October 1970, Simon was named to the firm's seven-man management committee, and his 1972 earnings reportedly totaled $3 million. In December 1972, Nixon appointed Simon Deputy Secretary of the Treasury, and at the height of the oil crisis promoted him to Energy Czar. In April 1974 Simon was appointed Secretary of the Treasury, replacing George Schultz.

The following day the trading of Equity Funding was halted by the New York Stock Exchange on Salomon's initiative. The Boston group has now filed a $16 million counterclaim charging that Salomon Brothers "held itself out as an expert and sophisticated in the buying and selling of blocks of stock and as a company in which Bristol Company and the public could place trust and confidence," and that Salomon owed Bristol and its clients a fiduciary duty to complete the transactions and make payment. See *Wall Street Journal,* May 9, 1973.

The Law Firm in Corporate Battles

Law firms play an important role in one of the basic steps in creating a monopoly—the merging, takeover and raiding of corporations. They provide the legal weaponry for the battles between corporations; and frequently they serve as advisers and coordinators during these corporate conflicts. Then, if transactions become suspect by government agencies, the corporate law firm is expected to use its influence in Washington to stop investigations and prosecutions. Nixon's law firm is, of course, highly qualified for this task.

In the case of Liquidonics Industries, the Nixon firm not only performed the functions mentioned above, but they, with the help of their banking client, actually took control of a company they had assisted in raiding. Liquidonics Industries, Inc., was a small electronics company in Westbury, New York, which had boosted its sales from $590,000 in 1962 to $9.4 million in 1967 by taking over smaller concerns. The firm's legal problems started when its eyes got bigger than its pocketbook. It wanted to take control of UMC Industries, Inc., a St. Louis company which had increased its 1967 sales to $124.3 million through diversification from matches into vending machines and military weapons. Starting in July 1968, Liquidonics bought 805,700 UMC shares (16 percent of the outstanding stock) from an investment company, United Corporation. The money for this purchase came from a public offering of $25.1 million in covertible debentures (IOU's convertible into stock).*

When merger negotiations were cut off by the UMC directors, Liquidonics decided to gain control by going directly to UMC stockholders to make them an offer they could not resist. Enter Mudge, Rose and its financial clients. Liquidonics now needed money to make an attractive offer to the UMC stockholders for their shares.

---

* Of which $10 million or nearly half the offering was bought by ITT, one of the companies in Bernie Cornfeld's IOS empire. *Forbes,* March 1, 1970, p. 42.

The secrecy of corporate dealings obscures some of the subsequent events, but the following is known. Liquidonics' president, N. Norman Muller, went to Studebaker-Worthington (whose board chairman at the time was law partner Randolph Guthrie) to inquire about either merging with Liquidonics, or helping finance Liquidonics' takeover of UMC. Nothing happened at Studebaker-Worthington; but what is interesting is that Liquidonics *then* went to two banks whose longstanding legal counsel was Guthrie's law firm, Mudge, Rose.*

First, Liquidonics went to Banque de Paris et des Pays-Bas in Geneva, and secured a $40.6 million loan which they used to pay UMC stockholders thirty dollars a share (almost double the market value) for up to 2,158,000 shares (22 percent of UMC outstanding shares). Liquidonics already held 18 percent, so their initial goal was not majority interest; but, when UMC stockholders offered to sell 2,300,000 shares, Liquidonics went to another Guthrie client, the Irving Trust Company of New York to borrow $15.1 million to buy the extra shares. Irving Trust had also handled the financial and administrative work in tendering the offer to stockholders. Finally, after nine months and an $80 million debt, Liquidonics controlled UMC.

This, however, did not end the maneuvering. Banque de Paris had made Liquidonics pay dearly for its short-term loan—which would have been illegal in the United States, since the company put up no collateral. Besides the 8.5 percent interest rate on the $40.6 million loan, the Banque de Paris charged $3.8 million in "placement fees." Whatever advantage Liquidonics gained from the takeover of UMC, the debt proved more than it could handle. Liquidonics had planned to repay these short-term loans with long-term Eurodollar loans, but the financing could not be

---

* When Guthrie was asked about Muller's choice of Banque de Paris, he said, "I knew Muller—I'd met him somewhere—and Muller knew the Banque de Paris. He asked me, when Studebaker turned him down, whether or not I thought the Banque de Paris might be interested in making him a loan. 'Well,' I told him, 'they're in business; go and see them.'"

arranged. With the threat of bankruptcy hanging over them, Liquidonics accepted Banque de Paris's $57.8 million offer to purchase its UMC stock, which allowed Liquidonics to pay off its debts. To show that there were no bad feelings, Banque de Paris loaned Liquidonics $7 million in Eurodollars for working capital. Guthrie's firm then drew up the contracts, just as they had done eight months before with the original loan. When Liquidonics signed on the dotted line, their venture had cost them $16.6 million on the stock sale to the bank (the difference between what they paid the stockholders and what the bank paid them), $4.7 million in placement fees, interest on the loans and their own legal expenses.

Liquidonics officers and directors immediately resigned their positions at UMC to make way for Randolph Guthrie as chairman of the board and his law partner H. Ridgely Bullock as secretary and director. As Mr. Guthrie puts it, "We'll obviously expand the board, put good people on it. . . . We didn't know *we* were going to make a deal here until December 24 [1969], when we actually closed [it]. . . . At the moment I am the chairman because they haven't got anybody else." As of 1973, Guthrie was still chairman and Bullock had become president. Guthrie added that UMC's new European owners "are first-class people. This is not some, you know, fellow sitting there in some little hole-in-the-wall bank or something. This is one of the great banks of Europe."

Officials of the Securities and Exchange Commission and Federal Reserve Board reportedly questioned the legality of Liquidonics's overseas borrowing, but decided not to try to block it after meeting with Mudge, Rose lawyers. U.S. Attorney Robert Morgenthau had also begun a preliminary investigation of Guthrie's involvement, but the other Mudge, Rose partner in Washington, Attorney General John Mitchell, fired him.

The Lucrative Business of Municipal Bonds

Municipal bonds are debt securities issued by cities and states to finance public projects. Billions of dollars of these bonds are

issued every year, and when they mature (come due) the municipal issuer redeems them through tax revenue or other income.
The very wealthy have a special interest in municipal bonds
because they offer a secure investment at a fixed interest rate
and they are exempt from income tax. They are inaccessible to
the small investor since each bond is usually priced at a thousand dollars or more.

John Mitchell's job at the law firm was to certify municipal
bonds. He served as counsel for many local and state governments, and worked for Governor Rockefeller in preparing New
York State bonds to finance a housing project. (One explanation for Mitchell's successful management of Nixon's campaigns
is the numerous contacts he had made with city and state officials through his work on municipal bonds.) After Nixon's 1968
election, the law firm picked up the following state and municipal clients: Nebraska, Kentucky, New Jersey, West Virginia, District of Columbia, and the Virgin Islands.

In 1971, Representative Morris Udall of Arizona charged im-
propriety when the U.S. Postal Service announced its $250 mil-
lion bond issue (the first in a $10 billion authorization as a
result of the reorganization of the Post Office into a semi-
private corporation) and revealed that it would retain Nixon
and Mitchell's former law firm to handle the legal work. Udall
quoted a Postal Service official as saying the five underwriters
of this bond issue had told the Service that Mudge, Rose,
Guthrie and Alexander "had to be hired." Udall said the legal
fees will amount to millions. The managing underwriter of the
bond issue was the law firm's longtime client Salomon Brothers.

Client's Counsel in the White House

It must bring a smile to a corporate executive's face when
two of his lawyers take over the White House and the Justice
Department. Although officially no longer counsel to the corporations, Nixon and Mitchell are now indebted to their clients
through campaign contributions. (See charts on law firm

clients.) Work on client problems began immediately after Nixon and Mitchell took office.

El Paso Natural Gas, while battling an anti-trust suit, had paid the law firm seven hundred seventy thousand dollars in legal fees (1961-67). Two months after Mitchell took office, the suit was dropped.*

Pepsico and six other soft-drink companies had been charged in 1971 with the anti-trust violation of restricting bottlers' sales. A spokesman for the Federal Trade Commission indicated it would be a long time before a decision was made.

Warner-Lambert Pharmaceutical's 1970 merger with the Parke-Davis drug company pushed their annual sales over the $1 billion mark. The Justice Department's anti-trust chief, Richard McLaren, had tried to block the merger; but, after Attorney General Mitchell disqualified himself "in order to avoid any possibility of or appearance of conflict of interest," Deputy Attorney General Richard Kleindienst stepped in to rule in favor of the merger.

The Penn Central Railroad, before its bankruptcy, had retained Mudge, Rose in an attempt to obtain a $200 million loan guarantee from the government. President Nixon, after initially supporting it, later withdrew his support when he realized the loan was insufficient to prevent bankruptcy.

ITT also retained Mudge, Rose from 1969 to 1971 to do legal work for its subsidiaries, Continental Baking Company, Hartford Fire Insurance Company, ITT Europe, Inc., and ITT World Communications. When ITT wanted to merge with the Hartford Insurance Company, Justice's anti-trust chief Richard McLaren tried to block it. Finally, after Mitchell again removed himself from the official decision, Kleindienst made a settlement which allowed ITT to keep the insurance company. McLaren was finally forced to leave his anti-trust position, and received a federal judgeship in Chicago.

Cargill, Inc., is one of the largest privately held multinational

---

* See *Lions in the Street*, p. 122.

companies engaged in grain trading and other agricultural ventures. It was a major participant in the Soviet wheat sale. In December 1971, President Nixon appointed Cargill vice president William Pearce to be his deputy special representative for trade negotiations. In 1963, the government had found Cargill guilty of manipulating the wheat futures market. The Department of Agriculture's Commodity Exchange Authority, after seven years, finally decided to place Cargill's top officers on probation for their crime. The ineffectiveness of the action was highlighted later when a Cargill trader admitted to a House subcommittee that he could not remember whether he was still on probation.

LAW PARTNERS IN WASHINGTON

When Nixon decided to enter the 1968 presidential race, Mudge, Rose became the base for campaign operations. After his election, some of his law partners were rewarded with government positions:

John N. Mitchell served as Nixon's campaign manager and chief political strategist for both the 1968 and 1972 campaigns. He was appointed U.S. Attorney General during Nixon's first administration. He returned to the law firm shortly after the 1972 re-election campaign, but withdrew again following his indictment for perjury, conspiracy and obstruction of justice for allegedly trying to block a criminal investigation of financier Robert Vesco in return for a two hundred thousand dollar campaign contribution. Mitchell was later indicted for his alleged role in the cover-up of Watergate.

Leonard Garment was Nixon's expert on minorities and civil rights during the campaign and at the White House under the title of Special Consultant to the President.

John P. Sears, one of the law firm's youngest partners, worked on delegate recruitment for the 1968 Republican convention because of his knowledge of local politics. After Nixon's nomination, Sears became his liaison to vice-presidential candidate Spiro Agnew, and subsequently joined the White House staff as a deputy counsel to the president. In 1970, he joined Charles Colson's law firm, Gadsby and Hannah. In May 1973, Sears surfaced as the attorney for White House cop John Caulfield when he testified at the Watergate hearings. In an attempt to stop the "national security" leaks, Sears's phone was tapped even though he claims he did not have access to uch information. Insiders noted that Sears, who dispensed federal patronage jobs for Nixon, became disliked by Mitchell during the 1968 campaign, and was suspected of leaking political information about the admiistration to the press.

Thomas W. Evans is a Nixon fundraiser and co-director of United Citizens for Nixon along with Washington attorney Charles Rhyne. He became co-chairman of the Republican National Committee. Two of the tasks he performed for Nixon were discovered during the Watergate investigation. First, he drafted the charters for one hundred fifty secret fundraising committees so that large contributors could avoid the gift tax by splitting up their donations. (These committees were established by Robert F. Bennett, president of Robert R. Mullen & Company, where E. Howard Hunt was employed before joining the White House staff.) The second operation which also involved Frances Raine, Jr. and Herbert Kalmbach, was the control and handling of $1,098,000 in cash and $570,000 in checking accounts left over from the 1968 presidential campaign.

Martin R. Pollner was the executive director of President Nixon's Advisory Council on Crime and Law Enforcement. In 1970 he got a chance to put his law practice behind a badge when Nixon named him director of the Treasury Department's Office of Law Enforcement. Pollner's deputy director was convicted Watergater G. Gordon Liddy. Pollner also supervised the Department's Alcohol, Firearms and Tobacco Bureau whose Assistant Director of Criminal Enforcement from July 1972 to May 1973 was John Caulfield. This group has been responsible for many acts of repression against the political left, such as the raid against the Black Panther party office in Seattle in 1970.

Joseph C. Daley served as a consultant to Attorney General Mitchell and the Justice Department.

Franklin B. Lincoln, Jr., a former Assistant Secretary of Defense under Eisenhower, handled the transition from the Johnson to the Nixon administration. Nixon appointed him to the Foreign Intelligence Advisory Board, a group composed primarily of the corporate elite which review government intelligence activities and make recommendations to the president. (President Kennedy had dissolved the board when he took office, but after the Bay of Pigs invasion failed, it was reconstituted with increased power to investigave the overall intelligence effort.)

Lincoln's corporate affiliations have included a vice-presidency of defense contractor Litton Industries, the presidency of its subsidiary Monroe Calculating Machine Company, and directorships of Barnes Engineering Company, Shelter Resources Corporation, Pacific Tin Consolidations Corporation, and ITEL Corporation. He is a vice president and director of United Cablevision, Inc., and Cypress Communications Corporation. And in February 1973 he took over the chairmanship of the Federal Home Loan Bank of New York, one of twelve regional banks set up by the government to regulate the financing of home mortgages.

John H. Alexander, the law firm's tax specialist, chaired Nixon's task force on business taxation.

Arthur H. Becker, an admiralty law expert, worked on a Nixon study of American shipbuilding. (In the first year of his administration, Nixon announced a ten-year $3.8 billion subsidy to finance the shipbuilding industry. Two concerns certain to benefit from the decision, American Shipbuilding Company and National Bulk Carriers, are law firm clients.)

Principal Sources:

New York Times, June 24, 1968; November 8, 1968; May 7, 1972; February 23, 1973; September 23, 1973; and October 15, 1973.
Wall Street Journal, May 14, 1973.
Washington Post, December 16, 1973.
Who's Who in Government, 1972–73.

LAW FIRM-CLIENT NEXUS

The accompanying chart of Nixon-Mitchell law firm clients demon-strates that the law firm (currently Mudge, Rose, Guthrie & Alexander) not only has clients in diverse sectors of the economy, but that the clients have interrelationships with each other. Even though there are un-doubtedly many more clients—Mudge, Rose will not reveal a complete list—the chart suggests the outline of an economic interest group which coordinates its activities in other ways.

The following is a list of known Mudge, Rose clients in addition to those listed on the chart. The chart lists only those clients which are interrelated with another client or have a director from the law firm on their board. An asterisk denotes companies discussed in this chapter.

Blair & Company: a national sales representative for television and radio stations to sell their air time to national advertisers.

Ridge Minerals Venture, Rock School Joint Venture, Wolf Joint Venture: operations seeking and holding concessions for the exploration of oil shale in Colorado and Utah.

Talisman Sugar Corporation: owned by William Pawley, who is a reac-tionary friend of Nixon. He supported Goldwater, was U.S. ambassador to Panama under Truman, assisted in the formation of the Flying Tigers Airline. The company grows sugar cane in Florida and Jamaica and hired the law firm in 1965 to be its registered lobbyist to gain required allot-ments and quotas. The company was recently bought out by Ed Ball, Florida banker for the DuPonts. (See *Congressional Quarterly*, August 27, 1965, p. 1743.)

Mitsui: one of the largest Japanese financial, industrial and trading com-bines.

American Shipbuilding Company*: the company and its chairman George M. Steinbrenner III contributed a hundred thousand dollars to Nixon's campaign.

National Bulk Carriers*: owned by Daniel K. Ludwig, whose personal fortune (close to $1 billion) was built on petroleum tankers in the 1940s and '50s. In the last decade, Ludwig has diversified his holdings into finance, petroleum, mining, hotels, agricultural and defense contracting. His latest investments are in the Amazon, where he has the support of the Brazilian dictatorship.

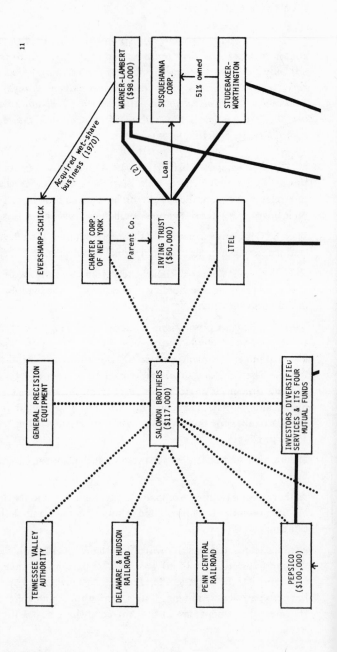

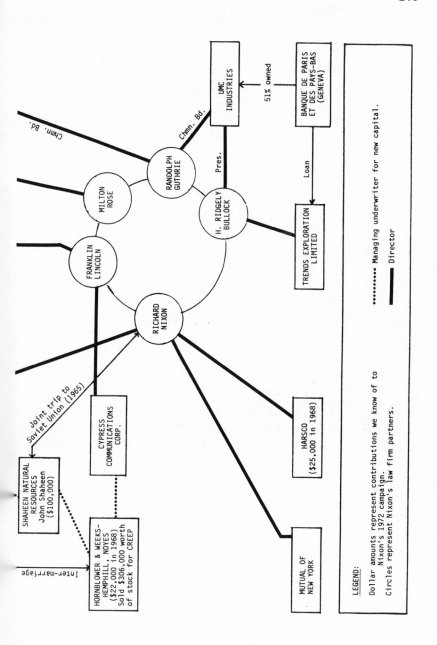

Atlas Sewing Centers, Inc. (Miami): filed suit in 1968 against Nixon, three other law firm partners, and the Irvinng Trust Company for their attempt to force the company to reorganize.

C. Arnholt Smith: long-time San Diego friend and contributor to Nixon. Mudge, Rose represented him in a suit filed by the Securities and Exchange Commission seeking an injunction against securities law violations and the removal of the Westgate-California conglomerate from Smith's control. He contributed at least fifty thousand dollars to Nixon.

Noranda Mines Ltd.

Stone & Webster, Inc.*

ITT*

El Paso Natural Gas Company*

General Cigar Company*

U.S. Postal Service*

Cargill, Inc.*: contributed twelve thousand dollars to Nixon.

Missouri-Kansas-Texas Railroad (Katy Industries)

Governments of District of Columbia, Kentucky, Nebraska, New Jersey, Virgin Islands, West Virginia, Wisconsin.*

Principal Sources:

Paul Hoffman, *Lions in the Street: The Inside Story of the Great Wall Street Law Firms* (Saturday Review Press, 1973).
Joseph C. Goulden, *The Superlawyers: The Small and Powerful World of the Great Washington Law Firms* (David McKay Co., 1971).
"Mitchell and His Law Firm," *New York Times*, May 7, 1972.
"Law Firm Changes as Nixon Departs," *Washington Post*, November 24, 1968.

*Colson was too much of a politician to believe that any-
thing could be learned of value at the Democratic National
Committee.* His own intelligence net *was far more
effective—but he would not share what he learned with
anyone except Haldeman and Nixon.*

—Theodore White,
The Making of the President, 1972

Charles Colson — Superspy

Stu Bishop

Who hired E. Howard Hunt, dispatched the "plumbers" to the
office of Daniel Ellsberg's psychiatrist, drew up the "enemies
list," arranged the release of former Teamster boss Jimmy Hoffa
from federal prison, and masterminded most of the secret missions against President Nixon's opponents? Who turned the
9:15 A.M. White House "Attack Group" into an elaborate intelligence network to plan sabotage against the Democrats and the
left?

The answer is no secret. It was Charles Colson, "Special
Counsel" to the president, "King of the White House Hard
Hats," and the president's own "hatchet man."

The original version of this essay, entitled "Colson: Agent in the White
House," appeared in NACLA's *Latin America & Empire Report*, November 1973. Reprinted by permission of NACLA.

But where did Charles Colson learn his "dirty tricks?" The answer to that is a mystery, though evidence suggests that the paunchy New England lawyer might have been a high-level operative of the Defense Intelligence Agency or the CIA. If true, it might help explain one of the smaller mysteries of the Watergate conspiracy: why Charles Colson was the only conspirator close to Nixon who escaped the Senate Watergate Committee.

To begin with, Colson had close ties to the military. At the age of twenty-two, he was the youngest Company Commander in the history of the Marine Corps, moving on to become assistant to the Assistant Secretary of the Navy in 1955-56. More recently, he reportedly led a workshop at the University of Virginia as part of the ongoing Inter-University Seminar on Armed Forces and Society sponsored by the Russell Sage Foundation. The title of Colson's workshop: "The Reorganization of Intelligence in the Military."

Colson also had an ongoing association with CIA veteran Howard Hunt, reaching back at least as far as 1961-63 when both men were officials of the Brown University Alumni Association. But far more convincing were the White House missions which Colson planned for Hunt and the lesser spooks. The choice of targets and diversity of tactics, smearing opponents, breaking and entering to gain evidence, forging documents, manufacturing phony propaganda, manipulating front groups—it was all strikingly similar to the way the CIA and military intelligence agencies have been operating abroad over the past decades. No novice could have initiated a program like that.

Colson the Lawyer

After engineering Saltonstall's re-election in 1960, despite a Democratic sweep in Massachusetts, Colson became a partner in the Boston law firm of Gadsby and Hannah. The Gadsby in the name is the former chairman of the Securities and Exchange Commission. When Colson joined the firm, it had twenty-two partners and specialized in "jungle law"—its clients were mainly corporations that had problems with the federal government's regulatory agencies. Colson also lobbied for such giants as Investors Diversified Services, the nation's largest mutual fund complex; Uniroyal, the giant rubber firm; Massachusetts Investors Trust; and Grumman Aircraft, one of the Navy's prime contractors and builders of the F-14 fighter.

Colson strengthened his links to the military during the mid-sixties through his corporate directorships of the Specialty Electronics Development Corporation (Spedcor) and the Loral Corporation. Colson was a director of Spedcor from 1964-68. According to its 1969 prospectus, the firm made between 84 percent and 97 percent of its sales through Defense Department contracts during Colson's last year as a director. Loral Corporation, of which Colson was also a director, is a New York-based firm specializing in the production of electronic systems for the military.

In the wake of the spring 1973 Watergate revelations, Colson resigned his post as Special Counsel and quietly slipped into his new Washington, D.C. law firm, Colson and Shapiro. It was Colson who was the prime mover behind former Teamster boss Jimmy Hoffa's release from prison. In return, the Teamsters switched their hundred-thousand-dollar (annual) legal account from Edward Bennet Williams's Democratic law firm to Colson's.

Colson the Ass-kicker

Colson once described his job as Special Counsel to the President as being "chief ass-kicker around the White House." One of his functions was to serve as chief White House liaison man with outside groups, including Hard Hats, wildlife societies, the League of Women Voters, homebuilders, Veterans, and an assortment of labor groups. It is Colson who was most credited with being the architect of Nixon's '72 campaign strategy that molded a new GOP majority by winning over Democratic constituencies: the coalition of ethnic-Catholic-Wallaceite groups that Nixon exploited through his appeals to racism and super-patriotism.

In a *Village Voice* article ("How's Charles Colson's Grandmother These Days," October 4, 1973), Martin Nolan gives an insight into how much power Colson exerted within the White House:

> Colson also swallowed-up the empire of Herb Klein, another long-time Nixon chum. Klein was dispatched to make speeches at Sigma Delta Chi luncheons while Colson took direct charge of communications and Klein's staff. . . . He . . . hired Ken Clawson of the *Washington Post* to become director of communications, theoretically under Klein but in reality lieutenant to Colson's command in 1972 of the Attack Group. . . .

Clawson reportedly fabricated the letter to the editor of the *Manchester Union Leader* (New Hampshire) contending that Senator Edmund Muskie condoned a slur on Americans of French-Canadian descent in which they were called "Canucks." The letter was one of the factors that led to Muskie's politically damaging "crying speech" outside the newspaper's offices.

Colson also "kicked ass' within the Nixon camp, including that of former Attorney General John Mitchell. Their rivalry and friction centered on a common problem in the Nixon White House: the competition between aides for the president's ear. However, there is evidence to suggest that the Colson-Mitchell tug-of-war was more complicated. When John Mitchell resigned as Attorney General and took over the job as chief of CREEP, he reportedly laid down two conditions: first, that Kleindeinst be appointed his successor as Attorney General; and second, that Colson be kept out of his way.

The first request was simple; the second out of the question. Part of the reason Mitchell hated Colson so much may have been that they ran competing intelligence operations. Judging from the quote at the beginning of this article, it appears that Colson viewed CREEP's operations as amateurish, and thought that his Attack Groups were much more effective in destroying

Nixon's "enemies." A friend of Mitchell's tells the story: "Normally, John [Mitchell] could call the President directly about anyone, and if John didn't like the guy, he would be gone the next morning. Not with Colson, though. Colson was there to stay."*

Colson the Agent

Next to Nixon, Colson was perhaps the most important single figure in the series of events now known as Watergate. In all, witnesses at the Senate Watergate Hearings credited him with over thirty secret missions. Even a partial listing makes the point:

Colson was responsible for the drafting of the "Enemies List" which contained the names of two hundred Nixon critics.

E. Howard Hunt testified at the Senate Watergate Hearings that it was Colson who mapped out and put into motion "Operation Gemstone," the code word for actions against Nixon's enemies.

Colson ordered a group of Cuban exiles, led by Bernard Barker, to attack Daniel Ellsberg and other demonstrators at J. Edgar Hoover's funeral in Washington, D.C.

Colson played a key role in the commutation of two prison sentences: those of former Teamster boss Jimmy Hoffa and Florida builder Calvin Kovens. At the suggestion of former Senator George Smathers, Colson arranged Kovens's release in the hope of winning more of Florida's Jewish vote for Nixon; in return for Hoffa's release, Nixon not only garnered the Teamster endorsement, but later Colson's new Washington, D.C., law firm received the Teamster's lucrative legal account.

Colson planned the Plumbers' mission that broke into Ellsberg's psychiatrist's office.

Colson and Nixon, through then Attorney General Kleindienst, had fraud charges dropped against Richard Fitzsimmons,

---

* Theodore White, *The Making of the President, 1972* (New York: Atheneum, 1973), p. 292.

son of Teamster president Frank Fitzsimmons.

Colson dispatched the Plumbers to a Las Vegas publisher's office, not to obtain evidence that would "blow Muskie out of the water," as reported, but to retrieve potentially dangerous papers summarizing Nixon's San Clemente land deal, in which he utilized three hundred fifty thousand dollars of campaign funds and three hundred thousand dollars of Syndicate money.

Colson ordered Hunt to Milwaukee to break into Arthur Bremer's appartment in an attempt to link Wallace's accused assailant to the left. Colson thought evidence could be obtained in the apartment that would substantiate such a link, thus discrediting the left.

Colson suggested the break-in and firebombing of the "liberal" Brookings Institution as a diversionary tactic for breaking into Leslie Gelb's Brooking's office to try to locate the source of the Pentagon Papers leak. His subordinate, John Caulfield, refused to carry through the plan.

When Nixon ordered the mining of Haiphong, telegrams running six to one in the president's favor began pouring into the White House. However, there was one small catch: the favorable telegrams were sent by CREEP's November Group, which was another of Colson's ideas.

Colson dispatched E. Howard Hunt in disguise to a hospital to visit the ailing Dita Beard. Beard was the ITT lobbyist who broke the story that ITT and Nixon had reached a settlement on an anti-trust action in which the GOP would receive four hundred thousand dollars to help finance its 1972 convention in San Diego. Colson wanted Hunt to get a confession that her allegations were false.

Colson doctored up a photograph that showed McGovern standing with what looked like a group of "weirdo longhairs" as part of the campaign tactic to link the Democrats with the "extremist left."

When members of the Vietnam Veterans Against the War (VVAW) were peacefully demonstrating in Washington, D.C., Colson quickly established a phony front group called

"Veterans for a Just Peace."

Colson attempted to influence the Securities and Exchange Commission by placing a law partner of his, King Mallory, in a key SEC post. The scheme fell through.

Colson worked closely with other government agencies in their operations against Nixon enemies. One was the Internal Revenue Service (IRS), which audits tax returns. Colson implied to the IRS that Teamster vice president Harold Gibbons's returns might be out of order. Gibbons was a McGovern supporter. Colson also attempted to do the same to chief McGovern fundraiser Henry Kimmelman.

Is it possible that Charles Colson is a linguist in addition to his various other talents? In 1967 he became vice-chairman of the Brazilian-American Cultural Development Institute, a non-profit organization which claims to teach Portuguese and English to U.S. and Brazilian businessmen. We do not know much about this group and would appreciate hearing from readers who have more information.*

If the Watergate witnesses were right, Charles Colson had chalked up a record worthy of the most savvy secret agent. But so far the grand jury has indicted him only for his alleged role in the cover-up.

---

* Send information to NACLA, P.O. Box 226, Berkeley, CA 94701.

Nixon and the Miami Connection

Jeff Gerth

Richard M. Nixon has been a central figure in American politics since the end of World War II. At the end of his third presidential campaign, he was the best-financed candidate in American history. Yet in many ways Nixon remains a profound enigma. Never a man of great personal popularity, he has nevertheless survived an almost endless series of personal crises and defeats to attain the pinnacle of American power.

Nixon's career has been continuously marred by scandal and controversy. From his smear campaigns in the late forties, to the secret slush fund that led to the Checkers speech in 1952, to the Hughes loan in 1960, to the four-hundred-thousand-dollar ITT scandal in 1972, to the Watergate break-in and the secret Republican war chest, Nixon's ascendancy to power has been surrounded by the stigma of suspicion.

Nixon's rise to wealth and power has required the silent loyalty of a wide range of personalities whose names only occasionally surface in the glare of scandal—with good reason.

The original version of this essay, entitled "Nixon and the Mafia," © 1972, appeared in *Sundance*, November-December 1972. Reprinted by permission of the author.

Richard Nixon would not be president were it not for his un-canny ability to thrive on political crisis. As much as anything else it is his self-proclaimed poker-playing instincts—the cautious, calculating, close-mouthed style and the ability to keep a stone face in rough as well as smooth times—that carried Nixon to the presidency.

"A hundred Navy officers will tell you Nix never lost a cent at poker," says a buddy from World War II. "It's a matter of being in the right place at the right time," says Nixon, "and I'm always willing to take a chance . . . maybe it's that old poker-playing instinct."

But it is in moments of vulnerability that the underworld inevitably makes contact. It is the loan shark who will lend you money when no one else will, and it is the mob that controls the pleasures and vices of escape—narcotics, gambling, pornography.

Accordingly, Nixon's closest contact with organized crime occurred during the most vulnerable periods of his political career—his start in the forties, and his years out of office in the sixties.

The Early Days in Florida

A major base for the wide network of organized crime is the Caribbean, and consequently a major capital is Miami. In the days of the Cuban dictatorship, Miami was the center of the "Havana connection"—a funnel for money flowing from the Caribbean gambling hotel, prostitution, and drug operations which centered in prerevolutionary Cuba. The control exercised by organized crime over the city of Miami dates back to the forties.

As of January 3, 1947, Richard Nixon was a congressman from southern California. Mr. Nixon and his biographers have always maintained that he never showed up in Florida—the site of so many of his later dealings—until the early fifties. Keeping Nixon out of Florida in the forties is essential to the Nixon

image, because in 1950 Senator Estes Kefauver opened his cele-
brated hearings on organized crime in Miami. In seven hundred
thirty pages of testimony Kefauver painted a shattering picture
of nationally known gangsters working in harmony with Florida
public officials ranging in rank from sheriff to governor. But
according to Richard Danner, a former head of the Miami FBI
office, and his FBI partner John Madala, Nixon did show up.
Many of Nixon's early Florida excursions found him fishing
with Bebe Rebozo, an unknown gas station operator, and
Tatum "Chubby" Wofford, whose Wofford Hotel Kefauver
identified as Syndicate-controlled.

During an hour and a half conversation in September 1972,
Danner recounted for me one of Nixon's Miami visits. The time
was 1948. Nixon was involved in prosecuting the Hiss case, in
which (in *Six Crises*) Nixon has confessed his "name, reputation, and career" were staked. In the middle of the prosecution,
George Smathers called Danner from Washington to tell him,
"Dick is on the verge of a physical breakdown. We're all concerned about him." Smathers put Nixon on the train and
Danner met him at the other end, in Miami. Danner remembers
he thought Nixon looked "like a northern hick" coming off the
train in his heavy overcoat. After a week in Vero Beach, where
Danner had a car dealership, the two headed for a Miami osteo-
path. Danner called Rebozo to say, "Bebe, get your boat and
meet us at the doctor's office." The three then went out on
Rebozo's yacht. From the sunny quiet of Miami Nixon returned
to Washington rested and ready to continue his attack on Alger
Hiss.

Danner's past was hardly free of scandal. There was his
friendship with corrupt officials like Dade County Sheriff James
Sullivan during his 1940-46 FBI days and there was his stint in
1946 at the Miami Beach Hotel Owners Association with his
friend Abe Allenberg, the association president. Allenberg also
happened to be booking manager of the Wofford Hotel and
local representative for the New York syndicate.

From 1946 to 1948 Danner was city manager of Miami, and

his term of office ended with him caught in the middle of a gangland dispute over control of the city police. In 1948 the city council dismissed Danner, accusing him of "playing both ends against the middle." Furthermore, one council member alleged that two years earlier Danner had accepted ten thousand dollars from gambling interests while managing the congressional campaign of George Smathers. In the early fifties Danner left Florida to join his friends in Washington. He opened shop as a lawyer and took out membership in the Burning Tree Country Club, where his golfing partners were Smathers and Nixon. Danner managed to keep out of the public eye until the mid-sixties, when General Motors used him to coordinate its snooping on Ralph Nader.

In 1968, Howard Hughes sent Nixon a hundred-thousand-dollar contribution through Danner and Rebozo. Danner was representing Hughes's Las Vegas casino interests at the time. Not long after Nixon had set himself up at Key Biscayne—with the help of Rebozo—Danner located himself in Nevada to oversee the Hughes empire there. Danner's friendship with former FBI buddy Robert Maheu put him there in the first place, and it was Nixon's influence that kept him safe during Maheu's stormy, well-publicized departure.

Bebe Rebozo, Nixon's closest friend, is probably the most mysterious. As *Life* said in 1970, "He's the only person Nixon really trusts. He can talk to Rebozo, ask him questions. He knows Bebe will give him honest answers. They can talk about anything . . . And nothing Nixon says is going to go any further." A man who knows both says, "Bebe and the president can sit together for hours and say practically nothing to each other."

Today Rebozo owns considerable real estate, has a financial interest in several small firms, and owns the only bank on Key Biscayne—the Key Biscayne Bank. Dubbed the unofficial mayor of the island, Rebozo drives around in his large green Continental with the bumper sticker that read, "The only issue is America."

While an American citizen (born of Cuban parents) Rebozo has close ties to the pre-Castro Cuban political scene. His business associates have included the former Cuban ambassador to Brazil under Batista, Burke Hedges (a heavy initial in Rebozo's bank), and the former mayor of Havana, Dr. Eduardo Buttari (who ran the "Cubans for Nixon" organization in 1968). Buttari now holds a plush twenty-five-thousand-dollar-a-year job in HEW doing little. According to a reliable source, Buttari— a Cuban refugee—had his citizenship papers okayed rather quickly in August 1971. He claims to have a "great friendship with Nixon and Rebozo."

Among Rebozo's business associates are Dick Fincher and "Big Al" Polizzi. Fincher, who invested in Lummus Island with Rebozo, has been a "character witness" for a number of underworld characters. Polizzi was convincted in 1943 of black market liquor violations arising from his and the Cleveland syndicate's efforts to smuggle rum from Cuba to Key West—with the help of Cuban President Batista. In 1968 Rebozo chose the Polizzi Construction Company to build a shopping center in the Cuban community in Miami. Among the uncorroborated testimony accumulated by the Miami Police Department is an intelligence report dated November 13, 1963, which lists the testimony of a gangster informant that Bebe Rebozo ran a numbers racket out of a coin laundry operation—Wash Well—and was "fronting in this operation for ex-Vice President Nixon."

Rebozo's capital for his land purchases came from his wartime service station business, and it was his sideline in tires that brings the supposedly unconnected forties careers of Smathers, Nixon, and Rebozo into curious intersection. Before the war had broken out, Rebozo was running a Shell gas station which also served as a hangout for such friends as Smathers and Sloan McCrea, a future Nixon finance chairman. By the end of 1941, with gas rationing already in effect for six months, service stations were not good investments. A few weeks after Pearl Harbor, the government banned construction of any new stations. Nevertheless, just two days after Pearl Harbor, Rebozo purchased the land next to his station to enlarge his facilities. In Washington, the Office of Price Administration (OPA) was one of two agencies charged with managing the tire scarcity. Since original tires were unavailable to the public, recaps and retreads became precious commodities. Bootleggers, thriving on the scarcity, were to enjoy many years of profit.

In the meantime, the OPA's tire rationing division had hired a few young attorneys to draft the multitude of necessary regulations and to set up regional offices to enforce these regulations. On January 9, 1942, Richard Nixon, just a few years out of Duke Law School, went to work in the interpretations unit of the legal section of the tire rationing branch of the OPA. For Nixon, the position must not have been a memorable one. He concealed his employment at the OPA until he became president. In his official biography in the Congressional Directory for the eightieth Congress, he listed his employer from January to August 1942 as the Office of Emergency Management. While this was not technically incorrect, it is the equivalent of an FBI agent saying he works for the Justice Department.

Charged with enforcing OPA policy on the local level was the tire allocation board of the Dade County Defense Council. The chairman of the council and at least one key member had direct links with members of organized crime. And three men who served on the board had ties to Rebozo. Frank Smathers, father of Rebozo's associate George Smathers; Lucien Renuart of Renuart Lumber, which had loaned Rebozo the money to expand his service station into the profitable tire recapping business; and C. W. Chase, Jr., of Chase Savings and Loan Association, which employed Rebozo's sister Margaret Barker in an executive position (and which was a few years later to provide Rebozo with capital for his real estate ventures)—all served in clear violation of OPA policy (3C-118) which stated, "Persons connected with the production or distribution of tires and tubes, or with the recapping or retreading of tires should not be selected to serve on the Boards."

On January 29, 1942 George Smathers was in federal court

for the matter of *United States v. Standard Oil of Kansas,* involving U.S. Customs confiscating American-made tires coming into the country from Cuba in an "attempt to circumvent national tire rationing." When Smathers encountered a delay in the case he sought a ruling from the OPA in Washington on the legality of bringing tires in from Cuba.

OPA records in the National Archives reveal that one of Nixon's duties was handling all correspondence involving tire rationing. It was therefore his responsibility to answer Smathers, and it is relevant to know what he said. Unfortunately, most OPA records were destroyed after the war. The court file for this case is supposed to be in the Atlanta Records Center, but a written request submitted to the clerk of the civil court in Miami on July 6, 1972 has not been honored, despite the usual one-week response time. Contradictory excuses for the delay have been given.

Written questions submitted to President Nixon and Bebe Rebozo have also gone unanswered. Among the relevant questions is whether Miami was one of the regional offices Nixon set up. In the context of their later friendship, one is forced to ask just when did Nixon, Rebozo, and Smathers come into contact with each other, and under what circumstances?

War profiteering was the pastime of Nixon's other yachting host, "Chubby" Wofford. Wofford's hotel was one of the two Miami Beach Hotels allowed to remain open during the war. According to Danner, Wofford made "tons of money" through the Navy's use of this hotel, but "that wild man blew it all away."

Over the years, one of the most powerful forces on the Miami-Havana axis was a secretive, informal investment group which we will call the Ansan group—after their primary real estate front, Ansan Corporation. The group's holdings in Florida real estate eventually amounted to over $50 million. Smathers's law firm protected the Ansan group from publicity, while the firm of Hunt, Salley and Roman held off the Internal Revenue Service.

In 1946 Richard Hunt resigned his position as a judge on the circuit court to become legal counselor for the corrupt Dade County Sheriff, Jim Sullivan. William Roman vacated the Miami office of the FBI and another lawyer named George Salley joined to form Hunt, Salley and Roman. According to a Miami Crime Commission memo (it was the Miami Crime Commission that did most of the investigative work for the Kefauver Committee in Miami) Hunt was the "brains for every public utterance made by [Sheriff] Sullivan." The source further alleged that Hunt was "involved with Sullivan in taking graft."

Roman also acted as attorney for the Keyes Realty Company. With a top Keyes official he set up a spin-off realty company to transact such deals as procuring a rent-free home for the sheriff. The IRS regarded the Keyes spin-off as a "dummy front for handling sub-rosa deals for Sullivan."

This wasn't the first time Keyes officials were involved in questionable ventures. Keyes himself—in conjunction with the Ansan group—set up a number of real estate fronts for acquiring land on Key Biscayne. Nor was it the last time. In 1971 a Keyes vice president named Eugenio Martinez helped form a Miami real estate company called Ameritas, which has been used as a cover for the principals of the Watergate break-in. Martinez and his boss at Ameritas—Bernard Barker—were two of the seven men indicted in the espionage case that leads from the White House to the Democratic National Committee headquarters. The offices of Ameritas were originally located one floor below the headquarters for Keyes Realty.

Richard Nixon is also quite close to the Keyes associates. Nixon and Rebozo have been close friends and occasional investment partners with the top executives of the Keyes organization. For example, Keyes's successor as president, a man named Allen Morris, joined with Nixon and Rebozo in a land deal brokered by a Keyes realtor. Another top Keyes officer has been a director of Bebe Rebozo's Key Biscayne Bank for the last few years, and it was to the Keyes company that the White House turned to transact some of the business involved in establishing the presidential compound at Key Biscayne.

The vast invesments which the Ansan group made in south Florida real estate in the forties are a good example of the unifying nature of the politics of corruption, Cuban style. The group's visible partners were the Minister of Education, Jose Aleman; his wife, Elena Santiero; and Dr. Anselmo Alliegro, Batista's close friend and finance minister. Aided by Miami allies like Smathers's law firm, Keyes company, and the Hunt firm, the Ansan group managed to buy large chunks of real estate in anonymity. By failing to register changes in stock ownership with the state incorporation office, by presenting false ownership information, by paying for the land in cash, and by shielding the real ownership behind an elaborate maze of real estate fronts, the real roots of the Ansan group and their capital remained a mystery.

Aleman is considered responsible for the siphoning of between $60 and $174 million from the Cuban Treasury in the years before his death in 1950. The story goes that Aleman simply pulled up to the Treasury with a truck and hauled off the loot. Aleman was guilty, of that there is no doubt. As for how much he took, that can never be answered, for all the pertinent records relating to the Cuban Treasury were later stolen and never recorded.

The Ansan group purse strings, swelled by the Cuban Treasury as well as Batista money (in the person of Alliegro) had one other source. That was what George C. Vilas, IRS Intelligence Special Agent, had in mind February 20, 1948 when he filed a report "with regard to large real estate purchases in the Miami area." The IRS report states:

1. At the time "Lucky" Luciano was on board a ship at a New York dock prior to his deportation to Italy [February 1946] he was visited by Frank Costello, who is alleged to have carried suitcases on board containing around $2,000,000, representing Luciano's share of gambling income during his incarceration. When Costello left the ship he did not have the suitcases.

2. When Luciano came to Cuba eighteen months ago [in violation of

his deportation proceedings] he was visited by a number of underworld characters prior to his deportation to Italy by Cuban authorities. In connection with Cuban deportation charges Luciano employed Cuban Senator Santiero, the father of Elena Santiero y
Garcia, the president of Ansan and other corporations that have
made large investments in real estate in this area. It is believed that
some of the funds being invested in this area by Mrs. Garcia may
belong to Luciano or other underworld characters, which was turned
over to Senator Santiero in Cuba.

Additional information reveals further contacts between leading underworld figures and Cuban political officials connected
to the Dade County investments. Meyer Lansky, who had
helped arrange Luciano's deportation, paved the way for
"Lucky's" illegal entry into Cuba, via Italy, then Mexico.
Lansky had made arrangements with the Cuban government "to
receive Luciano warmly, though unofficially."

During his brief stay in Cuba, "Lucky" managed to move in
all the right circles. A report by Federal Narcotics Bureau agent
operating undercover in Havana stated "that Luciano had already become friendly with a number of high Cuban officials
through the lavish use of expensive gifts."

The IRS noted that the funds used for Ansan's purchases,
"consisted entirely of currency in bills of one-thousand-dollar
denomination." The IRS tried to ask Elena Santiero about the
origin of the bills, many of which were consecutively numbered.
She referred them to her lawyers, Hunt and Salley, who gave a
simple response: they money had been "earned or acquired in
Cuba." Of course they didn't mention how it was earned or
acquired. The IRS's suspicions were increased when Vilas noticed that Elena was "transferring this sum to Miami in currency, rather than through [normal] banking channels." (The
money was deposited by the escrow agent in Ed Ball's Florida
National Bank and Trust of Miami. Ball figures later in the
development of Key Biscayne.)

Though shrouded in secrecy, the workings of the Ansan
group remain a model of how the Miami/Havana connection

operated. With the coming of Castro in 1959, and the subsequent emigration of gangsters and politicians alike, the Miami/Havana connection shifted its emphasis from corruption to espionage. Political espionage, be it gun-running, invasions of Cuba or snooping in Washington, or laundering money through Miami banks, is the byword since 1959 of the Miami/Havana connection.

The Pan American Bank in Miami is linked to this connection and to Richard Nixon. The bank was started in 1945 by George Salley of Hunt, Salley and Roman. Early directors included Kenneth Keyes and William Roman, and down through the years leading executives of Keyes have been directors as well as Salley and Roman. The top fifteen stockholders in the sixties included Anselmo, Alliegro, Hoke T. Maroon and Walter Frederich, the last two of whom are investment partners of Nixon and Smathers. In recent years, another Nixon/Smathers investment partner, Sloan McCrea, has been a director of the bank. In a 1960 stock suit involving his Pan American Bank stock, Alliegro was identified as fronting for Batista. The judge said, "All inferences point to the startling fact that—the stock may be in the property of Batista and is being held by the Plaintiff [Alliegro] to prevent Dictator Castro from seizing it." The bank was identified in the McClellan hearings as helping to finance in conjunction with some Teamster officials a proposed gun-running scheme that found weapons and ammunition going to Batista sympathizers in 1959.

The Key Biscayne Story

Before 1940 Key Biscayne was undeveloped and unlinked to the mainland, its land titles firmly in the hands of two wealthy northern estates—the Deerings, a family of Chicago industrialists, and the Mathesons, a family of New York financiers.

In the forties the Mathesons offered a large chunk of the island—eight hundred eight acres—as a county park if the county would finance a causeway to the mainland. Working behind the scenes to set up the details was Ed Ball.

Ball is the brother-in-law of Alfred I. duPont, manager of the billion-dollar duPont empire in Florida. In 1950 Ball helped finance and organize the election of his close friend and vicious anticommunist George Smathers to the U.S. Senate. Both men were friends with Smathers's old high-school buddy, Bebe Rebozo. In 1963 it was Ball, Rebozo, and another friend of Ball's—World War I flying ace, Eddie Rickenbacker—who "arranged the necessary introductions which led to Nixon joining a New York law firm" (Mudge, Rose, Guthrie and Alexander) according to a 1969 article on Rebozo in *Women's Wear Daily*. When the causeway was finished after World War II it bore the name Rickenbacker Causeway, and it also brought some shady land deals. In March 1943, the Matheson estate sold one hundred ninety-three acres (tract six) on the southern end of the island to the head of Keyes Realty Company—Kenneth Keyes. Keyes created a special company especially for this transaction, its principals being himself and three Cuban clients. Tract six was described in 1946 by the *Miami Herald* as "probably one of the most valuable pieces of land in the United States, not excepting the financial district of Manhattan."

Keyes and his friend paid only two hundred thousand dollars —barely 10 percent of the assessed value—for land whose value was conservatively estimated at $1,930,000. In 1946 Keyes set up a new affiliate company and transferred the title for ten dollars.

In 1947, a three-hundred-seventy-acre parcel of land owned by the Deerings—a parcel covering the southern tip of the island and adjacent to the Matheson tract six—passed to the Ansan group. The attorneys for the Deering estate "negotiated" a price of $1.7 million, well below the conservatively assessed value of $4 million. The First National Bank of Miami Beach—owned by the Smathers family—acted as trustee for the Ansan group. The Smathers law firm "convinced" the Miami newspapers in 1948 to withhold from the public information concerning land deals in the Miami area—including those on Key Biscayne—until after the Cuban elections of that year.

In 1952 the *American Mercury* magazine identified the Key Biscayne holdings of the Deering family as a front for "Capone interests."

Meanwhile, the three Mackle brothers—Robert, Bruce, and Frank—were making their first millions through the development of housing tracts on Key Biscayne. The Mackles had received their land in large chunks in suspicious deals from the Matheson Estate. By 1953, with the opening of the Mackles' Key Biscayne Inn and Villas, Richard Nixon had become a regular visitor. The series of intimate villas bordering the ocean have proved to be a favorite retreat and meeting place for Nixon down through the years. Another frequent guest was FBI Director J. Edgar Hoover.

In December 1953 Nixon and William Rogers, then Deputy Attorney General, held a meeting at Key Biscayne with Joe McCarthy, telling the Wisconsin senator to "ease off" on his attacks. (Interestingly enough, before the Key Biscayne resort opened, Nixon's visits to the Miami area, as well as those of Hoover, found them at two hotels owned by G. Meyer Schine, whose son David Schine was a prominent figure in the McCarthy hearings. Today the elder Schine is a director of the Boca Raton Bank through which one hundred fourteen thousand dollars in mysterious Watergate funds passed. Twenty years earlier, Schine, as a witness before the Kefauver Committee, reluctantly admitted that he had lease arrangements with bookmakers at his Miami Beach hotels.)

The Mackles had even closer connections with organized crime. In 1958 they entered into a partnership in the General Development Company with Lou Chesler, a business associate of Meyer Lansky. Other investors in the land development company included two other Lansky business associates, one of whom—"Trigger Mike" Coppola—was a notorious syndicate "hit" man. The year the Mackles sold out, 1961, one of those Lansky associates was involved in the fraudulent trading of the company's stock, for which he was later convicted.

In 1958 the Ansan group "found" a buyer for five hundred

forty-seven acres of Key Biscayne. His name was Arthur Desser, a close friend of Jimmy Hoffa. That year—1958—Desser got a $5 million loan from the Teamsters which probably went to help cover the $13 million price of the Key Biscayne acquisition.

About this time the Teamsters were taking control of the Miami National Bank and within a few years Desser and the real estate company he controlled had become closely connected with the bank.

Also connected to the bank was Meyer Lansky. According to a 1959 federal indictment of Lansky and some of his associates, the Miami National Bank was used between 1963 and 1969 as a depository for skimmed and illicit funds, money which also flowed in and out of the interlocking Exchange and Investment Bank of Switzerland.

In 1959—three years after its founding—the bank's control passed to the Teamsters Central, Southwest and Southeast States Pension Fund in the form of a loan. In 1964 a loan from Lansky front-man Sam Cohen (Cohen was indicted with Lansky in 1969) retired the Teamster loan and influence. With his foot already in the door, Cohen finished taking over the bank by 1966. Over that 1956-66 period of Hoffa-Lansky control, six top executives and three other directors of the bank were subjects of government indictments.

By 1964 a company called Worldwide Realty shared three common directors with the Miami National Bank as well as some mutual large stockholders. Worldwide also took loans from the Miami National for five of its subsidiaries and owned the building in which both companies operated.

Major figures in Worldwide had conducted numerous transactions with John Lansky (Meyer's brother) and other Lansky associates, and it is the belief of some organized crime investigators that these Worldwide figures are "respectable" business associates of Lansky's.

Through a number of joint ventures Worldwide was closely connected in the early sixties with another Florida realty company—Major Realty. In 1968, when the Lansky-connected people had disappeared from control of the company, it was revealed that a director and a large stockholder (ninety-four thousand shares) in Major Realty was then-Senator George Smathers.

The worlds of Major and Worldwide Realty are marginally linked to Richard Nixon, but Nixon's links to the Lansky-related Miami National Bank are more direct.

There is, for example, a man named William Pallot, a Smathers-type Florida Democrat who was a chief executive officer and director of the Miami National Bank from 1959 to 1963. After leaving the Miami National, Pallot founded the International Bank of Miami, one of whose directors, James Angleton, is a member of the CIA. In 1968 Pallot headed the Florida State Chapter of United Citizens for Nixon/Agnew.

Furthermore, Miami National was the chief creditor in a bankruptcy case that resulted in a $3 million damage suit against Nixon and other members of his New York law firm in 1968. The suit, which is still pending, involves the Atlas Sewing Company of Miami. It alleges that Nixon and his firm negotiated a contract between Atlas and Nixon clients, the Irving Trust and Beneficial Company. According to the suit, Irving assigned $20 million in Atlas accounts to Beneficial, which in turn "skimmed $5 to $6 million."

The key figure in the case, Irwin Ray, the court-appointed trustee, got his job through the efforts of the president of the Miami National Bank. (According to the court papers, the trustee had "underworld connections.") Before bankruptcy, Atlas turned to a small New York investment firm for its underwriting, a firm whose partners have given more than twenty-five thousand dollars to Nixon's presidential campaigns.

Nixon's dealings with the Miami National Bank may also have brought him into contact with one of its directors—one James Lawrence King—for in October 1970, Nixon appointed King to be a judge in the U.S. District Court for Southern Florida. King has said he has "no comment" on Lansky's use of the Miami National.

One of King's first cases as a judge involved a suit against Bebe Rebozo's Key Biscayne Bank. It involved the passage of some stolen stock through the bank, and, according to several Miami reporters, King was in the process of quietly dismissing the case until the *Miami News* began looking into it.

Not all the Key Biscayne corporations met with success. In 1962 Worldwide Realty lost most of its Key Biscayne holdings. The Ansan group foreclosed on Worldwide's Key Biscayne acreage after Worldwide failed to meet two year's mortgage payments. The Ansan group then put an $8 million price tag on their newly repossessed parcel.

Four years later the land was still unbought. That year Bebe Rebozo founded the Cape Florida Development Company. Other founders included Donald Berg, who became company president; Francisco Saralegui, a wealthy Cuban refugee newspaper publisher; Robert Haverfield, a Florida state senator; and three others.

Largely through the efforts of Haverfield, the state of Florida decided to create a park on the southern end of Key Biscayne, to be called Cape Florida State Park. The state of Florida then forked over twenty-five thousand dollars per acre for land assessed at fifteen thousand one hundred forty-five dollars per acre. Ansan and company received at least a million dollars more than their $8 million asking price, even though the land had gone unbought for four years. In keeping with their history of sound government relations, the Ansan principals and their lawyers "persuaded" Dade County officials to forgo taxes during the option period of the sale in return for the granting of permission for public use of some of the property.

Thus twenty years after its northern end became a park through a deal tainted by conflict of interest, Key Biscayne's southern end also became a public park in a similar manner. Both deals involved Ed Ball, and both centered on land prices considerably out of line with their assessed value. While the causeway-park swap in the forties benefited corrupt Cuban figures working within organized crime, the mid-sixties creation of the Cape Florida park benefited the organized-crime-tainted Ansan group, Worldwide Realty, and Bebe Rebozo's Cape Florida Development Company, which in 1966—the year the park was created—paid a million dollars to Worldwide for one hundred prime waterfront lots adjacent to the park.

For a short time Rebozo's development company claimed it was having trouble selling its high-priced lots. But in 1967 Rebozo brought in Richard Nixon for a promotional photo and sales picked up quickly. In return Nixon got two lots at a "substantial discount." In the usual care-and-feeding tradition, Nixon was allowed to pay a little more than twenty-five thousand dollars each for two lots worth seventy-five thousand dollars total at the time, and now worth well over a hundred thousand dollars.

Mysteriously, the yet-to-be president recorded only one of his new lots at the Dade County Courthouse. The other lot went unrecorded for four years—until June 1971. The reason Nixon concealed his ownership of the lot for those four years was that there were two previous mortgages on the Cape Florida development held by Arthur Desser, who was associated with Lansky and Jimmy Hoffa through the mob-controlled Miami National Bank. The first of these mortgages was satisfied in February 1971, and the second in March 1971. Nixon waited until both mortgages were satisfied before he recorded his lot, thereby avoiding the stigma of a connection with Desser.

Nixon made another strange land purchase in Cape Florida about this time. He bought George Smathers's house (next door to Rebozo's) in 1968 for one hundred twenty-five thousand dollars. This would seem fair enough, but the very next year, 1969, the house was assessed at a value of only seventy-six thousand dollars—just 60 percent of the president's buying price.

With Nixon's promotional photograph for Rebozo's development company and the establishment a year later of the Florida White House, the Nixonization of Key Biscayne was in full bloom.

The story of Key Biscayne is complex and shrouded in mystery, but there are some indisputable truths and some irrepressible suspicions.

Clearly, Nixon left one of his Cape Florida lots—on which the Florida White House now sits—unrecorded for four years because of the taint of a financial connection with Arthur Desser. He was therefore aware of Desser's connections with Mafia kingpin Lansky, and he did not want the public to know that the president would become involved with such a man. The unrecorded lot is a good example of Nixon's attempts to cover his tracks whenever there is a threat of major scandal.

One wonders whether this explains why he concealed his employment with the OPA for so many years, or why the crucial court file in the Atlanta Records Center is so mysteriously unavailable.

One also wonders about Don Berg, the man who sold Nixon his lots. The Secret Service found Berg's "background" questionable enough to tell the president to stop eating at his Key Biscayne restaurant. Berg told *Newsday* that he is "well acquainted" with Lou Chesler, a Mayer Lansky business associate, and once entered a deal with Chesler, only to have it collapse because a third party died. Chesler then went ahead with the deal by enlisting the aid of another Cape Floridian, whose lot bordered Nixon's.

Berg's relationship with organized crime is of particular interest in light of the fact that the two previous owners of his subdivision in the previous twenty years—the Ansan group and Worldwide Realty—both have significant links with organized crime.

Now Nixon's island paradise seems more like a closed compound of corruption than the innocent resort home of an elected official. With the two ends of the island "reserved" as parks, the central district of homes is reserved for an elite group at least a few of whom reserved their places in highly questionable fashion. If you talk to enough residents of Key Biscayne you realize how tight the island is, how everybody knows what everybody else is up to.

For example, one local resident recounted for me in a long-winded forty-five minute rap, the history of just about every parcel of land in the island. Large pieces of land change hands rarely, rarer still among strangers.

For Richard Nixon, like most of the other Key Biscayne property owners, life on the island is fat and secure. The only bank is owned by the president's closest friend, Rebozo. The largest landowners are also good friends: for example, Harold Geneen, president of ITT and recent purchaser of six new lots. The ITT conglomerate itself also became an official Nixon neighbor recently, purchasing the last large (thirty-eight acre) tract of undeveloped land there.

The rootless Mr. Nixon seems to have found a fitting home on Key Biscayne.

Nixon's Cape Florida deal wasn't his first private Floridian land venture, nor was it the first one cloaked in secrecy.

Sometime after his defeat in the 1962 California guberna-torial election, Richard Nixon began acquiring land in Fisher Island, Inc., a secretive investment syndicate headed by Bebe Rebozo, whose sole holding was Fisher Island, an undeveloped two-hundred-twenty-acre island just off the southern tip of Miami Beach. The dealings of Fisher Island Inc. are so secretive that there is no definite date as to when Mr. Nixon began buy-ing it. The common guess is 1962, but the authors of *American Melodrama* put the date at 1960.

Nixon's Fisher Island investment was apparently intended to be a long-range one. Seemingly out of politics, Mr. Nixon could afford to do a little wheeling and dealing, particularly as he had left the vice-presidency with only forty-nine thousand dollars.

As Nixon began to re-enter the national political scene in the late sixties, discontent broke out in the ranks of Nixon's fellow investors, most of whom were close associates of Smathers and Rebozo. By 1968 Nixon's presence in the syndicate and the exact circumstances surrounding his investments became a liability. One investor: Hoke T. Maroon, told friends: "I wanted Nixon out. How can you pull a political deal when the president of the United States is your partner? Everyone in the world is looking over your shoulder."

Immediately after becoming president, Nixon maintained he "had no plans to sell the stock." But soon thereafter leaks —presumably from fellow investors—found their way into the *Miami News*. By February 1969, Nixon sold his 185,291 shares in the Fisher Island venture. (It is said that despite stockholder resistance Nixon was paid two dollars per share, double his money. The exact circumstances of Nixon's "investment" and "return" in Fisher Island remain a mystery.)

The political deal that Hoke Maroon complained Nixon's presence would hamper involved the building of a causeway linking Fisher Island to the Florida mainland, a maneuver requiring taxpayer assistance, and one that would provide a spectacular increase in the value of the real estate.

Interest in the causeway was intensified when Rebozo acquired most of the island in 1957, and with the progress of his plans for a resort-style development there. Testimony in the Bobby Baker hearings a few years later disclosed that Baker's business associates, the Texas Murchisons, were involved in the proposed building of that causeway.

Clint and John Murchison are Texas multi-millionaires who multiplied their father's $300 million fortune in oil through construction, recreational concerns like the Dallas Cowboys, and publishing, among other ventures. The Murchisons were close friends of Lyndon Johnson and were featured guests at John Connally's Texas barbeque, held in the summer of 1972 for Nixon's benefit.

A Murchison associate named Thomas Webb testified at the Baker hearings that "we had been working on it [the causeway] for over a year. The purpose of the meetings [Webb's meetings with Murchison and others in the winter of 1959] there was with the city council and county commissioners whom we had been working with for quite a while . . . [sic] "

Fisher Island Inc. had a lot of good friends in government to help swing the deal. Members of Miami city council included Robert Haverfield, later a Rebozo business partner and principal in the Key Biscayne deals, and Grant Stockdale, an aide to George Smathers. The city manager was Ira Willard, who later became the first president of Rebozo's Key Biscayne Bank.

In his testimony, Webb identified a man named Leonard Bursten as "one of the people we were working with on this causeway."

Bursten's reputation as a man with "important connections" made him a logical choice for behind-the-scenes negotiating. Bursten was a Milwaukee attorney who was brought to Washington by Joe McCarthy to work on McCarthy's Senate Investigating Committee. The year 1959 was an exciting one for him, for while he was trying to swing the Fisher Island causeway deal he also concocted a scheme to get the ousted Cuban dictator Batista asylum in the United States and at the same time managed to get involved in an income tax evasion case which later led to his conviction. Bursten eventually gave up on the causeway, although Rebozo and his friends are still trying.

Bursten is also close friends with Jimmy Hoffa and helped found the Miami National Bank, which Hoffa and the Teamsters controlled while Bursten was a director. Bursten was indicted twice in 1972 in connection with the scandal-ridden Teamster-financed Beverly Ridge Estates project in Los Angeles.

The Beverly Ridge project is not far from another Teamster-financed project, the Truesdale Estates in Beverly Hills. This choice development, built by the Murchisons, was where Nixon established his California residence in 1961. Bursten thought enough of Nixon to distribute anti-Catholic literature in Nixon's 1960 campaign against John Kennedy.

While Bursten has strong links to the Fisher Island project and to the Teamster's dealings in the Miami National Bank and elsewhere, a man named Nathan Ratner has even closer links to both Nixon and organized crime.

The son of a prominent Cleveland builder, Ratner arranged

and brokered the sale of Fisher Island to Rebozo. He handled plans for its development, owned land with Nixon, and helped Nixon and Rebozo distribute pieces of Fisher Island as favors to friends. Ratner was also a broker for Keyes Realty, which was deeply involved in Key Biscayne land, and a former president of the Keyes Company was also an investor in the Fisher Island project.

But it is Ratner's holding of 3,140 shares in the Bank of Miami Beach that is most interesting.

The Bank of Miami Beach was organized in 1955 to service organized crime based in the Havana gambling empire. Its incorporation papers were drawn up in Havana the same year that Casino Internacional opened there under the guidance of the Cleveland syndicate. The stock in the casino was transferred to Mohawk Securities Corporation, a Panamanian company. Mohawk then opened an account at the Bank of Miami Beach, and thereafter cash from Havana and skimmed funds from the Las Vegas syndicate flowed into the account. There is considerable evidence that checks were drawn on Mohawk's account at the Bank of Miami Beach as a device for laundering black money and distributing it to syndicate members.

Meyer Lansky used the bank as a vehicle for funds from his Havana Riviera operations, among other things. On one occasion Meyer's brother Jake was searched by customs officials on returning to Miami from Cuba. Apparently Jake was on his way to make another deposit at the Bank of Miami Beach, as he was carrying fifty thousand dollars in checks.

Sworn testimony before the 1967 Royal Commission of Inquiry in the Bahamas showed that Lansky's Bahamian casinos continued to use the Bank of Miami Beach. For example, the Commission disclosed one case where over five hundred thousand dollars in checks laundered through the bank by Lansky couriers in 1964 turned up with different names on them after they were cashed.

By 1963 the bank had changed hands, but the new "owners" continued the bank's fine service to organized crime. An FBI memo dated July 29, 1964 details a story of Boston Mafia gangsters bringing "hot money" to the bank and arranging "loans" in return. In reality it was their own money they were getting back, but the "loans" made it possible for them to explain the possession of extra cash.

The Bank of Miami Beach had a fraternal relationship with another syndicate-favored Miami bank, the aforementioned Miami National Bank. Not only have the banks shared many of the same directors and stockholders, but one person has served as chairman of both banks simultaneously.

In 1965 Ratner, already a longstanding large stockholder, tried unsuccessfully to gain control of the Bank of Miami Beach. Like most mob-related ventures, the Bank of Miami Beach was a tight operation with very few stockholders. It would be difficult to believe that Ratner was unaware of, if not involved in, the activities of the bank in which he held so much stock and which he wanted to control.

In keeping with the traditions of Nixon business associates, Ratner has refused to comment on his role in the Bank of Miami Beach.

Organized Crime: The Ghost in the Machine

The predominant characteristic of organized crime today is its shift from the crimes of violence to the business of crime. Images of rough-looking thugs toting machineguns in their suitcases have been replaced by pin-striped executives carrying attaché cases stuffed with thousand dollar bills. A 1971 IRS report disclosed that fully 85 percent of the nation's gangsters have investments in legitimate businesses.

Although there may have been a reduction in violence, there has not been a reduction in crime.

Ralph Salerno, an expert on organized crime, explains that "throughout the progression from simple extortion and mayhem to the penetration and control of sophisticated larger businesses, there is never an abandonment of illegal enterprises. In organized crime a man never goes completely 'legit,' though he may well move out of direct operation of illegal business."

Thus today, the underworld consists of a shadowy empire held together by mutual arrangements, influence, and money. It uses various fronts—dummy corporations, attorneys, and accountants—to protect itself in a maze of paperwork. This network has led to the creation of the most successful business of all: with yearly revenues of $50 billion, organized crime takes in about two times as much money as General Motors.

With its economic power, international organization, and invisibility, organized crime is in business with everybody. Recent revelations have shown its involvement with the CIA in heroin traffic in Southeast Asia, with high supermarket prices in New York City, and with the billion-dollar frauds in U.S. and South Vietnamese military PXs and black market currency manipulations.

Since World War II, organized crime has been one step ahead of the major population shifts in the United States. Postwar Americans flocked to the sun, making California, Arizona, Nevada, Texas, and Florida the five fastest-growing states during the last twenty years. Accompanying these changes in population patterns were qualitative shifts in the economy. A decline in real wealth (i.e., equipment and raw materials) was paralleled by an increase in "paper" capital (stocks and finance). Organized crime again has been one step ahead, diversifying its products from the "vices" of gambling, liquor, and narcotics to the "services" of hotels, restaurants, insurance, real estate, and entertainment. The creation of a huge leisure industry—rooted in travel, recreation, entertainment, and escape—has further helped expand the coffers of organized crime.

As Donald Cressey, consultant to the presidential commission on violence, concluded, "The penetration of business and government by organized crime has been so complete that it is no longer possible to differentiate 'underworld' gangsters from 'upper-world' businessmen and government officials."

During Nixon's years in office the underworld empire in the United States has prospered almost unrestricted by the federal government. From its base in the gigantic resources of heroin traffic, gambling, prostitution, "protection," and a host of other enterprises of violence against society, organized crime has moved like a bulldozer into the world of legal, "respectable" business.

Every link between Richard Nixon and organized crime, however marginal, is of significance, if for no other reason because he is president. And there are people all over America, from government intelligence agents to hotel waiters, who have Nixon stories to tell. He covers his tracks well, but not well enough.

The full extent of Nixon's involvement with organized crime is just beginning to surface. The evidence in this article is merely the tip of a dirty iceberg that will slowly become visible over the coming years.

The milieu in which he has traveled for three decades, and in which so many of his friends, associates, and appointees have been related to the mob, throw a long and permanent shadow over everything Richard Nixon the "public servant" has ever said, and over everything his political life has ever meant.

For in light of his career, both past and present, Richard M. Nixon seems to be the factual embodiment of Ralph Salerno's prediction that organized crime would someday put its own man in the White House.

Yankees and Cowboys —
the World Behind Watergate

Kirkpatrick Sale

The bedfellows politics makes are never strange; it only seems that way to those who have not watched the courtship. In Richard Nixon's case, notwithstanding his presence in national politics for the last twenty-five years, those courtships have remained remarkably unexamined—or, when examined, remarkably misunderstood—and as a result the bedfellows he has acquired have remained unusually obscure both to the public and to the political pundits who are supposed to conjure with such things. Certain obvious relationships, to be sure, have been given attention—the back-scratching of Nixon and his old friend and Pepsico chairman Donald Kendall, for example, the latest evidence of which is Washington's gift of the Soviet soft-drink franchise to Pepsi-Cola. But the wider pattern of his associations, the character of his power base, remains essentially obscure. This seems particularly dangerous in view of the evidence that these people will be influential in American government not only for the next four years but for the foreseeable future.

The original version of this essay, entitled "The World Behind Watergate," © 1973, appeared in the *New York Review of Books,* May 3, 1973. Reprinted by permission of the author.

The Nixonian bedfellows, the people whose creed the president expresses and whose interests he guards, are, to generalize, the economic sovereigns of America's Southern rim, the "sunbelt" that runs from Southern California, through Arizona and Texas, down to the Florida keys. They are, for the most part, new-money people, without the family fortunes and backgrounds of Eastern wealth (Rockefellers, DuPonts, etc.), people whose fortunes have been made only in the postwar decades, mostly in new industries such as aerospace and defense contracting in oil, natural gas, and allied businesses, usually domestic rather than international, and in real-estate operations during the postwar sunbelt population boom.

They are "self-made" men and women, in the sense that they did not generally inherit great riches (though of course in another sense they are government-made, depending, as in oil and aerospace, on large favors from Washington, but they hardly like to think of it that way), and they tend to a notable degree to be politically conservative, even retrograde, usually anti-union, antiblack, anticonsumer, and antiregulation, and quite often associated with professional "anticommunist" organizations. Whether because of the newness of their position, their frontier heritage, or their lack of old-school ties, they tend to be without particular concerns about the niceties of business ethics and morals, and therefore to be connected more than earlier money would have thought wise with shady speculations, political influence-peddling, corrupt unions, and even organized crime.

The political ascendancy of these Southern-rim people—those whom Carl Oglesby once called "the Cowboys," as distinct from "the Yankees" of old Eastern money—has taken place coincidentally with their economic growth in the last generation. Their power on a state level was solidified a decade or so ago, and they made certain inroads to national influence with Johnson's assumption of the presidency in 1963.* But it was

* Johnson's assumption of power had several consequences beyond the enthronement of a man heavily in political debt to conservative Texas oil,

not until the election of Richard Nixon in 1968—and even more in his second term in which he seems far beyond mediating pressure from the press, Congress, and public—that the Southern-rim bedfellows were firmly installed in the bedrooms of political power in Washington. It is a fitting symbol of this that Nixon has established White Houses at the two extremes of the Southern rim, San Clemente and Key Biscayne.

Now it is certainly true that the Yankees retain considerable power in national politics, that the Wall Street investment houses and the family banks and the well-established holding and insurance companies still have influence throughout local and federal government. No one would want to suggest that David Rockefeller or the First National City Bank was inconsequential in guiding the affairs of state—and the important position of Henry Kissinger, a man with authentic Yankee ties (Harvard, Rockefeller Brothers Fund, Council on Foreign Relations) attests to their continuing influence. What is important to note, however, is the *relative* decline of the Yankees in recent years and their relinquishment of important powers to Cowboy hands. Moreover, as the economic importance of the Southern rim has increased, New York banks and investment houses (notably Loeb Rhoades and Lehman Brothers) have bought into its businesses, with the result that to a greater extent than before the interests and wishes of the Cowboys have become of serious concern to the moguls of Wall Street.

One rough measure of the political ascendancy of the Cowboys is the number of them who actually occupy high positions in Washington. Of the four members of what Nixon liked to call his "super-super cabinet," three of them—the three with the highest authority in domestic affairs (the fourth being Kissinger)—were from the Southern rim: Roy Ash (California: millionaire defense contractor), John Ehrlichman (California,

---

among them the squelching of the Bobby Baker and TFX-Convair (Dallas) investigations, the exercise of American pressure to forestall a threatened nationalization of American oil interests in Argentina, and the reversal of Kennedy's announced plans to begin withdrawing troops from Vietnam.

out of Seattle: lawyer, politico), and Bob Haldeman (California: PR man). On the cabinet level there were Anne Armstrong (Texas: Republican politico), Claude Brinegar (California: Union Oil executive), Frederick Dent (South Carolina: textile millionaire), Richard Kleindienst (Arizona: Goldwater crony), and Caspar Weinberger (California: Republican politico and ex-Reagan aide).

Of the five Nixon nominees to the Supreme Court, three (Rehnquist, Carswell, and Haynesworth) were wool-died Southern-rim conservatives and one (Powell) was a right-wing Virginian who was also a director of oil and gas corporations. The key appointments to the increasingly powerful Republican National Committee have all been from the Southern-rim—co-chairpersons George Bush (Texas: oil company co-founder) and Janet Johnson (California: rancher) and general counsel Harry Dent (South Carolina: lawyer, ex-GOP state head). The rim influence is here so strong that there have even been published complaints from Midwestern Republicans about a "Southern Mafia."

And peppered throughout the government are such key Cowboys as press secretary Ronald Ziegler (California: public relations), Frederic Malek, second-in-command of the budget (South Carolina: tool-manufacturing millionaire), Commissioner of Education John Ottina (California: defense industry consultant), Director of Communications Herbert Klein (California: Copley Press executive), Deputy Secretary of Defense William Clements (Texas: oil millionaire), Assistant Agriculture Secretary Robert Long (California: Bank of America executive), Undersecretary of State William Casey (a New Yorker, but director and counsel of a Southern-rim agribusiness corporation). . . . And on and on, scores more throughout the top levels of the administration, not even balanced this term by very many liberals and Easterners.

A second measure of Cowboy penetration is their preponderance among Nixon's major financial supporters. Though the loopholed campaign-spending laws permit only partial identification of the top money men, it seems clear at least that the chief sources of Nixon's campaign finances—and therefore presumably the people whose interests the president will try to keep dominant—are independent oil producers, defense contractors, right-wing unions, rich conservative businessmen, and various Southern-rim manufacturers. This does not mean, of course, that the more traditional sources of Republican money, such as the old-money families and Yankees new and old throughout the financial world, have been thoroughly displaced or no longer make big contributions, but only that their position is being steadily narrowed and their importance therefore steadily decreased.

Oil money, for example, has always found its way into politics, as much from the old corporations with chiefly international interests as from the new independents who have sprung up along the Southern rim. But it has been the latter who have been most important in Nixon's career, from such supporters as Union Oil, Superior Oil, and Texas ultraconservative H. L. Hunt, who helped finance his early campaigns, through California right-winger Henry Salvatori, the Texas Murchison family, and at least a third of the backers in the 1952 "slush fund." In this last campaign there were some large contributions from old oil—Richard Mellon Scaife (Gulf Oil, among other interests) gave a million dollars, the Phipps family (Texaco among others) gave at least fifty-five thousand—but the striking fact is the number of domestic oil donors, rimsters or with rim interests, people like Kent Smith (Lubrizol, $244,000), Francis Cappeart (Southern oil and agribusiness, $174,000), John Paul Getty (Getty Oil, $97,000), John J. Shaheen (Shaheen Natural Resources, $100,000), Elisha Walker (Petroleum Corporation of America, $100,000), Max Fisher (Marathon Oil, $60,000), the O'Connor family (Texas Oil, $60,000), and the Osea Wyatt family (Coastal States Gas, $41,000).*

---

* These figures are from the Citizens Research Foundation of Princeton, New Jersey, a group that tries to keep track of all the sources of campaign

Other major sources of support in the 1972 campaign can be traced, too, and they follow the same general pattern: some sizable donors from the old-money families and new-money Easterners, but surprising strength from the Southern rim. Among the largest donors with defense interests last year were Yankees like Arthur Watson (IBM, $303,000) and Saul Steinberg (Leasco, $250,000), but they were matched by the rimsters, people like Charles and Sam Wyly (Dallas computer company, $172,000), Thomas Marquez (Electronic Data Systems, Dallas, $88,000), Howard Hughes (Hughes Tool, etc., Houston, $100,000), Ling-Temco-Vought (Texas, $60,000), and Litton Industries ($18,000).

Southern-rim new-money businessmen included Walter T. Duncan (Texas, real estate, $305,000), Sam Schulman (California, National General conglomerate, $257,000), John and Charles Williams (Oklahoma manufacturers, $98,000), M. B. Seretean and Eugene Barwick (Southern textile manufacturers, $200,000), Anthony Rossi (Florida, Tropicana, $100,000), C. Arnholt Smith (California financier, $50,000), and L. B. Maytag (Florida, National Airlines, $50,000). Donors among the major organizations include three with extensive rim contracts, the Texas-based Associated Milk Producers ($782,000), and two right-wing unions, the Seafarers (with direct oil and agribusiness links, $100,000) and the Teamsters (with heavy investments from Southern California and Las Vegas to Miami, an estimated $100,000).

Perhaps an even more revealing measure of the rimsters' influence is their dominance of the Nixon inner circle. Now their numbers are hardly legion, because this president is an essentially friendless man, a distrustful person with few close cronies,

---

money. They are generally only estimates and often represent only a small part of what was actually given. Other major oil donors and fundraisers on the CRF lists include Arthur E. Johnson (Midwest Oil), Thomas Pappas (Esso-Pappas), the Pew family (Sun Oil), William Liedtke (Pennzoil), J. A. Vickers (Vickers Petroleum), and H. W. McCollum, Philip Kramer, and J. D. Callender (Amerada Hess).

but the few that exist are, almost to a man (no women), from the sunbelt states. The visible exceptions are Donald Kendall and former Secretary of State William Rogers, both solid Easterners, and even they are new-money, up-from-poverty types.

The rest are people like Southern California businessmen Jack Drown, Ray Arbuthnot and C. Arnholt Smith, California politician Robert Finch (a friend, apparently, even after his fall from office), and four men who seem to be closest of all to the president: Herbert Kalmbach, a rich Los Angeles lawyer who is the president's personal counsel and was his chief fundraiser during 1971; John Connally, the oil-tied Texas politician who is Nixon's financial guru and reportedly his choice as successor; Murray Chotiner, the California lawyer who was with Nixon from the beginning; and Bebe Rebozo, the Florida millionaire who is reckoned to be the most intimate of all with the president. All of these are fairly typical Southern rimsters, all are new-money people, all are well-off, and all of them (except maybe Finch) are politically conservative. Most disturbing of all, several of these people have had the taint, and sometimes the full stigma, of scandal around them.

This last attribute deserves somewhat more attention, for it is inevitably one of the most striking features of the political Cowboys and one with very serious implications for our national life. Without going into a full portrait of the noisome character of so much of the Southern rim—home of well-established organized-crime centers in such places as Las Vegas, New Orleans, and Miami, the last having lately become a veritable Marseille—one can still note that many of Nixon's closest friends from this region are, to a remarkable and unhealthy degree, guilty of improprieties in business, a certain disregard for public trust, a general lack of ethical sophistication, or in some cases direct association with criminal figures. To cite a few examples:

Herbert Kalmbach has been identified as one of the five people in charge of funds for the million-dollar Republican operation to sabotage the Democratic campaign last year, and according to the FBI he personally gave Republican funds to Donald Segretti, the California lawyer who by all accounts (none denied) was the West Coast leader of that operation; Kalmbach has also been identified in sworn court papers as the strong-man in the Republicans' efforts to squeeze some seven hundred thousand dollars out of the large milk producers in return for a government-approved price raise.

Connally, whose service on behalf of rich Texas oilmen has been well documented, was attorney for Texas millionaire Sid Richardson when he engineered a million-dollar payment to Texas oilman Robert Anderson in the mid-fifties;* and while governor of Texas he trickily denied the fact that he had received at least $225,000 from the multimillion-dollar Richardson estate, a payment that was possibly in violation of the Texas constitution.

Chotiner has also had a career of slimy dealings ever since he first invented the Pink-Lady attack on Helen Gahagan Douglas: between 1949 and 1952 he handled some two hundred twenty-one gambler-bookmaker cases in Los Angeles; he was instrumental in getting a deportation order rescinded for Philadelphia mobster Marco Reginelli in the 1950s; in 1956 the McClellan Senate committee investigated his role as attorney for a convicted clothing racketeer and exposed (but did not fully explore) his influence-peddling activities in Washington; and most recently he acknowledged in court papers his own role in the milk scandal by admitting he intervened with Ehrlichman and others in the White House to get the price increase for the milk producers and subsequently arranged the channeling of their contributions to the Nixon campaign.

Whatever else you want to say about these presidential pals, they hardly seem to be the kind that Billy Graham, let's say,

---

* Robert Sherrill, *The Accidental President* (New York: Pyramid, 1968), pp. 122, 236. The payment was to compensate Anderson for an anticipated salary cut he would take as vice president on the 1956 ticket, for which his Texas oil friends were then pushing.

should approve of.

Rebozo, the inscrutable man who is closest of all to Nixon—the latest example of his intimacy being the donation of his hundred-thousand-dollar Bethesda home to Julie Nixon Eisenhower—deserves a somewhat closer examination here, for in some ways he personifies the Cowboy type.* Rebozo, Cuban-born of American parents, grew up in relative poverty, and at the start of World War II he was a gas-station operator in Florida. With the wartime tire shortage Rebozo got it into his head to expand his properties and start a recapping business, so he got a loan from a friend who happened to be on the local OPA tire board (a clear conflict of interest) and before long was the largest recapper in Florida. In 1951, he met Richard Nixon on one of the latter's trips to Miami and the two seem to have hit it off: both the same age, both quiet, withdrawn, and humorless, both aggressive success-hunters, both part of the new Southern-rim milieu.

Rebozo later expanded into land deals and in the early 1960s established the Key Biscayne Bank, of which he is president and whose first savings-account customer was Nixon. This bank in 1968 was the repository of stolen stocks, originally taken and channeled to the bank by organized crime sources. Rebozo clearly suspected there was something dubious about these

---

* Rebozo's career has been examined in at least three recent studies which also spell out other unsavory aspects of those in the Nixon circle and cast doubt upon the president's own behavior. *Newsday* published a series of articles on Nixon's Florida connections in the fall of 1971 (available as a "Special Report" from *Newsday,* 550 Stewart Avenue, Garden City, New York 11530); a new leftish magazine called *Sundance* (now defunct) ran an article by journalist Jeff Gerth (excerpted in this volume) in its issue of November-December 1972; and the North American Congress on Latin America (Box 57, Cathedral Station, New York, New York 10025) published a booklet on Nixon's links to organized crime and the Watergate affair in October 1972. In constructing this portrait of Rebozo, as in other sections in this article, I have also used the copious and careful researches of Peter Dale Scott.

stocks (he even told an FBI agent that he had called up Nixon's brother Donald to check on their validity), but he subsequently sold them for cash, even after an insurance company circular was mailed out to every bank listing them as stolen. Small wonder that the bank was thereupon sued by the company which had insured those stocks. (The case was eventually tried before a Nixon-appointed federal judge, James Lawrence King, who himself had some interesting banking experience as a director in 1964 of the Miami National Bank, cited by the *New York Times* [December 1, 1969] as a conduit for the Meyer Lansky syndicate's "shady money" from 1963 to 1967. King decided against the insurance company, but the case is now being appealed to a higher court.)

At about the same time as the stolen stocks episode came the shopping-center deal. Rebozo, by now a very rich man, still managed to get a loan out of the federal Small Business Administration—one of five which he somehow was lucky enough to secure in the 1960s, perhaps because of his friendship with ex-Senator George Smathers (who had been on the Senate Small Business Committee and who wrote the SBA to help Rebozo get another loan), or perhaps because the chief Miami officer of the SBA also happened to be a close friend of Rebozo's and a stockholder in his bank. This, coupled with the fact that Rebozo never fully disclosed his business dealings in making applications to the SBA, led *Newsday* in a prominent editorial, to denounce the SBA for "wheeling and dealing ... on Rebozo's behalf," and it led Representative Wright Patman to accuse the SBA publicly of wrongdoing in making Rebozo a "preferred customer."

With one of the SBA grants Rebozo proceeded to build an elaborate shopping center, to be leased to members of the right-wing Cuban exile community, and he let out the contracting bid for that to one "Big Al" Polizzi, a convicted black marketeer and a man named by the Federal Bureau of Narcotics as "one of the most influential members of the underworld in the United States."

Rather unsavory, all that, if not precisely criminal, and a rather odd career for an intimate of our moralistic president. But Nixon seems not to mind. In fact he has even gone in with Rebozo on at least one of his deals, a Florida real-estate venture called Fisher's Island, Inc., in which Nixon invested some $185,891 around 1962, and which he sold for exactly twice the value, $371,782, in 1969. It seems to have been a peculiarly shrewd deal, since the going rate for Fisher's Island stock had not in fact increased by a penny during those years and certainly hadn't doubled for anyone else—but happily for the stockholders, Nixon shortly thereafter signed a bill paving the way for $7 million worth of federal funds for the improvement of the Port of Miami, in which Fisher's Island just happens to be located. In any case, that's small enough potatoes for a man in Nixon's position, and seems to reflect the fact that, no matter how many rich wheeler-dealers he has around him, Nixon himself is not out to make a vast personal fortune as his predecessor did.

But the unsavoriness surrounding Bebe Rebozo does not stop there. For in the mid-1960s Rebozo was also a partner in a Florida real-estate company with one Donald Berg, an acquaintance of Nixon's and the man from whom Nixon bought property in Key Biscayne less than a mile from the Florida White House. This same Donald Berg, who has been linked with at least one associate of mobster Meyer Lansky, has a background so questionable that after Nixon became president the Secret Service asked him to stop eating at Berg's Key Biscayne restaurant. Finally, according to Jack Anderson, Rebozo was "involved" in some of the real-estate deals of Bernard Barker—the former CIA operative who was the convicted payoff man for the Watergate operation in 1972.*

It is not surprising that *Newsday* concluded: "The deals made by Bebe Rebozo . . . have tarnished the Presidency."

Mention of Bernard Barker brings up the Watergate scandal,

---

* See Jack Anderson's Washington column for weekly newspapers, United Features Syndicate, June 26, 1972.

perhaps even more interesting because it is so complicated and revealing of the interlocking relations among the Southern rim. We are far from knowing all the details as yet, but an examination of the people known to have been involved does provide a clear window on the Nixon milieu.

Watergate, and at least some of the other operations against the Democrats and radical groups in 1972, was paid for by Cowboy money. Most of it came from Texas oil, channeled through Nixon fund-raiser Robert Allen (Gulf Resources), "laundered" in a Mexican bank, and then carried to Republican finance chairman Maurice Stans by an executive of Pennzoil. The rest came from a Minneapolis "soybean king," Dwayne Andreas, with a home and investments in Florida and ties to Southern money, and was delivered to Stans by a crony of Andreas's with Florida investments of his own.* The money stayed for a time in Stans's safe and then was deposited in a

---

* To get an idea of how complicated Southern-rim contacts can be, try this. Andreas's crony, Kenneth Dahlberg, a Nixon fundraiser, was also a director of a Florida bank whose co-chairman was a major stockholder in an investment group called Penphil and who has benefited enormously from Penphil's favors. Penphil has since been accused by a congressional committee of helping to bankrupt the Penn Central Railroad, and two of its organizers and one of its key shareholders have been indicted for criminal conspiracy in manipulating more than $85 million of Penn Central investments for their own personal profit. (*New York Times*, January 5, 1972)

Among Penphil's major investments were a Florida gas company, two Florida banks, and a Dallas investment corporation, which also owned a California real-estate operation—a rather neat sweep of the Southern rim. This last outfit, Macco Corporation, had—are you ready?—Herbert Kalmbach as its vice president, and Maurice Stans as an investor with stock options that turned out to be worth $570,000. How's that for full circle? (The Penphil story is told in full in Joseph R. Daughen and Peter Binzen, *The Wreck of the Penn Central* [Little, Brown, 1971], pp. 148-175. For the role of the congressional committee, see House Committee on Banking and Currency, *The Penn Central Failure and the Role of Financial Institutions*, Staff Report, January 3, 1972.)

Miami bank for Bernard Barker, Rebozo's business associate, a man who had worked for the CIA, had been paymaster of the Bay of Pigs operation, was close to the anti-Castro, pro-Batista Cuban community in Miami, and masterminded at least three forays by Cuban emigrés to attack antiwar protestors in Washington in the spring of 1972.

Barker was paymaster this time around, too, and personally recruited three others, all of whom subsequently pleaded guilty at the Watergate trial: Eugenio Martinez, another old CIA operative and a real-estate business partner of Barker's, and also vice president of another real-estate firm with which both Nixon and Rebozo have done business; Frank Sturgis, a CIA operative, who lost his citizenship at one time for his Caribbean gunrunning activities (first for Castro in 1958, then against him in 1962), and organizer of a "Cubans for Nixon" demonstration at Miami Beach last year;* and Virgilio Gonzalez, also a CIA operative in on the Bay of Pigs, and a member of a right-wing anti-Castro organization run by the same people who ran the "Cubans for Nixon" operation both in 1968 and in 1972.

These four men were guided in their operations by at least three others with close connections to the Nixon inner circle, all of whom have been convicted for their part in Watergate: Gordon Liddy, a former FBI agent who had worked on espionage matters in the White House under Ehrlichman, who was assigned by the White House counsel John Dean to Nixon's Committee to Re-Elect the President, and who thereupon, according to trial testimony, set up the Republican sabotage campaign;

---

* Senate Committee of the Judiciary, *Communist Threat to the United States through the Caribbean*. Hearings, 1965, pp. 918-920, 946, 951, 963-964; *New York Times,* June 28, 1972; NACLA, op. cit., p. 24; *Washington Post,* June 18, 1972. Sturgis (then using the name Fiorini) was also involved in a scheme—aborted by the Miami police—to supply arms for a Nicaragua rebellion in 1959, using planes bought in his name originally for Castro (Senate Hearings, pp. 963-964); that same year he also flew a plane over Havana to drop anti-Castro leaflets, provoking a major diplomatic incident (*New York Times,* October 3, 1959, p. 12).

James McCord, a twenty-year CIA agent with extensive contacts among the anti-Castro community, who was "security coordinator" for CREEP and who says that Dean cleared him for the job; and Howard Hunt, another career CIA agent (chief operations officer for the Bay of Pigs) and former White House consultant, who became a CREEP operative in 1971. Having spooks right in the White House seems bad enough, but the sorry trail goes on—in fact goes on for two more steps.

The first step involves at least three other men besides Dean who were White House aides to Nixon: Charles Colson, Hunt's supervisor at the White House and head of a White House anti-Democrat committee known as the "attack group"; Gordon Strachan, a Haldeman assistant who (according to an FBI file) was the chief link to the reported California saboteur, Donald Segretti and according to the *New York Times* was the White House contact for the Watergate people; and Dwight Chapin, another White House Californian and Haldeman aide who, according to L. Patrick Gray III, transmitted funds to his old college friend Segretti, mostly through—here he is again—Herbert Kalmbach. (In the hearsay testimony of McCord to the Senate Watergate Committee Haldeman himself is said to have known "what was going on" at CREEP.)

The second step leads to two men close to Nixon, personally and professionally, CREEP treasurer Stans and CREEP chairman John Mitchell. Though things get pretty shadowy at this point—partly because Nixon's FBI hasn't investigated much here—it seems obvious that both men condoned the anti-Democratic operations, and trial testimony indicates that both men approved specific payments to spymaster Liddy out of Stans's own office safe. In addition, Mitchell as CREEP chairman was so implicated in the scandal—not least by his loquacious wife, who complained of John's "dirty things"—that he resigned his CREEP position in July; it has since emerged that he met daily with McCord while running CREEP and according to McCord was the "overall boss" of the operation.

Stans, who stayed on, has since been shown to be directly

involved in at least one other piece of chicanery having to do with a secret two-hundred-thousand-dollar campaign gift he accepted in cash from Arthur Vesco of Investors Overseas Service (heavily invested, incidentally, in the Bahamas), a man then (and now) being sued by the SEC for having "spirited away" some $224 million from four mutual funds.

There can be little doubt finally that the entire sabotage campaign was at least tacitly approved, if not actually orchestrated, by the president himself—a conclusion which subsequent presidential actions seem only to confirm, from the hasty attempt at a "no-one-was-involved" cover-up to the testy erection of "executive privilege" barriers. And so there it is: from the top level of the government, through two of Nixon's closest advisers and the "California Mafia" in the White House, through CIA career men and right-wing Miami exiles, down to Florida businessmen and Texas oil millionaires. This is the world the of thirty-seventh president.

Maybe Nixon's Quaker brethren were right all along. One leader of the Whittier, California, Quaker meeting—of which Richard Nixon is still a member—has gone on record as being "quite concerned personally for the spiritual life of Richard Nixon"; the entire body once debated "the removal of Richard Nixon from membership" for his un-Quakerly prosecution of the Vietnam war; and his own mother, Hannah Milhous Nixon, a member of the committee charged with members' "spiritual health," even had serious enough doubts about her son to advise him "not to run for president."*

The purpose of examining all of this is not, of course, to sling more mud on a figure already as splattered as a happy hippopotamus, but to try to clarify the shadowy world of Nixon's bedfellows and to examine the extent of what is almost a second government, an unofficial but very important nexus of power behind the acknowledged civics-textbook institutions.

* *Minutes and Proceedings* of the 275th Session of the New York Yearly Meeting of the Religious Society of Friends, Silver Bay, New York, July 26-August 2, 1970, p. 37.

This second government, as we have begun to see, is a combination of vast and complicated interlocking forces, pulling in the CIA here and organized crime there, using politicians one time and emigré thugs the next, which seems to regard government as a tool for financial enrichment, and is to a large extent financed by and working to the benefit of the newer exploitative businesses, chiefly in the Southern rim.

Perhaps because they are new to the game, perhaps because they just feel they can get away with it, the more recent operatives of this second government seem to have been a little clumsy, inadvertently supplying several revealing glimpses into their world.*

Take the Soviet wheat deal, a bonanza for certain American shippers and agricultural middlemen, oddly enough with Republican ties. Or the cost-plus banditry which such defense giants as Litton and Ling-Temco-Vought have been allowed to get away with. Or the funny dealings of Undersecretary of State and former SEC chairman William Casey, who is one of seventeen defendants in a $2.1 million federal damage suit, charged, in the words of the court-appointed trustee, with "self-dealings among themselves for their own personal self-gain but to the utmost detriment and damage" to a Southern rim agribusiness corporation which went bankrupt a week after Casey was nominated for the SEC. Or the charges against California businessman and former Assistant Attorney General Robert Mardian, a leader of Nixon's CREEP whom McCord has linked to Watergate and whom the *New York Times* has accused of getting confidential information from the Justice Department to use in the Republican campaign.

---

* Even one of the old operators of this type has recently misstepped. ITT, which has been quietly cosy with the CIA since World War II, recented had to acknowledge its attempt to pay a million dollars to the White House and the CIA to prevent Allende's election in Chile, and this followed not long after its public embarrassment in being caught bribing and armtwisting to pave the way for its multibillion-dollar Hartford Fire Insurance merger.

Or the findings of "profound immorality and corruption" by a nonpartisan investigating committee by the Argentine legislature against Texan William Clements, now Deputy Secretary of Defense, for his very profitable role in a multimillion-dollar oil deal, a deal in which he was partners with one man who is suing him for fraudulent conspiracy and two others who have skipped the U.S. to avoid paying taxes on their profits. Or the neat little deal by which Director of the Budget Roy Ash and a partner in 1969 traded twenty-two acres of land in California with the Federal Bureau of Lands for 14,145 acres of government-owned land in Nevada, or his even neater dumping of some $2.6 million worth of Litton stock in 1970, not long before it became public that Litton's shipbuilding program was in deep trouble and the price of the stock dropped by half, the implications of which are now being looked into by the SEC. Or, . . . but just wait until tomorrow's morning paper.

All of these glimpses into the world of the second government—and they are obviously only tip-of-the-iceberg glimpses—suggest that there are important operations going on beyond the reach of ordinary citizens or of party politics, in many ways beyond even the control of Congress. And though these operations involve men at the top levels of government, they do not seem to indicate any great attachment to democratic processes, as the acknowledged campaign to sabotage one major political party bears witness, or to the constitutional exercise of foreign policy, as the acknowledged attempt to forestall Allende makes clear. Who knows what other schemes ITT may be hatching right now in some other part of the world? Who knows what other secret plans the Republican party has ready to serve its own narrow purposes?

On a somewhat less sordid level, we can also get a glimpse of how the second government operates by looking at the recent "energy crisis" furor. Now the fuel resources of this country are quite possibly being dangerously depleted—though, as James Ridgeway has pointed out, since few independent surveys have been made, it's almost impossible to tell—but the evidence indicates that the recent "crisis" was created not so much by diminishing supplies as by the oil interests, both those with international ties who wanted to increase shipments from abroad and domestic producers along the Southern rim. With winter coming on and the refineries having concentrated on gasoline rather than heating fuel over the summer, the industry launched a $3 million PR campaign to create panic buying at higher rates and force a relaxation of unwanted pollution standards ("buy dirty or freeze"). As a Ford Foundation energy consultant, S. David Freeman, recently put it, "The 'energy crisis' could well serve as a smokescreen for a massive exercise in picking the pocket of the American consumer to the tune of billions of dollars a year."

The Nixon Administration, as might be expected, considering its enormous debt to oil, bought the "energy crisis" line and pushed it upon the public with all the skill of the Petroleum Institute itself. It has made provisions in the new budget for considerable money to be given to domestic producers for "technical assistance"—especially to develop oil-from-coal extraction—and this is likely to increase in future budgets. It permitted a hefty 8 percent rise in heating-oil costs in mid-January 1973, right after price controls were lifted (thus making its ballyhooed 1 percent price freeze in March almost pointless). And it has just proposed a new energy program which, while allowing more foreign oil imports, to the benefit of the larger international concerns, is explicitly designed for the advantage of domestic producers through the imposition of a set of tariff-like "fees" on imports and the official encouragement of domestic resource development and refinery construction. Its net effect is to increase the value of in-ground resources in this country, which will be vital in case of future international troubles or eventual shortages.

More of the same governmental largesse can be expected in the future. The administration, disregarding its recent setback by the Supreme Court, will step up pressure in Congress to pass laws permitting the Alaskan pipe-line favored by oilmen and damned by environmentalists (one source has already said the latter are fighting a lost cause). It is likely to open up the Eastern seaboard's continental shelf to oil explorers and exploiters. It will press for the no-control strip-mining bill already in Congress on the grounds that quick coal-gathering, even if ecologically disastrous, is necessary to meet energy needs, a conclusion that chiefly benefits the Western and Southwestern coal operators. And it is more than likely to postpone enforcement of the federal pollution standards which, much to the dismay of the fuel corporations, were supposed to have gone into effect in 1975.

Other examples of the influence of the Southern rim, operating through this shadowy second government, are sure to emerge in the coming months: more money for defense industries, for example, following the $4.1 billion increase in the new budget even after the Vietnam cease-fire; support for road building over mass transportation, satisfying boom-area industry, right-wing construction unions, Detroit, oil interests, and the Teamsters all at once; continued encouragement for TV and radio licensing challenges from conservative Cowboys against Yankee-owned stations; expansion of American influence in the Caribbean, where so many of Nixon's friends have heavy investments (Connally, Rebozo, Robert Abplanalp, the Murchisons, etc.).

Other scandals—whether called by that name in the press or not, as with the Watergate "caper"— are also sure to follow, for it seems obvious that the kind of milieu in which the president has chosen to immerse himself will continue to produce policies self-serving at best, shady at average, and downright illegal at worst, and that at least some of this will break through to public attention. It also seems probable that the American public will continue to pay it all not much mind, despite worries from some Republicans now, and indeed that many people in the land identify themselves with—or at least dream themselves as—the new-money wheeler-dealers and seem to regard influence-peddling and back-scratching as the true stuff of the

American dream. But that's another story.

The real trouble with such oil stains, not to mention spots of fetid dirt, is that they are very hard to wash off your hands. Some liberals, clucking with glee over the new Watergate disclosures, might like to believe that the power of the Southern rimsters is going to vanish after Nixon and his immediate friends leave office. As I read it, however, this power is not likely to be washed away with a new administration, no matter what party it comes from, for the entrenched position of the Southern rim in the American economy is not likely to diminish—indeed, seems most likely to increase—in the decades to come.

There will certainly be more exploitation of its untapped energy resources, on shore and off, more dependence upon its defense expertise. There will be more reliance upon its (often) union-free labor, both in agriculture and textile manufacturing, more trade (legal and illegal) across its wide-open borders to Latin America. There will also continue to be more population growth in its undeveloped areas, automatically shifting political power (as with the House of Representatives), and more growth especially in its suburbs, where the Supreme Court's one-man-one-vote decision has so far had the largest effect and where political power has already been transferred to a considerable degree to Republicans and conservatives.

What is at work here is nothing less than Kevin Phillip's (and Richard Nixon's) Southern strategy, the creation of conservative forces within the Republican party so as to make it, for the first time since 1932, the majority party in the country. It is built on the population growth of the Southern rim, the increased *voting* population of the new-money suburbs, the galloping desertions from the ever-blackening Democratic party in the South, the rampant I'm-all-right-jackism of the established nonurban unions, and of course the financial wealth and shady dealings of the Cowboys. If that strategy is correct, and every indication from the last two elections suggests that it is, the reversal of power that it has brought is likely to last just as long as the one that brought Roosevelt to power.

Cowboys and Crooks

Steve Weissman

Who's to blame for Watergate? The President and his White House Guard? Or, as some critics claim, a bigger, badder scapegoat behind them: the nouveau riche defense contractors, oil men, land speculators, and Syndicate gangsters of the American South and Southwest—the Cowboys?

Reactionary right-wingers, fanatics, "nigger-haters," and crude capitalists lacking in the moral sensibilities of the older Eastern money, the Cowboys are supposedly the big wigs of the Southern rim—the part of America stretching from Bebe Rebozo's Key Biscayne through John Connally's Texas to Richard Nixon's San Clemente and Arnholt Smith's San Diego. They are the conspirators behind the assassination of President John F. Kennedy in the movie *Executive Action*, the money in the Military Industrial Complex, and the sponsors of the break-in at the Watergate offices of the Democratic National Committee.

As scapegoats go, the Cowboys are nearly perfect. They are defined so loosely that no one knows who's a Cowboy and who's not—from half the country to a cabal of Howard Hughes, Meyer Lansky, and the Teamsters Union. They are economic rather than "just political," which pleases the vulgar Marxists.

They are the source of all evil, which pleases the vulgar Mani-
cheans. And they are the promise that America would be okay
in the hands of some equally ill-defined Eastern Establishment,
the Yankees.

But the Cowboys don't exist, at least not as they are pictured. For all their oil wells and defense plants, the new money
of the sunbelt has never banded together to battle Wall Street,
nor have they dictated national policy—whether in Vietnam or
at Watergate. It is perhaps comforting to believe that there's a
"split in the ruling class." But American capitalists are not waging any regional economic war, and believing that they are only
blinds us to the real dangers of repression at home and intervention abroad.

The Cowboys were born in the spring of 1968, called into
being by Carl Oglesby, the past president of Students for a
Democratic Society (SDS). Oglesby wanted the new left to
form "a meaningful relationship to bewildered Kennedy liberals," arguing that the personal conflict between Robert Kennedy and Lyndon Johnson reflected a deeper, historical
cleavage. Behind Kennedy were the Ivy-aristocratic, cosmo-
politan, Europe-oriented, more dovish Eastern Establishment.
Behind Johnson, the more racist, Asia-first war hawks of the
South and Southwest. The Yankees versus the Cowboys.

Oglesby sketched out the idea in the *National Guardian* in
April, but his best evidence came that summer. As he told it, he
and a handful of other new left notables had been meeting with
the enemy—some high-powered executives from the biggest
multinational corporations, led by Eldridge Haynes, president
of Business International—a sophisticated corporate information
service. The businessmen were desperately unhappy with the
war in Vietnam, the threat of a new war against China, racism,
poverty, and the hysterical anticommunism of American foreign
policy. They feared that the national conventions of the Democratic and Republican parties would leave them with an un-
acceptable choice between the "rotten borough politics" of

Hubert Humphrey and the "obviously reactionary" stance of Richard Nixon. They favored the "more rational" candidates—Eugene McCarthy and Nelson Rockefeller.

The leftists and the businessmen continued to meet, and as the conventions approached some of the executives made "a vague proposal." They would do "whatever was possible" to help SDS stage a massive demonstration against Humphrey in Chicago and Nixon in Miami. SDS refused the offer, and left to others the leadership of the big Chicago protest. But Oglesby came away convinced that the Yankee Establishment was at war with the new-money Cowboys.

Given the probable ties between Business International and the intelligence community, Oglesby's friends could as easily have been part of a CIA conspiracy to provoke a reluctant SDS into a violent confrontation, justifying a major crackdown on the organization. But whoever the executives spoke for, they did not represent any Yankee Establishment. By summer the majority of big business leaders from all over the country were moving toward Richard Nixon, who was something less than the "obviously reactionary" anticommunist war hawk, especially in regard to China.

The businessmen backed Nixon for good reasons. From the riot in Watts in 1964 to those in Newark and Detroit in 1967, big business leaders had created summer job programs for ghetto youths, organized special funds for ghetto investment, and thrown their support to the Great Society programs of that supposed Cowboy, Lyndon Johnson. They also backed the Urban Coalition, headed by former HEW Secretary John Gardner, now of Common Cause, and committed themselves to bigger public and private spending on housing, education, and a heavily subsidized social-industrial complex. But by the middle of 1968 the same business leaders concluded that spending would spur inflation and further weaken the international standing of the dollar. Inevitably, they chose to cut back social spending, curb wages, raise unemployment, and back the presidential candidate who most favored those domestic priorities—

Richard Nixon.

According to available evidence, the top businessmen did not make their decision on the basis of Vietnam policy. Few of them liked the war or its cost; most seemed content with Johnson's March 31, 1968 decision to stop the build-up of American ground forces. But only a handful, if that, were willing to "cut and run." The vast majority wanted to get out of the war without getting out of Vietnam or compromising commitments to the more important Asian dominoes. Humphrey and Nixon agreed, and after the election Nixon committed himself to a "phased withdrawal" of ground troops over a two or three year period, abandoning hope for any "purely military victory." Hardly a Cowboy's call to arms.

Oglesby continued to talk up his Yankees and Cowboys, as did a few other writers and activists around the old SDS. But only after Watergate did the idea catch hold, as everyone from Eric Sevareid of CBS to the underground weeklies scapegoated the upstarts who had stolen the White House, while maintaining "a meaningful relationship" to Eastern good guys like Special Prosecutor Archibald Cox, Attorney General Elliot Richardson, and Connecticut Senator Lowell Weicker. Then came the clincher, an article in the *New York Review of Books* by Kirkpatrick Sale, author of *SDS.** An admirer of Carl Oglesby, Sale explicitly blamed Watergate on Nixon's Cowboy cronies.

The more general belief that America's corporate rich had seriously split over Vietnam also continued to gain ground, especially after the Moratorium against the war on October 15, 1969. The key organizers of the nationwide protest, a Boston envelope manufacturer and some former student supporters of Senator Eugene McCarthy, were themselves neither radical nor of the ruling class. They were mostly middle-class liberals with a lot of organizing skill and the gumption to demand an immediate and unconditional withdrawal from Vietnam. But as October 15 drew near, the TV networks and several national newspapers and magazines jumped on the bandwagon, along

---

* Reprinted in this volume.

with over eighty senators and congressmen, who endorsed Moratorium Day "as a positive, constructive, non-violent means of protesting the war." Wall Street joined in with its own Moratorium, attended by such notables as former Deputy Secretary of Defense Roswell Gilpatric of the Cravath, Swaine, and Moore law firm; John R. Lehman of the Lehman Brothers investment house; and Kennedy family financial adviser Andre Meyers of Lazard Frères.

The top-drawer turnout was impressive. But the Establishmentarians muted the Moratorium's demand for immediate withdrawal and dissociated themselves from the more radical November 13-15 Mobilization in Washington. Most of those in Congress fell back even further, supporting a resolution that applauded President Nixon's efforts to achieve "peace with Justice" in Vietnam—the first major congressional statement on the war since the 1964 Tonkin Gulf Resolution. The "split" seemed less about Vietnam than about the peace movement—whether to coopt it, as many of the Establishment doves wanted, or crush it, as the Nixon hawks wanted to do.

When Nixon invaded Cambodia and Ohio National Guardsmen shot four students at Kent State in the spring of 1970, more top-drawer doves turned out, including a flock of Wall Street lawyers. The protest was again anti-radical, turning a militant outpouring on the campuses and in the streets into a polite and unsuccessful effort to pass the McGovern-Hatfield antiwar amendment in the halls of Congress. But whatever the motivations, the split over Vietnam in the ruling class now *seemed* even deeper.

What was really happening was more interesting. The Business Executives Move for Vietnam Peace (BEM), the most active of the business groups, had been around since the end of 1966, drawing support from all over the country and helping to legitimize the more radical antiwar movement. But even at the time of Cambodia, BEM's sponsors included few executives from *Fortune*'s top 500 corporations or top fifty banks. The BEMers were rich, powerful in their own communities, and very decent human beings. But, with few exceptions, they were relatively small change, with little economic interest in America's Asian dominoes and little policy-making influence within the big business community.

Nor were the BEM members exclusively from one region. Many of the initial leaders came from the East, but one of the most active BEM groups was in Los Angeles, which was also the home of the Winsocket Club, the fat cats behind the presidential campaign of George McGovern. What kind of Cowboys were these?*

A few big businessmen did speak out, to be sure. The chairman of the Bank of America, the chairman of IBM, former Federal Reserve Chairman Marriner Eccles, Washington lawyer and former Defense Secretary Clark Clifford, investor and statesman Averell Harriman all added their voices to the antiwar protest. But they remained individual voices, representing a small minority of big business and no discernible economic or regional alignment. If anything, the greatest tie between some of the name opponents of the war was their leadership in the Democratic Party, which suggests that their motives might have been more narrowly political than economic.

The vast majority of big business leaders remained committed to Nixon and his strategy for winding down the role of American groundtroops in the war. Right at the time of the Cambodian protest, Lyndon Johnson's onetime Commerce Secretary John Connors denounced the invasion before a meeting of the blue-ribbon Business Council. According to the press, 90 percent of his listeners supported the president, and of the 10 percent who did not, several thought Connors wrong to criticize him publicly.

If the split in the ruling class was a mirage, why did so many people see it as real? One reason is that few businessmen ac-

---

* Many of these same people also backed the successful campaign for mayor of Thomas Bradley, a liberal black. But so did Howard Hughes. Were the Cowboys confused? Or was it the theorists?

tually applauded the war, except perhaps for the initial boost to the economy in 1964 and 1965. Most found it a necessary and costly evil, as reflected in the on-the-one-hand, on-the-other-hand editorials of the *Wall Street Journal* or the "peace rallies" on the stock market whenever the news suggested that Washington might stop the communists at the conference table rather than on the battlefields.

Another reason was the media, much of which did split with the administration over the war, and over a lot more. This was especially true of CBS, NBC, the *New York Times* and the *Washington Post*—the nub of what the administration called the Eastern Establishment. The term was again vague and made it sound as if the media were speaking for Eastern Money, or the Yankees. But they were not, and that's not what the Nixon people were trying to imply. This Eastern Establishment was a cultural establishment, and the split with Nixon a part of what sophisticated economic determinists see as a very real super-structure of culture and politics.

"Virtually every element of the Nixon coalition dislikes the Sixties cultural hegemony of the *New York Times,* CBS, Harvard, the Ford Foundation, Norman Mailer, Oh! Calcutta!, and the *Portnoy's Complaint*-mongers," explained Kevin Phillips, author of the *Emerging Republican Majority.* The conflict was real. But instead of Cowboy versus Yankee money, it was *Readers Digest* versus *Newsweek,* the Grand Old Opry versus Camelot, and the votes of the middle class of the South and Southwest, as well as the Eastern suburbs, against the "limousine liberals" of Manhattan *and* Los Angeles.

The cultural establishment didn't think too highly of Nixon in return, and the media did kick him around. Where newsmen had gone along with the government in the past, they grew restive in the last years of the Johnson administration and widened the credibility gap under Nixon. But this was hardly the Eastern snobbery which both Nixon and Johnson suspected. The media responded almost magically to the charismatic John Connally, while Nixon's number one nemesis Dan Rather of

CBS is himself a Texan. More than any cultural bias, or even personal dislike, Nixon and Johnson simply suffered from the erosion of the national consensus, particularly over Vietnam and domestic dissent.

This is especially important in understanding the media's coverage of Watergate, which both Nixon and his more radical critics tend to see as the spearhead of a not-so-secret campaign to oust him from office. But, it was not the media which uncovered most of Watergate. The first inside story of the break-in came from wiretap monitor Alfred Baldwin III, who told his tale to federal prosecutors sometime before October 1972. The story of the money which paid for the break-in came from the Government Accounting Office, an arm of Congress. The story of the cash payments and offers of executive clemency to the defendants came from James McCord, frightened by the heavy provisional sentence imposed by a conservative Republican judge, "Maximum John" Sirica. The story of the Ellsberg break-in, the enemies list, the Huston Plan, and other White House Horrors came from former counsel John Dean, under pressure from congressional investigators and fearful that the White House would make him the Watergate scapegoat. Only with Donald Segretti's campaign sabotage and perhaps one or two other stories did the media do more than leak information which government investigators, the Ervin Committee, and the grand juries had unearthed and would later make public themselves.*

The leaks did create a sense of excitement, and the newsmen did show an obvious bias against Nixon and for Cox and Richardson (as well as for Leon Jaworski, a Cowboy). But for the most part, the media was responding, not initiating, and it is hard to see how anything short of a unified effort to suppress the story could have kept it from becoming a cause célèbre, especially when the credibility gap was already so wide.

Nor is there any evidence that the Watergate coverage or the cultural conflict reflected any deeper economic cleavage, as the

* See Edward Jay Epstein, "How Press Handled Watergate Scandal," *Los Angeles Times*, September 14, 1973, p. 1.

Yankee-Cowboy theorists suggest. Many of the Eastern media magnates and managers—like the Paleys of CBS, the Sulzbergers of the *Times,* and Katherine Graham of *Post-Newsweek*—came from Jewish or part-Jewish families, hardly old Yankee, and they were evidently independent of any economic interest groups on Wall Street or anywhere else. The Harriman family, long considered a major behind-the-scenes force in CBS, was Yankee and did control a lot of old money. But that could hardly be the cause of Averell Harriman's politics or Walter Cronkite's bias, since Averell's brother E. Roland Harriman remained a rock-ribbed Republican. Pushing the search for economic explanations even farther, the Trust Department of the Rockefeller family's Chase Manhattan Bank controlled large blocks of stock in all three networks. No one was more Eastern Establishment economically, and the family was the heart and pocketbook of the old Eastern Internationalist wing of the Republican Party, which had battled with the provincial and isolationist Taft Republicans, whose voting base was chiefly in the Midwest. This split, which was real, was probably the source of Oglesby's idea of a Yankee-Cowboy split. But the Midwesterners had become internationalists as they expanded their stake in overseas trade and investment, and they were hardly nouveau riche Cowboys. In any case, after the failure of Nelson Rockefeller's candidacy, Chase Manhattan Chairman David Rockefeller and Nelson both became staunch backers of Richard Nixon. Why not? Henry Kissinger was their foreign policy adviser.

But East-West, North-South notions should probably be shelved altogether, at least in the case of media. Even in the old Republican Party split, many of the leading Eastern Internationalists came from the heart of the Midwest. Colonel Frank Knox, who brought Republican pro-war sentiment into the Roosevelt government in 1940, ran the *Chicago Daily News,* while the Cowles still run their old family newspapers in Minneapolis and Des Moines. Today, one of the more anti-Nixon papers is the Knight chain's *Herald* in Miami, while the East

Coast *Newsday*, which did investigative reporting on Nixon's links to organized crime, belongs to the big-on-Watergate *Los Angeles Times*, which also owns the *Dallas Times-Herald* and TV station KRLD in Dallas-Fort Worth.

Another reason for the belief that economic blocs had split over Vietnam was the liberal attack on the Military Industrial Complex. To the liberal critics, many of them in the media, the MIC was the key cause of bloated defense budgets, hysterical anticommunism, and the war in Vietnam. The military industrialists were the number one bad guys, and they were generally pictured as suntanned executives from aerospace, all profitably paranoid about the commie threat and ready to blow us all to Kingdom Come.

In fact, the computerized Cowboys of aerospace were only a small group among the Merchants of Death. According to the Pentagon's annual lists of the Top 100 Defense Contractors, the key killers included the big four automakers, seven or eight of the international oil giants, the top tire and rubber companies, GE, Westinghouse and the consumer electronics people, even Western Union, Eastman Kodak, and Ma Bell (AT&T). All the supposed sheep were goats, and a lot of Eastern sheep at that. Far from a small group on the outskirts of the American economy, the military industrial complex turned out to be the brand names.

The Cowboys didn't even dominate the big aerospace companies, so many of which did have their plants in the sunbelt. The Wall Street bankers and their allies around the country held the financially faltering Lockheed in hock, while the dean of the Harvard Business School and a blue-blood director of CBS sat on the board of directors. Chicago industrialist Henry Crown and his friend Nathan Cummings of Consolidated Food topped General Dynamics, together with the ostensibly antiwar Andre Meyer of Lazard Frères and the partners of Cravath, Swaine, and Moore, who were also active in CBS and *Time-Life*. The East Coast financial community had a tight hold on United

Aircraft and Boeing as well, and the leading venture capitalist in several of the smaller firms and also McDonnel Aircraft was Laurence Rockefeller. The military industrial complex turned out to be the cream of the corporate establishment, but the Cowboy image lived on.

On a more sophisticated level, the Yankee-Cowboy theorists borrowed from the Marxists, most obviously in seeing the economy divided into a series of "financial groups," bringing together key corporations, banks, and families through interlocking directors, common stockholdings, and long-standing financial ties. It was an old idea. Lenin had commented on the Morgan and Rockefeller groups, while the American Marxist Victor Perlo catalogued "several major empires and a series of minor duchies." But the notion got new life in 1969 when the Russians published a new book by S. Menshikov, *Millionaires and Managers.*

A leading Soviet scholar, Menshikov consulted all of the standard business periodicals and studies. But he also took advantage of having lived in the United States as the son of a Soviet ambassador, using his family ties to gain personal interviews with several of the country's biggest businessmen. This gave his "scientific socialism" the flavor of inside dope, which was especially important in that he never gave the evidence to prove his case.

As Menshikov saw it, financial groups were still a basic building block of the American economy. He discussed Wall Street, including the Morgan, Rockefeller, First National City Bank, and Harriman groups, as well as the older regional alliances in Boston, Cleveland, Chicago and San Francisco. But he also highlighted the newer concentrations of capital, especially those in Texas and California, and suggested that this new provincial bourgeoisie might challenge the financial superiority of the old.

Menshikov said that the new *might* challenge the old; the Yankee-Cowboy theorists assumed that the two were already locked in mortal combat. But along with the vagueness of the two armies the few reported battles seemed like the normal economic competition that always goes on, within and across geographical boundaries. There was even less proof that those within any financial group actually worked together more than with firms outside, and no consideration of the welter of counter examples which suggest that American capital is coming together nationally, not splitting apart. It seemed as though the theorists had started out with real or imagined political conflicts and found some economic conflicts to go along with them.

In the theory, rich Texans were the foes of Wall Street. Back in the 1950s, for example, Texas money joined in the effort to take over the New York Central Railroad. In the 1960s the Murchisons of Texas managed to wrest temporary control of Investors Diversified Services from a group headed by Woolworth heir Allan Kirby, and there was a long-simmering feud between Eastern finance and Howard Hughes for control of TWA. One other example might be Texas computer king Ross Perot's purchase of the DuPont Walston brokerage firm, which went under despite Perot's millions.

But there were few examples of this kind, and even they raised problems for the Yankee-Cowboy theorists. Among Howard Hughes's chief Eastern foes were two firms which worked closely with Nixon's law firm and his administration—Dillon, Read and the Irvine Trust Bank. Nixon's Commerce Secretary Maurice Stans had been president of one of the firms that merged into DuPont Walston, which Perot took over. And even more pointed, when Woolworth heir Kirby regained Investors Diversified from the Murchisons he named Nixon to his board of directors.

More generally, the Texas Cowboys worked in close alliance with Wall Street, especially several predominantly Jewish investment firms—Lazard Frères, Lehman Brothers, Goldman Sachs, Carl M. Loeb, Rhoades, and Kuhn, Loeb. The Cowboys and Jews stood together in the new conglomerates, and as William Domhoff shows in *Fat Cats and Democrats,* they were the key financial groups within the Democratic Party. A symbol of this alliance was Robert B. Anderson, who moved from managing the cattle and oil of the Waggoner estate to Eisenhower's Defense and Treasury Departments to a Wall Street partnership in Loeb, Rhoades. The Harriman group also owned a big chunk of at least one prominent Cowboy corporation, El Paso Natural Gas, which received some favorable rulings from the Nixon administration.

The theory similarly ignored the historic economic ties between Northern finance and the Old South, the new Northern investments in Florida, the integration of California banks into a system dominated by Wall Street and the like. In fact, a few well chosen examples could show that Wall Street and the Yankees were consistently beating out the Cowboys, but that too would oversimplify the increasing financial integration of all parts of the country.

Perhaps the most interesting contribution of the Yankee-Cowboy theory was its treatment of organized crime. In this view, the Syndicate is far more than the old Sicilian Mafia and has expanded far beyond the older, largely Democratic cities of the North to encompass the legalized gambling of Las Vegas and the Caribbean, the new opium trade from Southeast Asia, and a growing portfolio of more legitimate investments, particularly in the rapidly growing areas of the South and Southwest. This expansion has enlarged the Syndicate's political connections, and also its financial resources, both from its own, often cash, profits and through control of other people's money, like the Teamsters' pension funds. And, as might be expected, many of these illegitimate capitalists do show up near Richard Nixon and his closest friends, especially in South Florida.

The facts spoke for themselves. Nixon's old political crony Murray Chotiner represented a long line of hoodlums, while Charles Colson worked closely with the Teamsters, both in securing Jimmy Hoffa's release from prison and in private law practice. Nixon had also been an honored guest at gambling clubs in the Bahamas. His friends and investment partners Bebe

Rebozo and former Senator George Smathers worked alongside Syndicate figures, as did his steady contributors Arnholt Smith and Howard Hughes.

But the story could be read the other way as well. The Justice Department prosecuted a large number of gangland figures, especially in the Democratic strongholds, and Nixon downplayed his anticommunism, which the gangsters were supposed to favor. In fact, there was little evidence that the gangsters ever got more than a few favors from the White House, and it was absurd to think that their influence could rival that of the somewhat cleaner capitalists, North and South. It was good that would-be Marxists had discovered crime. But they were bending the facts to suggest that it was more closely tied to Southern capital than to Northern, or they forgot that gangsters are supposed to have exercised great power in earlier administrations, particularly with Harry Truman of the old Pendergast machine in Missouri.

Normal economic competition, increased intra-regional cooperation, few major conflicts, and a sprinkling of Organized Crime throughout—that's a far better picture of the upper reaches of the American political economy than the supposed Yankee-Cowboy conflict. No region or clique of capitalists created Vietnam, Watergate, or the Nixon administration. They are all to blame, and unless the people stop them, they'll do a lot worse next time.

But whatever the evidence, most people will continue to believe that the crooks and the Cowboys, the military industrial complex, or some other special group is causing the country's problems. As long as the scapegoats remain shadowy and vague, no one will ever be able to knock them over. And as long as there are devils, people can go on believing that some others up there might not be so bad.

GLOSSARY of Government Espionage terms

From the Department of Defense *Dictionary of Military and Related Terms* (JCS Pub. 1):

Counterintelligence is "That aspect of intelligence activity which is devoted to destroying the effectiveness of inimical foreign intelligence activities and to the protection of information against espionage, individuals against subversion, and installations or material against sabotage."*

Countersubversion is "That aspect of counterintelligence designed to detect, destroy, neutralize or prevent subversive activities through the identification, exploitation, penetration, manipulation, deception and repression of individuals, groups or organizations conducting or suspected of conducting subversive activities." [The definitions of counterespionage and countersabotage are similar. NATO, SEATO, CENTO, and the Inter-American Defense Board drop "suspected of conducting" and substitute "capable of conducting"—a much broader definition.]

Espionage is "Actions directed toward the acquisition of information through clandestine operations."

Espionage against the United States is "Overt, covert or clandestine activity designed to obtain information relating to the national defense with intent or reason to believe that it will be used to the injury of the United States or to the advantage of a foreign nation."

Sabotage is "An act or acts with the intent to injure, interfere with, or obstruct the national defense of a country by willfully injuring or destroying, or attempting to injure or destroy material, premises, or utilities, to include human and natural resources."

---

* Approved for interdepartmental usage. The other terms are approved by the Department of Defense.

Penetration (intelligence) is "The recruitment of agents within or the infiltration of agents or technical monitoring devices in an organization or group for the purpose of acquiring information or of influencing its activities."

Subversion is "Action designed to undermine the military, economic, psychological, morale, or political strength of a regime."*

Overt operation is "The collection of intelligence openly, without concealment."

Covert operations are "Operations which are so planned and executed as to conceal the identity of or permit plausible denial by the sponsor. They differ from clandestine operations in that emphasis is placed on concealment of identity of sponsor rather than on concealment of the operation."*

Clandestine operations are "Activities to accomplish intelligence, counterintelligence, and other similar activities sponsored or conducted by governmental departments or agencies, in such a way as to assure secrecy or concealment. (It differs from covert operations in that emphasis is placed on concealment of the operations rather than on concealment of identity of sponsor.)"*

Internal security is "The state of law and order prevailing within a nation."*

—*Compiled by Herb Borock,*
Pacific Studies Center

COINTELPRO Documents

FBI Disruption of the New Left

Mailed May 14, 1968

SAC, Albany

Director, FBI

COUNTERINTELLIGENCE PROGRAM
INTERNAL SECURITY
DISRUPTION OF NEW LEFT

Effective immediately, the Bureau is instituting a Counterintelligence Program directed against the New Left movement and its Key Activists. All offices are instructed to immediately open an active control file, captioned as above, and to assign responsibility for this program to an experienced and imaginative Special Agent who is well versed in investigation of the New Left and its membership.

The purpose of this program is to expose, disrupt, and otherwise neutralize the activities of the various New Left organizations, their leadership and adherents. It is imperative that the activities of these groups be followed on a continuous basis so we may take advantage of all opportunities for counterintelligence and also inspire action in instances were circumstances warrant. The devious maneuvers and duplicity of these activists must be exposed to public scrutiny through the cooperation of reliable news media sources, both locally and at the Seat of Government. We must frustrate every effort of these groups and individuals to consolidate their forces or to recruit new or youthful coherents [sic]. In every instance, consideration should be given to disrupting the organized activity of these groups and no opportunity should be missed to capitalize upon organizational and personal conflicts of the leadership.

On or before June 1, 1968, all offices are instructed to submit to the Bureau a detailed analysis of potential counter-intelligence action against New Left organizations and Key Activists within their respective territories. Specific recommendations should be included for any logical immediate counter-intelligence action. Recommendations submitted under this program must include all necessary facts to enable the Bureau to intelligently pass upon the feasibility of the proposed action. In instances where a reliable and cooperative news media representative or other source outside the Bureau is to be contacted or utilized in connection with a proposed counterintelligence operation, it will be incumbant [sic] upon the recommending office to furnish assurances the source will not reveal the Bureau's interest or betray our confidence.

Offices which have investigative responsibility for Key Activists should specifically comment in the initial letter to the Bureau regarding these individuals. As these offices are aware, these individuals have been identified as the moving forces behind the New Left.

A counterintelligence action may be initiated by the field without specific Bureau authorization.

Commencing July 1, 1968, and every three months thereafter, each participating office should submit to the Bureau a status letter covering the prior 3-month period, including comments under the following captions.

1) Potential Counterintelligence Action
2) Pending Counterintelligence Action
3) Tangible Results

If necessary, a fourth caption "Miscellaneous" may be utilized for additional commments.

Recommendations for counterintelligence action should not be included in the 90-day status letters to the Bureau, but should be submitted individually by separate letter.

All Special Agent personnel responsible for the investigation of the New Left and the Key Activists should be alerted to our counterintelligence plans relating to these groups. Counterintelligence action directed at these groups is intended to complement and stimulate our accelerated intelligence investigations. Each investigative Agent has a responsibility to call to the attention of the counterintelligence coordinator suggestions and possibilities for implementing the program. You are cautioned that the nature of this new endeavor is such that under no circumstances should the existence of the program be made known outside the Bureau and appropriate within-office security should be afforded this sensitive operation.

The Bureau has been very closely following the activities of the New Left and the Key Activists and is highly concerned that the anarchistic activities of a few can paralyze institutions of learning, induction centers, cripple traffic, and tie the arms of law enforcement officials all to the detriment of our society. The organizations and activists who spout revolution and unlawfully challenge society to obtain their demands must not only be contained, but must be neutralized. Law and order is mandatory for any civilized society to survive. Therefore, you must approach this new endeavor with a forward look, enthusiasm, and interest in order to accomplish our responsibilities. The importance of this new endeavor cannot and will not be overlooked.

COINTELPRO Documents

FBI Disruption of the Black Panthers

5/11/70

SAC, San Francisco

Director, FBI

COUNTERINTELLIGENCE AND SPECIAL OPERATIONS
(RESEARCH SECTION)

The Bureau would like to offer for your consideration a proposal for a disruptive-disinformation operation targeted against the national office of the Black Panther Party (BPP). This proposal is not intended to be all inclusive or binding in any of its various phases, but only is a guide for the suggested action. You are encouraged to submit recommendations relating to revisions or innovations of the proposal.

1. The operation would be effected through close coordination on a high level with the Oakland or San Francisco Police Department.

2. Xerox copies of true documents, documents subtly incorporating false information, and entirely fabricated documents would be periodically mailed to the residence of a key Panther leader. These documents would be on the stationery and in the form used by the police department or by the FBI in disseminating information to the police. FBI documents, when used, would contain police routing or date received notations, clearly indicating they had been pilfered from police files.

3. An attempt would be made to give the Panther recipient the impression the documents were stolen from police files by a disgruntled police employee sympathetic to the Panthers. After initial mailings, brief notes by the alleged disgruntled employee would be included with the mailed documents. These notes

would indicate the motive and sympathy of the police employee, his bitterness against his department, and possibly a request for money.

4. Depending on developments, at a propitious time, consideration would be given to establishing a post office box or other suitable "drop" address for the use of the alleged disgruntled employee to receive responses, funds, and/or specifications relating to the documents from the Panthers.

5. Although the operation may not require inclusion of a live source to represent the disgruntled employee, circumstances might warrant the use of such a source for face-to-face meetings with the Panthers. During early stages of the operation, an effort should be made to locate and brief a suitable police employee to play the role of the alleged disgruntled employee.

6. A wide variety of alleged authentic police or FBI material could be carefully selected or prepared for furnishing to the Panthers. Reports, blind memoranda, LHMs, and other alleged police or FBI documents could be prepared pinpointing Panthers as police or FBI informants; ridiculing or discrediting Panther leaders through their ineptness or personal escapades; espousing personal philosophies and promoting factionalism among BPP members; indicating electronic coverage where none exists; outlining fictitious plans for police raids or other counteractions; revealing misuse or misappropriation of Panther funds; pointing out instances of political disorientation; etc. The nature of the disruptive material and disinformation "leaked" would only be limited by the collection ability of your sources and the need to insure the protection of their security.

Effective implementation of this proposal logically could not help but disrupt and confuse Panther activities. Even if they were to suspect FBI or police involvement, they would be unable to ignore factual material brought to their attention through this channel. The operation would afford us a continuing means to furnish the Panther leadership true information which is to our interest that they know and disinformation which, in their interest, they may not ignore.

Although this proposal is a realtively simple technique, it has been applied with exceptional results in another area of intelligence interest where the target was of far greater sophistication. The Bureau believes with careful planning this technique has excellent long-range potential to disrupt and curtail Panther activity.

San Francisco is requested to submit comments and/or recommendations relating to the implementation of this proposal.

Copies of this letter have been designated for Los Angeles for background and information purposes. Any suggestion Los Angeles may have for strengthening or further implementing the technique will be appreciated.

The Huston Plan

The Huston Plan

The now infamous "Huston Plan" was a series of national security proposals presented to President Nixon in July 1970. The proposals were approved by the president, but on the objection of FBI director J. Edgar Hoover the memo conveying presidential approval was recalled, although never technically rescinded. In August and September 1970 Huston attempted to circumvent Hoover, as well as to step up the political use of federal agencies such as the Internal Revenue Service. The final memo included in this section, from White House Counsel John Dean to Attorney General John Mitchell, shows the ongoing implementation of Huston's counterintelligence strategy after the recall of the White House Decision Memo on Huston's formal proposals.

John Dean's copies of these documents were accepted from Dean's bank safety-deposit box by U.S. District Judge John J. Sirica, who later made copies available to the Senate Watergate Committee and to federal prosecutors. The New York Times *published the Huston memos on June 7, 1973.*

—Ed.

RECOMMENDATIONS
TOP SECRET

Handle via Comint Channels
Only
*Operational Restraints
on Intelligence Collection*

A. Interpretive Restraints on Communications Intelligence.
RECOMMENDATION: Present interpretation should be broadened to permit and program for coverage by N.S.A. of the communications of U.S. citizens using international facilities.

RATIONALE: The F.B.I. does not have the capacity to monitor international communications. N.S.A. is currently doing so on a restricted basis, and the information is particularly useful to the White House and it would be to our disadvantage to allow the F.B.I. to determine what N.S.A. should do in this area without regard to our own requirements. No appreciable risk is involved in this course of action.

B. Electronic Surveillance and Penetrations. RECOMMENDATION: Present procedures should be changed to permit intensification of coverage of individuals and groups in the United States who pose a major threat to internal security.

Also, present procedures should be changed to permit intensification of coverage of foreign nationals and diplomatic establishments in the United States of interest to the intelligence community.

At the present time, less than (unclear) electronic penetrations are operative. This includes coverage of the C.P.U.S.A. and organized crime targets, with only a few authorized against subject of pressing internal security interest.

Mr. Hoover's statement that the F.B.I. would not oppose other agencies seeking approval for the operating electronic surveillances is gratuitous since no other agencies have the capability.

Everyone knowledgeable in the field, with the exception of
Mr. Hoover concurs that existing coverage is grossly inadequate.
C.I.A. and N.S.A. note that this is particularly true of diplomatic establishments, and we have learned at the White House
that it is also true of new Left groups.

C. Mail Coverage. RECOMMENDATION: Restrictions on
legal coverage should be removed.

Also, present restrictions on covert coverage should be relaxed on selected targets of priority foreign intelligence and
internal security interest.

RATIONALE: There is no valid argument against use of legal
mail covers except Mr. Hoover's concern that the civil liberties
people may become upset. This risk is surely an acceptable one
and hardly serious enough to justify denying ourselves a valuable and legal intelligence tool.

Covert coverage is illegal and there are serious risks involved.
However, the advantages to be derived from its use outweigh
the risks. This technique is particularly valuable in identifying
espionage agents and other contact of foreign intelligence
services.

D. Surreptitious Entry. RECOMMENDATION: Present restrictions should be modified to permit procurement of vitally
needed foreign cryptographic material.

Also, present restrictions should be modified to permit selective use of this technique against other urgent security targets.

RATIONALE: Use of this technique is clearly illegal: it
amounts to burglary. It is also highly risky and could result in
great embarrassment if exposed. However, it is also the most
fruitful tool and can produce the type of intelligence which
cannot be obtained in any other fashion.

The F.B.I., in Mr. Hoover's younger days, used to conduct
such operations with great success and with no exposure. The
information secured was invaluable.

N.S.A. has a particular interest since it is possible by this
technique to secure material with which N.S.A. can break foreign cryptographic codes. We spend millions of dollars attempt-

ing to break these codes by machine. One successful surreptitious entry can do the job successfully at no dollar cost.

Surreptitious entry of facilities occupied by subversive elements can turn up information about identities, methods of operation, and other invaluable investigative information which is not otherwise obtainable. This technique would be particularly helpful if used against the Weathermen and Black Panthers.

The deployment of the executive protector force has increased the risk of surreptitious entry of diplomatic establishments. However, it is the belief of all except Mr. Hoover that the technique can still be successfully used on a selective basis.

E. *Development of Campus Sources.* RECOMMENDATION: Present restrictions should be relaxed to permit expanded coverage of violence-prone campus and student-related groups.

Also, C.I.A. coverage of American students (and others) traveling or living abroad should be increased.

RATIONALE: The F.B.I. does not currently recruit any campus sources among individuals below 21 years of age. This dramatically reduced the pool from which sources may be drawn. Mr. Hoover is afraid of a young student surfacing in the press as an F.B.I. source, although the reaction in the past to such events has been minimal. After all, everyone assumes the F.B.I. has such sources.

The campus is the battleground of the revolutionary protest movement. It is impossible to gather effective intelligence about the movement unless we have campus sources. The risk of exposure is minimal, and where exposure occurs the adverse publicity is moderate and short-lived. It is a price we must be willing to pay for effective coverage of the campus scene. The intelligence community, with the exception of Mr. Hoover, feels strongly that it is imperative the (was unclear) increase the number of campus sources this fall in order to forestall widespread violence.

C.I.A. claims there are not existing restraints on its coverage of over-seas activities of U.S. nationals. However, this coverage has been grossly inadequate since 1965 and an explicit directive to increase coverage is required.

F. Use of Military Undercover Agents. RECOMMENDA-
TION: Present restrictions should be retained.

RATIONALE: The intelligence community is agreed that the
risks of lifting these restraints are greater than the value of any
possible intelligence which would be acquired by doing so.

Budget and Manpower Restrictions

RECOMMENDATION: Each agency should submit a detailed
estimate as to projected manpower needs and other costs in the
event the various investigative restraints herein are lifted.

RATIONALE: In the event that the above recommendations
are concurred in, it will be necessary to modify existing budgets
to provide the money and manpower necessary for their implementation. The intelligence community has been badly hit in
the budget squeeze. (I suspect the foreign intelligence operations are in the same shape) and it may be will be necessary to
make some modifications. The projected figures should be reasonable, but will be subject to individual review if this recommendation is accepted.

Measures to Improve Domestic Intelligence Operations

RECOMMENDATION: A permanent committee consisting
of the F.B.I., C.I.A., N.S.A., D.I.A. and the military counterintelligence agencies should be appointed to provide evaluations
of domestic intelligence estimates, and carry out the other objectives specified in the report.

RATIONALE: The need for increased cooperation, joint estimates, and responsiveness to the White House is obvious to the
intelligence community. There are a number of operational
problems which need to be worked out since Mr. Hoover is
fearful of any mechanism which might jeopardize his auton-
omy. C.I.A. would prefer an ad hoc committee to see how the
system works, but other members believe that this would

merely delay the establishment of effective coordination and joint operations. The value of lifting intelligence collection restraints is proportional to the availability of joint operations and evaluation, and the establishment of this interagency group is considered imperative.

HALDEMAN TO HUSTON

July 14, 1970

TOP SECRET

MEMORANDUM FOR: MR. HUSTON
SUBJECT: *Domestic Intelligence Review*

The recommendations you have proposed as a result of the review have been approved by the President.

He does not, however, want to follow the procedure you outlined on page 4 of your memorandum regarding implementation. He would prefer that the thing simply be put into motion on the basis of this approval.

The formal official memorandum should, of course, be prepared and that should be the device by which to carry it out.

I realize this is contrary to your feeling as to the best way to get this done. If you feel very strongly that this procedure won't work you had better let me know and we'll take another stab at it. Otherwise let's go ahead.

H. R. HALDEMAN

T O P   S E C R E T
Decision Memorandum
The White House
Washington
July 15, 1970

T O P   S E C R E T
Handle via Comint Channels only

Subject: Domestic Intelligence

The President has carefully studied the special report of the Interagency Committee on Intelligence (ad hoc) and made the following decisions:

1. Interpretive Restraint on Communications Intelligence. National Security Council Intelligence Directive Number 6 (NSCID-6) is to be interpreted to permit N.S.A. to program for coverage the communications of U.S. citizens using international facilities.

2. Electronic Surveillances and Penetrations. The intelligence community is directed to intensify coverage of individuals and groups in the United States who pose a major threat to the internal security. Also, coverage of foreign nations and diplomatic establishments in the United States of interest to the intelligence community is to be intensified.

3. Mail Coverage. Restrictions on legal coverage are to be removed, restrictions on covert coverage are to be relaxed to permit use of this technique on selected targets of priority foreign intelligence and internal security interest.

4. Surreptitious Entry. Restraints on the use of surreptitious entry are to be removed. The technique is to be used to permit procurement of vitally needed foreign cryptographic material and against other urgent and high priority internal security targets.

5. *Development of Campus Sources.* Coverage of violence-prone campus and student-related groups is to be increased. All restraints which limit this coverage are to be removed. Also, C.I.A. coverage of American students (and others) traveling or living abroad is to be increased.

6. *Use of Military Undercover Agents.* Present restrictions are to be retained.

7. *Budget and Manpower.* Each agency is to submit a detailed estimate as to projected manpower needs and other costs required to implement the above decisions.

8. *Domestic Intelligence Operations.* A committee consisting of the directors or other appropriate representatives appointed by the directors, of the F.B.I., C.I.A., N.S.A., D.I.A., and the military counterintelligence agencies is to be constituted effective August 1, 1970, to provide evaluations of domestic intelligence, prepare periodic domestic intelligence estimates, carry out the other objectives specified in the report, and perform such other duties as the President shall, from time to time, assign. The director of the F.B.I. shall serve as chairman of the committee. Further details on the organization and operations of this committee are set forth in an attached memorandum.

The President has directed that each addressee submit a detailed report, due on September 1, 1970, on the steps taken to implement these decisions. Further such periodic reports will be requested as circumstances merit.

The President is aware that procedural problems may arise in the course of implementing these decisions. However, he is anxious that such problems be resolved with maximum speed and minimum misunderstanding. Any difficulties which may arise should be brought to my immediate attention in order that an appropriate solution may be found and the President's directives implemented in a manner consistent with his objectives.

Tom Charles Huston

THE WHITE HOUSE
WASHINGTON

September 18, 1970

TOP SECRET

MEMORANDUM FOR
THE ATTORNEY GENERAL

Pursuant to our conversation yesterday, September 17, 1970, I suggest the following procedures to commence our domestic intelligence operation as quickly as possible.

1. *Interagency Domestic Intelligence Unit.* A key to the entire operation will be the creation of a interagency intelligence unit for both operational and evaluation purposes. Obviously, the selection of persons to this unit will be of vital importance to the success of the mission. As we discussed, the selection of the personnel for this unit is an appropriate first step for several reasons. First, effective coordination of the different agencies must be developed at an early stage through the establishment of the unit. Second, Hoover has indicated a strong opposition to the creation of such a unit and, to bring the FBI fully on board, this seems an appropriate first step to guarantee their proper and full participation in the program. Third, the unit can serve to make appropriate recommendations for the type of intelligence that should be immediately pursued by the various agencies. In regard to this third point, I believe we agreed that it would be inappropriate to have any blanket removal of restrictions; rather, the most appropriate procedure would be to decide on the type of intelligence we need, based on an assessment of the recommendations of this unit, and then to proceed to remove the restraints as necessary to obtain such intelligence.

To proceed to create the interagency intelligence unit, particularly the evaluation group or committee, I recommend that we request the names of four nominees from each of the intelligence agencies involved. While the precise composition of the unit may vary as we gain experience, I think that two members should be appointed initially from each agency in addition to your personal representative who should also be involved in the proceedings. Because of the interagency aspects of this request, it would probably be best if the request came from the White House. If you agree, I will make such a request of the agency heads; however, I feel that it is essential that you work this out with Hoover before I have any dealings with him directly.

2. *Housing.* We discussed the appropriate housing of this operation and, upon reflection, I believe that rather than a White House staffer looking for suitable space, that a professional intelligence person should be assigned the task of locating such space. Accordingly, I would suggest that a request be made that Mr. Hoover assign an agent to this task. In connection with the housing problem, I think serious consideration must be given to the appropriate Justice Department cover for the domestic intelligence operation. We discussed yesterday using IDIU as a cover and as I indicated I believe that that is a most appropriate cover. I believe that it is generally felt that IDIU is already a far more extensive intelligence operation than has been mentioned publicly, and that the IDIU operation cover would eliminate the problem of discovering a new intelligence operation in the Department of Justice. However, I have reservations about the personnel in IDIU and its present operation activities and would suggest that they either be given a minor function within the new intelligence operation or that the staff be completely removed. I have had only incidental dealings with the personnel, other than Jim Devine, and cannot speak to their discretion and loyalty for such an operation. I do not believe that Jim Devine is capable of any major position within the new intelligence operation. However, I do believe that he could help perpetuate the cover and he has evidenced a loyalty to you, the

Deputy and other key people in the Department of Justice, despite his strong links with the prior Administration. I would defer to your judgement, of course, on any recommendation regarding Jim Devine's continued presence in such an intelligence operation.

3. *Assistant to Attorney General.* We also discussed the need for you to have a right hand man to assist in running this operation. It would seem that what is needed is a man with administrative skills, a sensitivity to the implications of the current radical and subversive movements within the United States, and preferably, some background in intelligence work. To maintain the cover, I would think it appropriate for the man to have a law degree in that he will be a part of the Department of Justice. You suggested the possibility of using a prosecutor who had had experience with cases of this type. Accordingly, I have spoken with Harlington Wood to ask him to submit the names of five Assistant U.S. Attorneys who have had experience in dealing with demonstrations or riot type cases and who are mature individuals that might be appropriately given a sensitive assignment in the Department of Justice. I did not discuss the matter in any further detail with Wood other than to request the submission of some nominees. I would also like to suggest that we request names from the various intelligence agencies involved for personnel that might be appropriately involved in this activity or who might serve as your assistant.

In summary, I recommend the following immediate action:

(1) You meet with Hoover, explain what must be done, and request his nominees for the interagency unit.

(2) You request that   Hoover assign an agent to the task of locating appropriate housing for the operations.

(3) I request that other involved intelligence agencies submit nominees for the interagency unit.

(4) I request from the agencies names of appropriate personnel for assignment to the operation.

Finally, I would suggest that you call weekly meetings to

monitor the problems as they emerge and to make certain that we are moving this program into implementation as quickly as possible.

John Dean

N.B.: Bob Haldeman has suggested to me that if you would like him to join you in a meeting with Hoover he will be happy to do so.

BIBLIOGRAPHY

Documentation for these essays can be found in the hearings of the Senate Watergate Committee and the House Judiciary Committee on Impeachment, the *New York Times* edition of *The Watergate Hearings* (Bantam, 1973), the *Congressional Quarterly,* and articles in the leading newspapers and magazines, especially the *New York Times, Washington Post, Wall Street Journal,* and *Los Angeles Times.* The authors also interviewed participants, consulted the standard bibliographic and business references, and utilized the more specialized literature on power and politics, organized crime, political surveillance and "dirty tricks." For those interested in reading more on these subjects, this abbreviated bibliography should provide a good start.

Books

Anderson, Jack. *The Anderson Papers.* Ballantine Books, 1974.

Anslinger, Harry J. *The Protectors.* Farrar, Straus, 1964.

Belfrage, Cedric, *The American Inquisition 1945-1960,* Bobbs-Merrill, 1973.

Bernstein, Carl and Woodward, Bob. *All the President's Men.* Simon & Shuster, 1974.

Burns, James MacGregor. *The Deadlock of Democracy.* Prentice-Hall, 1967.

Chevigny, Paul. *Cops and Rebels: A Study of Provocation.* Curtis Books, 1972.

Citizens Research and Investigating Committee and Tackwood, Louis. *The Glass House Tapes.* Avon, 1973.

Cressey, Donald R.. *Theft of a Nation: The Structure and Operations of Organized Crime in America.* Harper & Row, 1969.

Domhoff, G. William. *Fat Cats and Democrats.* Prentice-Hall, 1972.

———. *The Higher Circles.* Random House, 1971.

———. *Who Rules America?* Prentice-Hall, 1967.

Dorman, Michael. *Pay-Off.* Berkeley Medallion, 1973.

Friendly, Fred W. *Due to Circumstances Beyond Our Control.* Random House, 1968.

Goulden, Joseph C. *The Superlawyers: The Small and Powerful World of the Great Washington Law Firms.* McKay, 1971.

Green, Mark J. et al. *The Closed Enterprise System: Ralph Nader's Study Group Report on Anti-Trust Enforcement.* Bantam Books, 1972.

Harris, Richard. *Justice.* Dutton, 1970.

Hess, Stephen and Broder, David. *The Republican Establishment.* Harper & Row, 1967.

Hoffman, Paul. *Lions in the Street: The Inside Story of the Great Wall Street Law Firms.* Saturday Review Press, 1973.

———. *The New Nixon.* Tower Publications, 1970.

Hunt, E. Howard. *Give Us This Day.* [Hunt also wrote fiction under several *noms de plume,* including John Baxter, Robert Dietrich, Gordon Davis, and David St. John.]

Johnson, Lyndon Baines. *The Vantage Point.* Holt, Rinehart and Winston, 1971.

Kefauver, Estes. *Crime in America.* Doubleday, 1951. [This is a summary of the hearings and reports of the Senate's Special Committee to Investigate Organized Crime in Interstate Commerce in the early 1950s.]

Lewis, Norman. *The Honored Society.* Putnam, 1964.

Lundberg, Ferdinand. *The Rich and the Super-rich.* Bantam, 1969.

McClellan, John L. *Crime Without Punishment.* Duell, Sloan, and Pearce, 1962. [McClellan was chairman of the Senate's Select Committee on Improper Activities in the Labor and Management Field and the Permanent Subcommittee on Investigations of the Senate Committee on Government Operations in the late 1950s and into the 1960s.]

McCord, Jr., James W.. *TA Piece of Tape.* Washington Media, 1974.

McCoy, Alfred W. *The Politics of Heroin in Southeast Asia.* Harper & Row, 1973.

MacNeil, Robert. *The People Machine: The Influence of Television on American Politics.* Harper & Row, 1968.

Magruder, Jeb Stuart. *An American Life: One Man's Road to Watergate.* Atheneum, 1974.

Mass, Peter. *The Valachi Papers.* Bantam, 1969.

Mazo, Earl and Hess, Stephen. *Nixon: A Political Portrait.* Popular Library, 1968.

Menshikov, S. *Millionaires and Managers: Structure of U.S. Financial Oligarchy.* Moscow: Progress Publishers, 1969.

Messick, Hank. *Lansky.* Putnam, 1971.

—— and Goldblatt, Burt. *The Mobs and the Mafia.* Crowell, 1972.

Mintz, Morton and Cohen, Jerry. *America, Inc.* Dell, 1971.

Mollenhoff, Clark. *Strike Force: Organized Crime and the Government.* Prentice-Hall, 1972.

Nixon, Richard M. *Six Crises.* Doubleday, 1962.

Ollestad, Norman. *Inside the FBI.* Lancer Books, 1967.

Perlo, Victor. *The Empire of High Finance.* International Publishers, 1957.

Phillips, Kevin P. *The Emerging Republican Majority.* Arlington House, 1969.

President's Commission on Law Enforcement and Administration of Justice. *The Challenge of Crime in a Free Society.* Government Printing Office, 1967.

——. *Task Force Report: Organized Crime.* Government Printing Office, 1967.

Prouty, L. Fletcher. *The Secret Team: The CIA and its Allies in Control of the United States and the World.* Prentice-Hall, 1973.

Reid, Ed. *The Grim Reapers.* Bantam, 1970.

Sheridan, Walter. *The Fall and Rise of Jimmy Hoffa.* Saturday Review Press, 1972.

Smith, R. Harris. *OSS: The Secret History of America's First Intelligence Agency.* University of California Press, 1972.

Socialist Workers Party. *Watergate: The View From the Left.* Pathfinder Press, 1973.

Sondern, Jr., Frederic. *Brotherhood of Evil: The Mafia.* Manor Books, 1972.

Gay Talese. *Honor Thy Father.* Norlo Publishing, 1971.

Turkus, Burton, and Feder, Sid. *Murder, Inc.* Farrar, Straus and Young, 1951.

Turner, William Wa. *Hoover's FBI: The Man and the Myth.* Sherbourne Press, 1970.

——. *Power on the Right.* Ramparts Press, 1971.

Volz, Joseph and Bridge, Peter. *The Mafia Talks.* Fawcett, 1969.

White, Theodore. *The Making of the President 1960.* Pocket Books, 1961.

——. *The Making of the President 1964.* Signet, 1965.

———. *The Making of the President 1968.* Atheneum, 1969.

———. *The Making of the President 1972.* Atheneum, 1973.

Winter-Berger, Robert N. *The Washington Pay-Off.* Dell, 1972.

Wise, David. *The Politics of Lying.* Random House, 1973.

Wise, David and Ross, Thomas B. *The Invisible Government.* Bantam, 1964.

Witcover, Jules. *The Resurrection of Richard Nixon.* Putnam, 1970.

Zeitlin, Maurice, ed. *American Society, Inc.* Markham, 1970.

Articles

Donner, Frank J. "The Theory and Practice of American Political Intelligence." *New York Review of Books,* April 22, 1971.

——— and Eugene Cerruti. "The Grand Jury Network." *The Nation,* January 3, 1972.

——— and Richard I. Lavine. "Kangaroo Grand Juries: From the Watergate Perspective." *The Nation,* November 19, 1973.

Drew, Elizabeth. "The New Men at Justice." *Atlantic,* May 1969.

Epstein, Edward J. "How the Press Handles Watergate Scandal." *Los Angeles Times,* September 14, 1973.

Farrell, Barry. "The Ellsburg Mask." *Harper's Magazine,* October 1973.

Foley, Charles. "Ronald Reagan's Secret 'Game Plan' for Saving America." *The Observer* (London), October 99, 1970.

Goulden, Joseph C. "Tooling Up for Repression: The Cops Hit the Jackpot." *The Nation,* November 23, 1970.

———. "Warming Up for Watergate." *The Nation,* May 28, 1973.

Hamer, John. "Intelligence Community." *Educational Research Reports,* July 25, 1973.

Herman, Edward S. "Do Bankers Control Corporations?" *Monthly Review,* June 1973.

Israel, Lee. "Helen Gahagan Douglas." *Ms.,* October 1973.

Kopkind, Andrew. "Cleaning Up the Act: The Politics of Police Reform." *Ramparts,* October 1973.

Lang, Frances. "Internal Security Makes a Comeback." *Ramparts,* January 1972.

Litterman, Bob. "Who Owns the Media?" *Pacific Research,* January-February 1973.

Newsday. "Special Report on Nixon, Rebozo, and Smathers." October 6-13, 1971.

Phillips, Kevin P. "Conservative Chic." *Harper's Magazine,* June 1973.

Powers, Thomas. "The Government Is Watching." *Atlantic,* October 1972.

Pyle, Christopher H. "CONUS Intelligence: The Army Watches Civilian Politics." *Washington Monthly,* January 1970.

———. "CONUS Revisited: The Army Covers Up." *Washington Monthly,* July 1970.

O'Connor, James. "Question: Who Rules the Corporations. Answer: The Ruling Class." *Socialist Revolution,* January-February 1971.

Oppenheimer, Mary and Fitch, Robert. "Who Rules the Corporations?" *Socialist Revolution,* Summer 1970, September-October 1970, November-December 1970, and "Reply," January-February 1971.

Sweezy, Paul M. "The Resurgence of Financial Control: Fact or Fancy." *Socialist Revolution,* March-April 1972.

Wall, Robert. "Special Agent for the FBI." *New York Review of Books,* January 27, 1972.

INDEX

DATE DUE	
JAN 1 0 1980	JAN 0 4 1994
LR FEB - 1 1983	
LR DEC 1 0 1987	FEB 1 5 1994
DEC 9 1988	APR 0 9 1995
APR 1 0 1992	
1 2 1992	
NOV 2 3 1993	
DEC 0 7 1996	

MP 728